Blackstone's Statutes on

# CONTRACT & TORT

Blackstone's Statutes on

# CONTRACT & TORT

Edited by

## F. D. Rose MA, BCL, PhD

of Gray's Inn, Barrister-at-Law
Senior Lecturer in Laws, University College London

BLACKSTONE
PRESS LIMITED

This edition published in Great Britain 1989 by Blackstone Press Limited, 9-15 Aldine Street, London W12 9AW. Telephone: 01-740 1173

First edition 1987
Second edition 1989

ISBN: 1 85431 050 X

British Library Cataloguing in Publication Data.
A CIP catalogue record for this book is available from the Britsh Library

Typeset by Murdoch Evans Partnership, London EC1
Printed by LR Printing Services Ltd., Burgess Hill, West Sussex

# CONTENTS

To Josephine

# PREFACE

Amongst the first impressions acquired by a student new to English law is of the common law system as one constructed from the decisions of the judges and best represented by, indeed often spoken of as synonymous with the law of contract and the law of tort. He or she also learns that legislation is one of the two most important sources of law, indeed that it overrides case law. But statutes are not uncommonly seen as aberrations, tinkering with what is essentially a case law system or establishing self-contained regimes, distinct from other areas within the same subject of study. Their hostility is manifest in areas where they have to be faced in strength, most prominently in land law, habitually studied after the foundation year, where their potential for impenetrability is made manifest.

If the discerning student should ever gain such a picture of English law, he will hopefully soon realise that, whatever glimmer of truth it may contain, it is at least superficial and misleading. The arrangement of the curriculum should not be permitted to obscure the fact that contract and tort, as is being increasingly stressed, with their overlapping and fluctuating boundaries, are but major categorisations together with others, in particular the law of restitution, of a broader subject of civil liability. Moreover, statutory contributions to this subject are at least as valid as, and in some areas increasingly more important than, those of judicial decisions. In part, this book recognises that and seeks to give some indication of the different ways in which statutes have helped to shape modern law. Some, though necessarily limited, account is also taken of the intending practitioner's need to realise that individual 'fact situations' prompt not only consideration of the law of civil liability but also of elements of property law, criminal law, commercial law, public law and so on.

One skill that all students and all lawyers must have is the ability to research. That requires not only finding the right books in the library, which in the case of statutory materials can be quickly achieved, but also of reading through those materials to find the relevant answers. Hopefully, the convenience of the present collection will encourage more extensive, even if only casual, reading of the statutory materials, particularly those that would otherwise be passed by, and in doing so, enhance the student's appreciation of the legislative sources of the law as well as making it apparent that those sources need not be as intimidating or demanding as they are sometimes believed to be. This book attempts to concentrate on the core statutory provisions and examples of some of the principal legislative devices in this area. It does not attempt to be complete or definitive. Where a provision is not included or a question remains unanswered, the answer to a query is as in all cases: look it up elsewhere.

Since most, if not all, students with a substantial legal content in their courses will have to study both contract and tort, and will have at least some contact with the increasingly prominent and usually related law of restitution, this collection ranges over the three areas. Hopefully, it will facilitate their study jointly. Moreover, recognising the increasing practice of candidates' being permitted to take primary source materials into their examinations, it provides a more economical means of doing so than having to acquire the relevant main sources individually. Indeed, more material is provided than a candidate would normally wish to purchase, particularly for one subject alone, but, as with all such materials, the candidate will not benefit from either the basic materials or relevant additional materials unless they have been digested in advance. With that in mind, hardly any supplementary notes are included.

The principal aim in selecting from the much wider range of potential material available has been to provide as much substantive material as possible. In general, therefore, apart from the title of the statute, the marginal note providing the title of the relevant section, and the material parts of those sections that are included, the statutes are printed without preambles, headings, provisions as to commencement, extent and citation, or references to the previous law. Provisions are printed as amended, amendments being indicated in square brackets, but details of the amending provisions are omitted. The occasional excision of, for present purposes, unnecessary words from the provisions included is marked by three dots, without brackets. Specific provisions for Scotland and Northern Ireland are in most cases also omitted. For ease of consultation, the statutes are arranged chronologically, although alphabetically within a given year. Following the primary statutory material, the book also includes a small section of some of the more significant secondary legislation, part of the Treaty of Rome and the EC product liability directive, the provisions of which are interesting to compare with their enacted form in the Consumer Protection Act 1987.

The present collection incorporates material which received the Royal Assent before 1 January, 1989.

*Francis Rose*
*May Day 1989*

# THE LIMITATION ACT 1623
## (21 Jac. I, c. 16)

**5. After judgment for defendant, etc., in trespas quare clausum fregit, upon disclaimer of defendant, etc., plaintiff barred of his action.**

And in all accions of trespas quare clausum fregit hereafter to be brought, wherein the defendant or defendants shall disclaime in his or their plea to make any title or claime to the land in which the trespasse is by the declaracion supposed to be done, and the trespas be by negligence, or involuntary, the defendant or defendants shalbe admitted to pleade a disclaymer, and that the trespas was by negligence, or involuntary, and a tender or offer of sufficient amends for such trespase before the accion brought, whereuppon or uppon some of them, the plaintiffe or plaintiffes shalbe enforced to joyne issue; and if the said issue be found for the defendant or defendants, or the plaintiffe or plaintiffes shalbe nonsuted, the plaintiffe or plaintiffes shalbe clearlie barred from the said accion or accions and all other suite concerning the same.

# THE STATUTE OF FRAUDS 1677
## (29 Chas. II, c. 3)

**4. No action against executors, etc. upon a special promise, or upon any agreement, or contract for sale of lands, etc. unless agreement, etc. be in writing and signed.**

No action shall be brought [. . .] whereby to charge the defendant upon any speciall promise to answere for the debt default or miscarriages of another person [. . .] unlesse the agreement upon which such action shall be brought or some memorandum or note thereof shall be in writeing and signed by the partie to be charged therewith or some other person thereunto by him lawfully authorised.

# THE FIRES PREVENTION (METROPOLIS) ACT 1774
## (14 Geo. III, c. 78)

**86. No action to lie against a person where the fire accidentally begins.**

And no action, suit or process whatever shall be had, maintained or prosecuted against any person in whose house, chamber, stable, barn or other building, or on whose estate any fire shall [. . .] accidentally begin, nor shall any recompence be made by such person for any damage suffered thereby, any law, usage or custom to the contrary notwithstanding; [. . .] provided that no contract or agreement made between landlord and tenant shall be hereby defeated or made void.

# THE LIBEL ACT 1792
## (32 Geo. III, c. 60)

**1. On the trial of an indictment for a libel the jury may give a general verdict upon the whole matter put in issue, and shall not be required by the court to find the defendant guilty merely on proof of the publication, and of the sense ascribed to it in the information.**

On every such trial the jury sworn to try the issue may give a general verdict of guilty or not guilty upon the whole matter put in issue upon such indictment or information, and shall not be required or directed by the court or judge before whom such indictment or information shall be tried to find the defendant or defendants guilty merely on the proof of the publication by such defendant or defendants of the paper charged to be a libel, and of the sense ascribed to the same in such indictment or information.

**2.    But the court shall give their opinion and directions on the matter in issue as in other criminal cases.**
Provided always, that on every such trial the court or judge before whom such indictment or information shall be tried shall, according to their or his discretion, give their or his opinion and directions to the jury on the matter in issue between the King and the defendant or defendants, in like manner as in other criminal cases.

## THE STATUTE OF FRAUDS AMENDMENT ACT 1828
### (9 Geo. IV, c. 14)

**6.    Action not maintainable on representations of character, etc., unless they be in writing signed by the party chargeable.**
No action shall be brought whereby to charge any person upon or by reason of any representation or assurance made or given concerning or relating to the character, conduct, credit, ability, trade, or dealings of any other person, to the intent or purpose that such other person may obtain credit, money, or goods upon, unless such representation or assurance be made in writing, signed by the party to be charged therewith.

## THE PARLIAMENTARY PAPERS ACT 1840
### (3 & 4 Vict., c. 9)

**1.    Proceedings, criminal or civil, against persons for publication of papers printed by order of Parliament, to be stayed upon delivery of a certificate and affidavit to the effect that such publication is by order of either House of Parliament.**
It shall and may be lawful for any person or persons who now is or are, or hereafter shall be, a defendant or defendants in any civil or criminal proceeding commenced or prosecuted in any manner soever, for or on account or in respect of the publication of any such report, paper, votes, or proceedings by such person or persons, or by his, her, or their servant or servants, by or under the authority of either House of Parliament, to bring before the court in which such proceeding shall have been or shall be so commenced or prosecuted, or before any judge of the same (if one of the superior courts at Westminster), first giving twenty-four hours notice of his intention so to do to the prosecutor or plaintiff in such proceeding, a certificate under the hand of the lord high chancellor of Great Britain, or the lord keeper of the great seal, or of the speaker of the House of Lords, for the time being, or of the clerk of the Parliaments, or of the speaker of the House of Commons, or of the clerk of the same house, stating that the report, paper, votes, or proceedings, as the case may be, in respect whereof such civil or criminal proceeding shall have been commenced or prosecuted, was published by such person or persons, or by his, her, or their servant or servants, by order or under the authority of the House of Lords or of the House of Commons, as the case may be, together with an affidavit verifying such certificate; and such court or judge shall thereupon immediately stay such civil or criminal proceeding; and the same, and every writ or process issued therein, shall be and shall be deemed and taken to be finally put an end to, determined, and superseded by virtue of this Act.

**2.    Proceedings to be stayed when commenced in respect of a copy of an authenticated report, etc.**
In case of any civil or criminal proceeding hereafter to be commenced or prosecuted for or on account or in respect of the publication of any copy of such report, paper, votes, or proceedings, it shall be lawful for the defendant or defendants at any stage of the proceedings to lay before the court or judge such report, paper, votes, or proceedings, and such copy, with an affidavit verifying such report, paper, votes, or proceedings, and the correctness of such copy, and the court or judge shall immediately stay such civil or criminal proceedings; and the same, and every writ or process issued therein, shall be and

shall be deemed and taken to be finally put an end to, determined, and superseded by virtue of this Act.

**3.    In proceedings for printing any extract or abstract of a paper, it may be shewn that such extract was bona fide made.**
It shall be lawful in any civil or criminal proceeding to be commenced or prosecuted for printing any extract from or abstract of such report, paper, votes, or proceedings, to give in evidence [. . .] such report, paper, votes, or proceedings, and to show that such extract or abstract was published bona fide and without malice; and if such shall be the opinion of the jury, a verdict of not guilty shall be entered for the defendant or defendants.

**4.    Act not to affect the privileges of Parliament.**
Provided always, that nothing herein contained shall be deemed or taken, or held or construed, directly or indirectly, by implication or otherwise, to affect the privileges of Parliament in any manner whatsoever.

## THE LIBEL ACT 1843
### (6 & 7 Vict., c.96)

**1.    Offer of an apology admissible in evidence of mitigation of damages in action for defamation.**
In any action for defamation it shall be lawful for the defendant (after notice in writing of his intention so to do, duly given to the plaintiff at the time of filing or delivering the plea in such action,) to give in evidence, in mitigation of damages, that he made or offered an apology to the plaintiff for such defamation before the commencement of the action, or as soon afterwards as he had an opportunity of doing so, in case the action shall have been commenced before there was an opportunity of making or offering such apology.

**2.    In an action against a newspaper for libel, the defendant may plead that it was inserted without malice and without neglect and may pay money into court as amends.**
In an action for libel contained in any public newspaper or other periodical publication it shall be competent to the defendant to plead that such libel was inserted in such newspaper or other periodical publication without actual malice, and without gross negligence, and that before the commencement of the action, or at the earliest opportunity afterwards, he inserted in such newspaper or other periodical publication a full apology for the said libel, or, if the newspaper or periodical publication in which the said libel appeared should be ordinarily published at intervals exceeding one week, had offered to publish the said apology in any newspaper or periodical publication to be selected by the plaintiff in such action; [. . .] and to such plea to such action it shall be competent to the plaintiff to reply generally, denying the whole of such plea.

## THE GAMING ACT 1845
### (8 & 9 Vict., c. 109)

**18.    Wages not recoverable at law.**
All contracts or agreements, whether by parole or in writing, by way of gaming or wagering, shall be null and void; and no suit shall be brought or maintained in any court of law and equity for recovering any sum of money or valuable thing alleged to have been won upon any wager, or which shall have been deposited in the hands of any person to abide the event on which any wager shall have been made: Provided always, that this enactment shall not be deemed to apply to any subscription or contribution, or agreement to subscribe or contribute, for or towards any plate, prize or sum of money to be awarded to the winner or winners of any lawful game, sport, pastime, or exercise.

## THE LIBEL ACT 1845
### (8 & 9 Vict., c. 75)

**2.  Defendant not to file such plea without paying money into court by way of amends.**
It shall not be competent to any defendant in such action, whether in England or Ireland, to file any such plea, without at the same time making a payment of money into court by way of amends [. . .], but every such plea so filed without payment of money into court shall be deemed a nullity, and may be treated as such by the plaintiff in the action.

## THE BILLS OF LADING ACT 1855
### (18 & 19 Vict., c. III)

**1.  Rights under bills of lading to vest in consignee or endorsee.**
Every Consignee of Goods named in a Bill of Lading, and every Endorsee of a Bill of Lading to whom the Property in the Goods therein mentioned shall pass, upon or by reason of such Consignment or Endorsement, shall have transferred to and vested in him all Rights of Suit, and be subject to the same Liabilities in respect of such Goods as if the Contract contained in the Bill of Lading had been made with himself.

## THE OFFENCES AGAINST THE PERSON ACT 1861
### (24 & 25 Vict., c. 100)

**44.  If the magistrates dismiss the complaint, they shall make out a certificate to that effect.**
If the Justices, upon the Hearing of any [. . .] Case of Assault or Battery upon the Merits, where the Complaint was preferred by or on the Behalf of the Party aggrieved, [. . .], shall deem the Offence not to be proved, or shall find the Assault or Battery to have been justified, or so trifling as not to merit any Punishment, and shall accordingly dismiss the Complaint, they shall forthwith make out a Certificate under their Hands stating the Fact of such Dismissal, and shall deliver such Certificate to the Party against whom the Complaint was preferred.

**45.  Certificate or conviction shall be a bar to any other proceedings.**
If any Person, against whom any such Complaint as [is mentioned in section 44 of this Act] shall have been preferred by or on the Behalf of the Party aggrieved, shall have obtained such Certificate, or, having been convicted, shall have paid the whole Amount adjudged to be paid, or shall have suffered the Imprisonment or Imprisonment with Hard Labour awarded, in every such Case he shall be released from all further or other Proceedings, Civil or Criminal, for the same Cause.

## THE APPORTIONMENT ACT 1870
### (33 & 34 Vict., c. 35)

**2.  Rents, &c. to accrue from day to day and be apportionable in respect of time.**
From and after the passing of this Act all rents, annuities, dividends, and other periodical payments in the nature of income (whether reserved or made payable under an instrument in writing or otherwise) shall, like interest on money lent, be considered as accruing from day to day, and shall be apportionable in respect of time accordingly.

**3.  Apportioned part of rent, &c. to be payable when the next entire portion shall have become due.**
The apportioned part of any such rent, annuity, dividend, or other payment shall be payable or recoverable in the case of a continuing rent, annuity, or other such payment

when the entire portion of which such apportioned part shall form part shall become due and payable, and not before, and in the case of a rent, annuity, or other such payment determined by re-entry, death, or otherwise when the next entire portion of the same would have been payable if the same had not so determined, and not before.

## 5.    Interpretation of terms.

In the construction of this Act—

The word "rents" includes rent service, rentcharge, and rent seck, and also tithes and all periodical payments or renderings in lieu of or in the nature of rent or tithe.

The word "annuities" includes salaries and pensions.

The word "dividends" includes (besides dividends strictly so called) all payments made by the name of dividend, bonus, or otherwise out of the revenue of trading or other public companies, divisible between all or any of the members of such respective companies, whether such payments shall be usually made or declared at any fixed times or otherwise; and all such divisible revenue shall, for the purposes of this Act, be deemed to have accrued by equal daily increment during and within the period for or in respect of which the payment of the same revenue shall be declared or expressed to be made, but the said word "dividend" does not include payments in the nature of a return or reimbursement of capital.

## 6.    Act not to apply to policies of assurance.

Nothing in this Act contained shall render apportionable any annual sums made payable in policies of assurance of any description.

## 7.    Nor where stipulation made to the contrary.

The provisions of this Act shall not extend to any case in which it is or shall be expressly stipulated that no apportionment shall take place.

## THE LAW OF LIBEL AMENDMENT ACT 1888
### (51 & 52 Vict., c. 64)

## 3.    Newspaper reports of proceedings in court privileged.

A fair and accurate report in any newspaper of proceedings publicly heard before any court exercising judicial authority shall, if published contemporaneously with such proceedings, be privileged: Provided that nothing in this section shall authorise the publication of any blasphemous or indecent matter.

## 4.    Newspaper reports of proceedings of public meetings and of certain bodies and persons privileged.

A fair and accurate report published in any newspaper of the proceedings of a public meeting, or (except where neither the public nor any newspaper reporter is admitted) of any meeting of a vestry, town council, school board, board of guardians, board or local authority formed or constituted under the provisions of any Act of Parliament, or of any committee appointed by any of the above-mentioned bodies, or of any meeting of any commissioners authorised to act by letters patent, Act of Parliament, warrant under the Royal Sign Manual, or other lawful warrant or authority, select committees of either House of Parliament, justices of the peace in quarter sessions assembled for administrative or deliberative purposes, and the publication at the request of any Government office or department, officer of state, commissioner of police, or chief constable of any notice or report issued by them for the information of the public, shall be privileged, unless it shall be proved that such report or publication was published or made maliciously: Provided that nothing in this section shall authorise the publication of any blasphemous or indecent matter: Provided also, that the protection intended to be afforded by this section shall not be available as a defence in any proceedings if it shall be proved that the defendant has been requested to insert in the newspaper in which the report or other publication complained of appeared a reasonable letter or statement by way of contradiction or explanation of such report or other publication, and has refused or neglected to insert the same: Provided further, that nothing in this section contained shall be deemed or construed to limit or abridge any privilege now by law existing, or to protect the publication of any matter not of public concern and the publication of which is not for the public benefit.

For the purposes of this section "public meeting" shall mean any meeting bonâ fide and lawfully held for a lawful purpose, and for the furtherance or discussion of any matter of public concern, whether the admission thereto be general or restricted.

## THE SLANDER OF WOMEN ACT 1891
### (54 & 55 Vict., c. 51)

**1.   Amendment of law.**
Words spoken and published which impute unchastity or adultery to any woman or girl shall not require special damage to render them actionable.

Provided always, that in any action for words spoken and made actionable by this Act, a plaintiff shall not recover more costs than damages, unless the judge shall certify that there was reasonable ground for bringing the action.

## THE GAMING ACT 1892
### (55 & 56 Vict., c. 9)

**1.   Promises to repay sums paid under contracts void by 8 & 9 Vict. c. 109. to be null and void.**
Any promise, express or implied, to pay any person any sum of money paid by him under or in respect of any contract or agreement rendered null and void by the [Gaming Act 1845] or to pay any sum of money by way of commission, fee, reward, or otherwise in respect of any such contract, or of any services in relation thereto or in connexion therewith, shall be null and void, and no action shall be brought or maintained to recover any such sum of money.

## THE MERCHANT SHIPPING ACT 1894
### (57 & 58 Vict., c. 60)

**513.   Power to pass over adjoining lands.**
   (1)   Whenever a vessel is wrecked, stranded, or in distress as aforesaid, all persons may, for the purpose of rendering assistance to the vessel, or of saving the lives of the shipwrecked persons, or of saving the cargo or apparel of the vessel, unless there is some public road equally convenient, pass and repass, either with or without carriages or horses, over any adjoining lands without being subject to interruption by the owner or occupier, so that they do as little damage as possible, and may also, on the like condition, deposit on those lands any cargo or other article recovered from the vessel.

   (2)   Any damage sustained by an owner or occupier in consequence of the exercise of the rights given by this section shall be a charge on the vessel, cargo, or articles in respect of or by which the damage is occasioned, and the amount payable in respect of the damage shall, in case of dispute, be determined and shall, in default of payment, by recoverable in the same manner as the amount of salvage is under this Part of this Act determined or recoverable.

**514.   Power of receiver to suppress plunder and disorder by force.**
   (1)   Whenever a vessel is wrecked, stranded, or in distress as aforesaid, and any person plunders, creates disorder, or obstructs the preservation of the vessel or of the shipwrecked persons or of the cargo or apparel of the vessel, the receiver may cause that person to be apprehended.

(2)    The receiver may use force for the suppression of any such plundering, disorder, or obstruction, and may command all Her Majesty's subjects to assist him in so using force.

(3)    If any person is killed, maimed, or hurt by reason of his resisting the receiver or any person acting under the orders of the receiver in the execution of the duties by this Part of this Act committed to the receiver, neither the receiver nor the person acting under his orders shall be liable to any punishment, or to pay any damages by reason of the person being so killed, maimed or hurt.

**566.    Appointment of receivers of wreck.**
. . . (in this Part of this Act referred to as a receiver) . . .

## THE MARINE INSURANCE ACT 1906
### (6 Edw. VII, c. 41)

**4.    Avoidance of wagering or gaming contracts.**

(1)    Every contract of marine insurance by way of gaming or wagering is void.

(2)    A contract of marine insurance is deemed to be a gaming or wagering contract—

(a)    where the assured has not an insurable interest as defined by this Act, and the contract is entered into with no expectation of acquiring such an interest; or

(b)    where the policy is made "interest or no interest", or "without further proof of interest than the policy itself", or "without benefit of salvage to the insurer", or subject to any other like term:

Provided that, where there is no possibility of salvage, a policy may be effected without benefit of salvage to the insurer.

**17.    Insurance is uberrimae fidei.**
A contract of marine insurance is a contract based upon the utmost good faith, and, if the utmost good faith be not observed by either party, the contract may be avoided by the other party.

**18.    Disclosure by assured.**

(1)    Subject to the provisions of this section, the assured must disclose to the insurer, before the contract is concluded, every material circumstance which is known to the assured, and the assured is deemed to know every circumstance which, in the ordinary course of business, ought to be known by him. If the assured fails to make such disclosure, the insurer may avoid the contract.

(2)    Every circumstance is material which would influence the judgment of a prudent insurer in fixing the premium, or determining whether he will take the risk.

(3)    In the absence of inquiry the following circumstances need not be disclosed, namely:

(a)    any circumstance which diminishes the risk;

(b)    any circumstance which is known or presumed to be known to the insurer. The insurer is presumed to know matters of common notoriety or knowledge, and matters which an insurer in the ordinary course of his business, as such, ought to know;

(c)    any circumstance as to which information is waived by the insurer;

(d)    any circumstance which it is superfluous to disclose by reason of any express or implied warranty.

(4)    Whether any particular circumstance, which is not disclosed, be material or not is, in each case, a question of fact.

**20.    Representations pending negotiation of contract.**

(1)    Every material representation made by the assured or his agent to the insurer during the negotiations for the contract, and before the contract is concluded, must be true. If it be untrue the insurer may avoid the contract.

(2)    A representation is material which would influence the judgment of a prudent insurer in fixing the premium, or determining whether he will take the risk.

(3)    A representation may be either a representation as to a matter of fact, or as to a matter of expectation or belief.

(4)    A representation as to a matter of fact is true, if it be substantially correct, that is to say, if the difference between what is represented and what is actually correct would not be considered material by a prudent insurer.

(5)    A representation as to a matter of expectation or belief is true if it be made in good faith.

(6)    A representation may be withdrawn or corrected before the contract is concluded.

(7)    Whether a particular representation be material or not is, in each case, a question of fact.

## 22.    Contract must be embodied in policy.

Subject to the provisions of any statute, a contract of marine insurance is inadmissible in evidence unless it is embodied in a marine policy in accordance with this Act. The policy may be executed and issued either at the time when the contract is concluded, or afterwards.

## 30.    Construction of terms in policy.

(1)    A policy may be in the form in the First Schedule to this Act.

(2)    Subject to the provisions of this Act, and unless the context of the policy otherwise requires, the terms and expressions mentioned in the First Schedule to this Act shall be construed as having the scope and meaning in that schedule assigned to them.

## 33.    Nature of warranty.

(1)    A warranty, in the following sections relating to warranties, means a promissory warranty, that is to say, a warranty by which the assured undertakes that some particular thing shall or shall not be done, or that some condition shall be fulfilled, or whereby he affirms or negatives the existence of a particular state of facts.

(2)    A warranty may be express or implied.

(3)    A warranty, as above defined, is a condition which must be exactly complied with, whether it be material to the risk or not. If it be not so complied with, then, subject to any express provision in the policy, the insurer is discharged from liability as from the date of the breach of warranty, but without prejudice to any liability incurred by him before that date.

## 34.    When breach of warranty excused.

(1)    Non-compliance with a warranty is excused when, by reason of a change of circumstances, the warranty ceases to be applicable to the circumstances of the contract, or when compliance with the warranty is rendered unlawful by any subsequent law.

(2)    Where a warranty is broken, the assured cannot avail himself of the defence that the breach has been remedied, and the warranty complied with, before loss.

(3)    A breach of warranty may be waived by the insurer.

## 35.    Express warranties.

(1)    An express warranty may be in any form of words from which the intention to warrant is to be inferred.

(2)    An express warranty must be included in, or written upon, the policy, or must be contained in some document incorporated by reference into the policy.

(3)    An express warranty does not exclude an implied warranty, unless it be inconsistent therewith.

### 48. Delay in voyage.

In the case of a voyage policy, the adventure insured must be prosecuted throughout its course with reasonable dispatch, and, if without lawful excuse it is not so prosecuted, the insurer is discharged from liability as from the time when the delay became unreasonable.

### 49. Excuses for deviation or delay.

(1)    Deviation or delay in prosecuting the voyage contemplated by the policy is excused—

(a)    where authorised by any special term in the policy; or

(b)    where caused by circumstances beyond the control of the master and his employer; or

(c)    where reasonably necessary in order to comply with an express or implied warranty; or

(d)    where reasonably necessary for the safety of the ship or subject-matter insured; or

(e)    for the purpose of saving human life, or aiding a ship in distress where human life may be in danger; or

(f)    where reasonably necessary for the purpose of obtaining medical or surgical aid for any person on board the ship; or

(g)    where caused by the barratrous conduct of the master or crew, if barratry be one of the perils insured against.

(2)    When the cause excusing the deviation or delay ceases to operate, the ship must resume her course, and prosecute her voyage, with reasonable dispatch.

### 87. Implied obligations varied by agreement or usage.

(1)    Where any right, duty, or liability would arise under a contract of marine insurance by implication of law, it may be negatived or varied by express agreement, or by usage, if the usage be such as to bind both parties to the contract.

## THE MARITIME CONVENTIONS ACT 1911
### (1 & 2 Geo. V, c. 57)

### 1. Rule as to division of loss.

(1)    Where, by the fault of two or more vessels, damage or loss is caused to one or more of those vessels, to their cargoes or freight, or to any property on board, the liability to make good the damage or loss shall be in proportion to the degree in which each vessel was in fault:

Provided that—

(a)    if, having regard to all the circumstances of the case, it is not possible to establish different degrees of fault, the liability shall be apportioned equally; and

(b)    nothing in this section shall operate so as to render any vessel liable for any loss or damage to which her fault has not contributed; and

(c)    nothing in this section shall affect the liability of any person under a contract of carriage or any contract, or shall be construed as imposing any liability upon any person from which he is exempted by any contract or by any provision of law, or as affecting the right of any person to limit his liability in the manner provided by law.

### 2. Damages for personal injuries.

Where loss of life or personal injuries are suffered by any person on board a vessel owing to the fault of that vessel and of any other vessel or vessels, the liability of the owners of the vessels shall be joint and several:

Provided that nothing in this section shall be construed as depriving any person of any right of defence on which, independently of this section, he might have relied in an action brought against him by the person injured, or any person or persons entitled to sue in respect of such loss of life, or shall affect the right of any person to limit his liability in cases to which this section relates in the manner provided by law.

### 3. Right of contribution.

(1)   Where loss of life or personal injuries are suffered by any person on board a vessel owing to the fault of that vessel and any other vessel or vessels, and a proportion of the damages is recovered against the owners of one of the vessels which exceeds the proportion in which she was in fault, they may recover by way of contribution the amount of the excess from the owners of the other vessel or vessels to the extent to which those vessels were respectively in fault:

Provided that no amount shall be so recovered which could not, by reason of any statutory or contractual limitation of, or exemption from, liability, or which could not for any other reason, have been recovered in the first instance as damages by the persons entitled to sue therefor.

### 4. Abolition of statutory presumptions of fault.

(2)   The failure of the master or person in charge of a vessel to comply with the provisions of section four hundred and twenty-two of the Merchant Shipping Act 1894 (which imposes a duty upon masters and persons in charge of vessels after a collision to stand by and assist the other vessel) shall not raise any presumption of fault that the collision was caused by his wrongful act, neglect, or default, and accordingly subsection (2) of that section shall be repealed.

### 6. General duty to render assistance to persons in danger at sea.

(1)   The master or person in charge of a vessel shall, so far as he can do so without serious danger to his own vessel, her crew and passengers (if any), render assistance to every person, even if such person be a subject of a foreign State at war with His Majesty, who is found at sea in danger of being lost, and, if he fails to do so, he shall be guilty of a misdemeanour.

(b)   Compliance by the master or person in charge of a vessel with the provisions of this section shall not affect his right or the right of any other person to salvage.

### 8. Limitation of actions.

No action shall be maintainable to enforce any claim or lien against a vessel or her owners in respect of any damage or loss to another vessel, her cargo or freight, or any property on board her, or damages for loss of life or personal injuries suffered by any person on board her, caused by the fault of the former vessel, whether such vessel be wholly or partly in fault, or in respect of any salvage services, unless proceedings therein are commenced within two years from the date when the damage or loss or injury was caused or the salvage services were rendered, and an action shall not be maintainable under this Act to enforce any contribution in respect of an overpaid proportion of any damages for loss of life or personal injuries unless proceedings therein are commenced within one year from the date of payment:

Provided that any court having jurisdiction to deal with an action to which this section relates may, in accordance with the rules of court, extend any such period, to such extent and on such conditions as it thinks fit, and shall, if satisfied that there has not during such period been any reasonable opportunity of arresting the defendant vessel within the jurisdiction of the court, or within the territorial waters of the country to which the plaintiff's ship belongs or in which the plaintiff resides or has his principal place of business, extend any such period to an extent sufficient to give such reasonable opportunity.

## THE LAW OF PROPERTY ACT 1925
### (15 & 16 Geo. V, c. 20)

**40.    Contracts for sale, etc., of land to be in writing.**

(1)    No action may be brought upon any contract for the sale or other disposition of land or any interest in land, unless the agreement upon which such action is brought, or some memorandum or note thereof, is in writing, and signed by the party to be charged or by some other person thereunto by him lawfully authorised.

(2)    This section applies to contracts whether made before or after the commencement of this Act and does not affect the law relating to part performance, or sales by the court.

**41.    Stipulations not of the essence of a contract.**

Stipulations in a contract, as to time or otherwise, which according to rules of equity are not deemed to be or to have become of the essence of the contract, are also construed and have effect at law in accordance with the same rules.

**49.    Applications to the court by vendor and purchaser.**

(2)    Where the court refuses to grant specific performance of a contract, or in any action for the return of a deposit, the court may, if it thinks fit, order the repayment of any deposit.

(3)    This section applies to a contract for the sale or exchange of any interest in land.

**56.    Persons taking who are not parties and as to indentures.**

(1)    A person may take an immediate or other interest in land or other property, or the benefit of any condition, right of entry, covenant or agreement over or respecting land or other property, although he may not be named as a party to the conveyance or other instrument.

**136.    Legal assignments of things in action.**

(1)    Any absolute assignment by writing under the hand of the assignor (not purporting to be by way of charge only) of any debt or other legal thing in action, of which express notice in writing has been given to the debtor, trustee or other person from whom the assignor would have been entitled to claim such debt or thing in action, is effectual in law (subject to equities having priority over the right of the assignee) to pass and transfer from the date of such notice—

    (a)    the legal right to such debt or thing in action;

    (b)    all legal and other remedies for the same; and

    (c)    the power to give a good discharge for the same without the concurrence of the assignor:

Provided that, if the debtor, trustee or other person liable in respect of such debt or thing in action has notice—

    (a)    that the assignment is disputed by the assignor or any person claiming under him; or

    (b)    of any other opposing or conflicting claims to such debt or thing in action;

he may, if he thinks fit, either call upon the persons making claim thereto to interplead concerning the same, or pay the debt or other thing in action into court under the provisions of the Trustee Act 1925.

(2)    This section does not affect the provisions of the Policies of Assurance Act 1867.

**146.    Restrictions on and relief against forfeiture of leases and underleases.**

(1)    A right of re-entry or forfeiture under any proviso or stipulation in a lease for a breach of any covenant or condition in the lease shall not be enforceable, by action or otherwise, unless and until the lessor serves on the lessee a notice—

    (a)    specifying the particular breach complained of; and

(b)    if the breach is capable of remedy, requiring the lessee to remedy the breach; and

(c)    in any case, requiring the lessee to make compensation in money for the breach;

and the lessee fails, within a reasonable time thereafter, to remedy the breach, if it is capable of remedy, and to make reasonable compensation in money, to the satisfaction of the lessor, for the breach.

(2)    Where a lessor is proceeding, by action or otherwise, to enforce such a right of re-entry or forfeiture, the lessee may, in the lessor's action, if any, or in any action brought by himself, apply to the court for relief; and the court may grant or refuse relief, as the court, having regard to the proceedings and conduct of the parties under the foregoing provisions of this section, and to all the other circumstances, thinks fit; and in case of relief may grant it on such terms, if any, as to costs, expenses, damages, compensation, penalty, or otherwise, including the granting of an injunction to restrain any like breach in the future, as the court, in the circumstances of each case, thinks fit.

(11)    This section does not, save as otherwise mentioned, affect the law relating to re-entry or forfeiture or relief in case of non-payment of rent.

(12)    This section has effect notwithstanding any stipulation to the contrary.

## 205.    General definitions.

(1)    In this Act unless the context otherwise requires, the following expressions have the meanings hereby assigned to them respectively, that is to say: . . .

(xvii)    "Notice" includes constructive notice;

(xx)    "Property" includes any thing in action, and any interest in real or personal property;

## THE RESERVOIRS (SAFETY PROVISIONS) ACT 1930
### (20 & 21 Geo. V, c. 51)

### 7.    Liability for damage and injury.

Where damage or injury is caused by the escape of water from a reservoir constructed after the commencement of this Act under statutory powers granted after the passing of this Act, the fact that the reservoir was so constructed shall not exonerate the undertakers from any indictment, action or other proceedings to which they would otherwise have been liable.

## THE THIRD PARTIES (RIGHTS AGAINST INSURERS) ACT 1930
### (20 & 21 Geo. V, c. 25)

### 1.    Rights of third parties against insurers on bankruptcy, etc., of the insured.

(1)    Where under any contract of insurance a person (hereinafter referred to as the insured) is insured against liabilities to third parties which he may incur, then

(a)    in the event of the insured becoming bankrupt or making a composition or arrangement with his creditors; or

(b)    in the case of the insured being a company, in the event of a winding-up order [or an administration order] being made, or a resolution for a voluntary winding-up being passed, with respect to the company, or of a receiver or manager of the company's business or undertaking being duly appointed, or of possession being taken, by or on behalf of the holders of any debentures secured by a floating charge, of any property comprised in or subject to that charge [or of a voluntary arrangement proposed for the purposes of Part I of the Insolvency Act 1986 being approved under that Part];

if, either before or after that event, any such liability as aforesaid is incurred by the insured, his rights against the insurer under the contract in respect of the liability shall, notwithstanding anything in any Act or rule of law to the contrary, be transferred to and vest in the third party to whom the liability was so incurred.

(2)    Where [the estate of any person falls to be administered in accordance with an order under section 421 of the Insolvency Act 1986], then, if any debt provable in bankruptcy is owing by the deceased in respect of a liability against which he was insured under a contract of insurance as being a liability to a third party, the deceased debtor's rights against the insurer under the contract in respect of that liability shall, notwithstanding anything in [any such order], be transferred to and vest in the person to whom the debt is owing.

(3)    In so far as any contract of insurance made after the commencement of this Act in respect of any liability of the insured to third parties purports, whether directly or indirectly, to avoid the contract or to alter the rights of the parties thereunder upon the happening to the insured of the events specified in paragraph (a) or paragraph (b) of subsection (1) of this section or upon the [estate of any person falling to be administered in accordance with an order under section 421 of the Insolvency Act 1986], the contract shall be of no effect.

(4)    Upon a transfer under subsection (1) or subsection (2) of this section, the insurer shall, subject to the provisions of section three of this Act, be under the same liability to the third party as he would have been under to the insured, but—

(a)    if the liability of the insurer to the insured exceeds the liability of the insured to the third party, nothing in this Act shall affect the rights of the insured against the insurer in respect of the excess; and

(b)    if the liability of the insurer to the insured is less than the liability of the insured to the third party, nothing in this Act shall affect the rights of the third party against the insured in respect of the balance.

(5)    For the purposes of this Act, the expression "liabilities to third parties", in relation to a person insured under any contract of insurance, shall not include any liability of that person in the capacity of insurer under some other contract of insurance.

(6)    This Act shall not apply—

(a)    where a company is wound up voluntarily merely for the purposes of reconstruction or of amalgamation with another company; or

(b)    to any case to which subsections (1) and (2) of section seven of the Workmen's Compensation Act 1925 applies.

## 2.    Duty to give necessary information to third parties.

(1)    In the event of any person becoming bankrupt or making a composition or arrangement with his creditors, or in the event of [the estate of any person falling to be administered in accordance with an order under section 421 of the Insolvency Act 1986], or in the event of a winding-up order [or an administration order] being made, or a resolution for a voluntary winding-up being passed, with respect to any company or of a receiver or manager of the company's business or undertaking being duly appointed or of possession being taken by or on behalf of the holders of any debentures secured by a floating charge of any property comprised in or subject to the charge it shall be the duty of the bankrupt, debtor, personal representative of the deceased debtor or company, and, as the case may be, of the trustee in bankruptcy, trustee, liquidator, [administator], receiver, or manager, or person in possession of the property to give at the request of any person claiming that the bankrupt, debtor, deceased debtor, or company is under a liability to him such information as may be reasonably required by him for the purpose of ascertaining whether any rights have been transferred to and vested in him by this Act and for the purpose of enforcing such rights, if any, and any contract of insurance, in so far as it purports, whether directly or indirectly, to avoid the contract or to alter the rights of the parties thereunder upon the giving of any such information in the events aforesaid or otherwise to prohibit or prevent the giving thereof in the said events shall be of no effect.

[(1A) The reference in subsection (1) of this section to a trustee includes a reference to the supervisor of a voluntary arrangement proposed for the purposes of, and approved under, Part I or Part VIII of the Insolvency Act 1986.]

(2)     If the information given to any person in pursuance of subsection (1) of this section discloses reasonable ground for supposing that there have or may have been transferred to him under this Act rights against any particular insurer, that insurer shall be subject to the same duty as is imposed by the said subsection on the persons therein mentioned.

(3)     The duty to give information imposed by this section shall include a duty to allow all contracts of insurance, receipts for premiums, and other relevant documents in the possession or power of the person on whom the duty is so imposed to be inspected and copies thereof to be taken.

## 3.    Settlement between insurers and insured persons.

Where the insured has become bankrupt or where in the case of the insured being a company, a winding-up order [or an administration order] has been made or a resolution for a voluntary winding-up has been passed, with respect to the company, no agreement made between the insurer and the insured after liability has been incurred to a third party and after the commencement of the bankruptcy or winding-up [or the day of the administration order], as the case may be, nor any waiver, assignment, or other disposition made by, or payment made to the insured after the commencement [or day] aforesaid shall be effective to defeat or affect the rights transferred to the third party under this Act, but those rights shall be the same as if no such agreement, waiver, assignment, disposition or payment had been made.

## THE LAW REFORM (MISCELLANEOUS PROVISIONS) ACT 1934
### (24 & 25 Geo. V, c. 41)

## 1.    Effect of death on certain causes of action.

(1)     Subject to the provisions of this section, on the death of any person after the commencement of this Act all causes of action subsisting against or vested in him shall survive against, or, as the case may be, for the benefit of, his estate. Provided that this subsection shall not apply to causes of action for defamation [. . .]

[(1A) The right of a person to claim under section 1A of the Fatal Accidents Act 1976 (bereavement) shall not survive for the benefit of his estate on his death.]

(2)     Where a cause of action survives as aforesaid for the benefit of the estate of a deceased person, the damages recoverable for the benefit of the estate of that person:—

     [(a)    shall not include—

          (i)       any exemplary damages;

          (ii)      any damages for loss of income in respect of any period after that person's death;]

     (b)    [. . .]

     (c)    where the death of that person has been caused by the act or omission which gives rise to the cause of action, shall be calculated without reference to any loss or gain to his estate consequent on his death, except that a sum in respect of funeral expenses may be included.

(4)     Where damage has been suffered by reason of any act or omission in respect of which a cause of action would have subsisted against any person if that person had not died before or at the same time as the damage was suffered, there shall be deemed, for the purposes of this Act, to have been subsisting against him before his death such cause of action in respect of that act or omission as would have subsisted if he had died after the damage was suffered.

(5)   The rights conferred by this Act for the benefit of the estates of deceased persons shall be in addition to and not in derogation of any rights conferred on the dependants of deceased persons by [the Fatal Accidents Act 1976 . . .] and so much of this Act as relates to causes of action against the estates of deceased persons shall apply in relation to causes of action under the said Act as it applies in relation to other causes of action not expressly excepted from the operation of subsection (1) of this section.

(6)   In the event of the insolvency of an estate against which proceedings are maintainable by virtue of this section, any liability in respect of the cause of action in respect of which the proceedings are maintainable shall be deemed to be a debt provable in the administration of the estate, notwithstanding that it is a demand in the nature of unliquidated damages arising otherwise than by a contract, promise or breach of trust.

## THE LAW REFORM (MARRIED WOMEN AND TORTFEASORS) ACT 1935
### (25 & 26 Geo. V, c. 30)

**3.   Abolition of husband's liability for wife's torts and ante-nuptial contracts, debts and obligations.**
Subject to the provisions of this Part of this Act, the husband of a married woman shall not, by reason only of his being her husband, be liable—
(a)   in respect of any tort committed by her whether before or after the marriage, or in respect of any contract entered into, or debt or obligation incurred, by her before the marriage; or
(b)   to be sued, or made a party to any legal proceeding brought, in respect of any such tort, contract, debt, or obligation.

**4.   Savings.**
(2)   For the avoidance of doubt it is hereby declared that nothing in this Part of this Act—
(a)   renders the husband of a married woman liable in respect of any contract entered into, or debt or obligation incurred, by her after the marriage in respect of which he would not have been liable if this Act had not been passed;
(b)   exempts the husband of a married woman from liability in respect of any contract entered into, or debt or obligation (not being a debt or obligation arising out of a commission of a tort) incurred, by her after the marriage in respect of which he would have been liable if this Act had not been passed;
(c)   prevents a husband and wife from acquiring, holding, and disposing of, any property jointly or as tenants in common, or from rendering themselves, or being rendered, jointly liable in respect of any tort, contract, debt or obligation, and of suing and being sued either in tort or in contract or otherwise, in like manner as if they were not married;
(d)   prevents the exercise of any joint power given to a husband and wife.

## THE LAW REFORM (FRUSTRATED CONTRACTS) ACT 1943
### (6 & 7 Geo. VI, c. 40)

**1.   Adjustment of rights and liabilities of parties to frustrated contracts.**
(1)   Where a contract governed by English law has become impossible of performance or been otherwise frustrated, and the parties thereto have for that reason been discharged from the further performance of the contract, the following provisions of this section shall, subject to the provisions of section two of this Act, have effect in relation thereto.
(2)   All sums paid or payable to any party in pursuance of the contract before the time when the parties were so discharged (in this Act referred to as "the time of discharge") shall, in the case of sums so paid, be recoverable from him as money received by him for the

use of the party by whom the sums were paid, and, in the case of sums so payable, cease to be so payable:

Provided that, if the party to whom the sums were so paid or payable incurred expenses before the time of discharge in, or for the purpose of, the performance of the contract, the court may, if it considers it just to do so having regard to all the circumstances of the case, allow him to retain or, as the case may be, recover the whole or any part of the sums so paid or payable, not being an amount in excess of the expenses so incurred.

(3)    Where any party to the contract has, by reason of anything done by any other party thereto in, or for the purpose of, the performance of the contract, obtained a valuable benefit (other than a payment of money to which the last foregoing subsection applies) before the time of discharge there shall be recoverable from him by the said other party such sum (if any), not exceeding the value of the said benefit to the party obtaining it, as the court considers just, having regard to all the circumstances of the case and, in particular,—

(a)    the amount of any expenses incurred before the time of discharge by the benefited party in, or for the purpose of, the performance of the contract, including any sums paid or payable by him to any other party in pursuance of the contract and retained or recoverable by that party under the last foregoing subsection, and

(b)    the effect, in relation to the said benefit, of the circumstances giving rise to the frustration of the contract.

(4)    In estimating, for the purposes of the foregoing provisions of this section, the amount of any expenses incurred by any party to the contract, the court may, without prejudice to the generality of the said provisions, include such sum as appears to be reasonable in respect of overhead expenses and in respect of any work or services performed personally by the said party.

(5)    In considering whether any sum ought to be recovered or retained under the foregoing provisions of this section by any party to the contract, the court shall not take into account any sums which have, by reason of the circumstances giving rise to the frustration of the contract, become payable to that party under any contract of insurance unless there was an obligation to insure imposed by an express term of the frustrated contract or by or under any enactment.

(6)    Where any person has assumed obligations under the contract in consideration of the conferring of a benefit by any other party to the contract upon any other person, whether a party to the contract or not, the court may, if in all the circumstances of the case it considers it just to do so, treat for the purposes of subsection (3) of this section any benefit so conferred as a benefit obtained by the person who has assumed the obligations as aforesaid.

## 2.    Provision as to application of this Act.

(1)    This Act shall apply to contracts, whether made before or after the commencement of this Act, as respects which the time of discharge is on or after the first day of July, nineteen hundred and forty-three, but not to contracts as respects which the time of discharge is before the said date.

(2)    This Act shall apply to contracts to which the Crown is a party in like manner as to contracts between subjects.

(3)    Where any contract to which this Act applies contains any provision which, upon the true construction of the contract, is intended to have effect in the event of circumstances arising which operate, or would but for the said provision operate, to frustrate the contract, or is intended to have effect whether such circumstances arise or not, the court shall give effect to the said provision and shall only give effect to the foregoing section of this Act to such extent, if any, as appears to the court to be consistent with the said provision.

(4)    Where it appears to the court that a part of any contract to which this Act applies can properly be severed from the remainder of the contract, being a part wholly performed

before the time of discharge, or so performed except for the payment in respect of that part of the contract of sums which are or can be ascertained under the contract, the court shall treat that part of the contract as if it were a separate contract and had not been frustrated and shall treat the foregoing section of this Act as only applicable to the remainder of that contract.

(5)    This Act shall not apply—

(a)    to any charterparty, except a time charterparty or a charterparty by way of demise, or to any contract (other than a charterparty) for the carriage of goods by sea; or

(b)    to any contract of insurance, save as is provided by subsection (5) of the foregoing section; or

(c)    to any contract to which [section 7 of the Sale of Goods Act 1979] (which avoids contracts for the sale of specific goods which perish before the risk has passed to the buyer) applies, or to any other contract for the sale, or for the sale and delivery, of specific goods, where the contract is frustrated by reason of the fact that the goods have perished.

### 3.    Short title and interpretation.

(1)    This Act may be cited as the Law Reform (Frustrated Contracts) Act, 1943.

(2)    In this Act the expression "court" means, in relation to any matter, the court or arbitrator by or before whom the matter falls to be determined.

## THE LAW REFORM (CONTRIBUTORY NEGLIGENCE) ACT 1945
### (8 & 9 Geo. VI, c. 28)

### 1.    Apportionment of liability in case of contributory negligence.

(1)    Where any person suffers damage as the result partly of his own fault and partly of the fault of any other person or persons, a claim in respect of that damage shall not be defeated by reason of the fault of the person suffering the damage, but the damages recoverable in respect thereof shall be reduced to such extent as the court thinks just and equitable having regard to the claimant's share in the responsibility of the damage:

Provided that—

(a)    this subsection shall not operate to defeat any defence arising under a contract;

(b)    where any contract or enactment providing for the limitation of liability is applicable to the claim, the amount of damages recoverable by the claimant by virtue of this subsection shall not exceed the maximum limit so applicable.

(2)    Where damages are recoverable by any person by virtue of the foregoing subsection subject to such reduction as is therein mentioned, the court shall find and record the total damages which would have been recoverable if the claimant had not been at fault.

(5)    Where, in any case to which subsection (1) of this section applies, one of the persons at fault avoids liability to any other such person or his personal representative by pleading the Limitation Act, 1939, or any other enactment limiting the time within which proceedings may be taken, he shall not be entitled to recover any damages [. . .] from that other person or representative by virtue of the said subsection.

(6)    Where any case to which subsection (1) of this section applies is tried with a jury, the jury shall determine the total damages which would have been recoverable if the claimant had not been at fault and the extent to which those damages are to be reduced.

### 4.    Interpretation.

The following expressions have the meanings hereby respectively assigned to them, that is to say—

"court" means, in relation to any claim, the court or arbitrator by or before whom the claim falls to be determined;

"damage" includes loss of life and personal injury; [. . .]

"fault" means negligence, breach of statutory duty or other act or omission which gives rise to liability in tort or would, apart from this Act, give rise to the defence of contributory negligence.

## THE CROWN PROCEEDINGS ACT 1947
### (10 & 11 Geo. VI, c. 44)

**2.   Liability of the Crown in tort.**

(1)   Subject to the provisions of this Act, the Crown shall be subject to all those liabilities in tort to which, if it were a private person of full age and capacity, it would be subject:—

(a)   in respect of torts committed by its servants or agents;

(b)   in respect of any breach of those duties which a person owes to his servants or agents at common law by reason of being their employer; and

(c)   in respect of any breach of the duties attaching at common law to the ownership, occupation, possession or control of property:

Provided that no proceedings shall lie against the Crown by virtue of paragraph (a) of this subsection in respect of any act or omission of a servant or agent of the Crown unless the act or omission would apart from the provisions of this Act have given rise to a cause of action in tort against that servant or agent or his estate.

(2)   Where the Crown is bound by a statutory duty which is binding also upon persons other than the Crown and its officers, then, subject to the provisions of this Act, the Crown shall, in respect of a failure to comply with that duty, be subject to all those liabilities in tort (if any) to which it would be so subject if it were a private person of full age and capacity.

## THE LAW REFORM (PERSONAL INJURIES) ACT 1948
### (11 & 12 Geo. VI, c. 41)

**1.   Common employment.**

(1)   It shall not be a defence to an employer who is sued in respect of personal injuries caused by the negligence of a person employed by him, that that person was at the time the injuries were caused in common employment with the person injured.

(3)   Any provision contained in a contract of service or apprenticeship, or in an agreement collateral thereto, (including a contract or agreement entered into before the commencement of this Act) shall be void in so far as it would have the effect of excluding or limiting any liability of the employer in respect of personal injuries caused to the person employed or apprenticed by the negligence of persons in common employment with him.

**2.   Measure of damages.**

(1)   In an action for damages for personal injuries (including any such action arising out of a contract), there shall in assessing those damages be taken into account, against any loss of earnings or profits which has accrued or probably will accrue to the injured person from the injuries, one half of the value of any rights which have accrued or probably will accrue to him therefrom in respect of [any of the following benefits under [the Social Security Act 1975, the Social Security Pensions Act 1975 or any corresponding provisions in force in Northern Ireland,] namely sickness benefit, invalidity benefit, non-contributory invalidity pension, injury benefit, disablement benefit], for the five years beginning with the time when the cause of action accrued.

This subsection shall not be taken as requiring both the gross amount of the damages before taking into account the said rights and the net amount after taking them into account to be found separately.

(2)   In determining the value of the said rights there shall be disregarded any increase of an industrial disablement pension in respect of the need of constant attendance.

(3) The reference in subsection (1) of this section to assessing the damages for personal injuries shall, in cases where the damages otherwise recoverable are subject to reduction under the law relating to contributory negligence or are limited by or under any Act or by contract, be taken as referring to the total damages which would have been recoverable apart from the reduction or limitation.

(4) In an action for damages for personal injuries (including any such action arising out of a contract), there shall be disregarded, in determining the reasonableness of any expenses, the possibility of avoiding those expenses or part of them by taking advantage of facilities available under the National Health Service Act, 1977, or the National Health Service (Scotland) Act, 1978, or of any corresponding facilities in Northern Ireland.

[(6) For the purposes of this section disablement benefit in the form of a gratuity is to be treated as benefit for the period taken into account by the assessment of the extent of the disablement in respect of which it is payable.]

### 3. Definition of "personal injury".
In this Act the expression "personal injury" includes any disease and any impairment of a person's physical or mental condition, and the expression "injured" shall be construed accordingly.

## THE NATIONAL PARKS AND ACCESS TO THE COUNTRYSIDE ACT 1949
### (12, 13 & 14 Geo. VI, c. 97)

### 60. Rights of public where access agreement or order in force.
(1) Subject to the following provisions of this Part of this Act, where an access agreement or order is in force as respects any land a person who enters upon land comprised in the agreement or order for the purpose of open-air recreation without breaking or damaging any wall, fence, hedge or gate, or who is on such land for that purpose after having so entered thereon, shall not be treated as a trespasser on that land or incur any other liability by reason only of so entering or being on the land:

Provided that this subsection shall not apply to land which for the time being is excepted land as hereinafter defined.

(2) Nothing in the provisions of the last foregoing subsection shall entitle a person to enter or be on any land, or to do anything thereon, in contravention of any prohibition contained in or having effect under any enactment.

(3) An access agreement or order may specify or provide for imposing restrictions subject to which persons may enter or be upon land by virtue of subsection (1) of this section, including in particular, but without prejudice to the generality of this subsection, restrictions excluding the land or any part thereof at particular times from the operation of the said subsection (1); and that subsection shall not apply to any person entering or being on the land in contravention of any such restriction or failing to comply therewith while he is on the land.

### 66. Effect of access agreement or order on rights and liabilities of owners.
(1) A person interested in any land comprised in an access agreement or order, not being excepted land, shall not carry out any work thereon whereby the area to which the public are able to have access by virtue of the agreement or order is substantially reduced:

Provided that nothing in this subsection shall affect the doing of anything whereby any land becomes expected land.

(2) The operation of subsection (1) of section sixty of this Act in relation to any land shall not increase the liability, under any enactment not contained in this Act or under any rule of law, of a person interested in that land or adjoining land in respect of the state thereof or of things done or omitted thereon.

## THE RESERVE AND AUXILIARY FORCES (PROTECTION OF CIVIL INTERESTS) ACT 1951
### (14 & 15 Geo. VI, c. 65)

### 13. Effect of failure to observe restrictions under Part I.

(2)  In any action for damages for conversion or other proceedings which lie by virtue of any such omission, failure or contravention, the court may take account of the conduct of the defendant with a view, if the court thinks fit, to awarding exemplary damages in respect of the wrong sustained by the plaintiff.

## THE DEFAMATION ACT 1952
### (15 & 16 Geo. VI & 1 Eliz. II, c. 66)

### 1. Broadcast statements.

For the purposes of this law of libel and slander, the broadcasting of words by means of wireless telegraphy shall be treated as publication in permanent form.

### 2. Slander affecting official, professional or business reputation.

In an action for slander in respect of words calculated to disparage the plaintiff in an office, profession, calling, trade or business held or carried on by him at the time of the publication, it shall not be necessary to allege or prove special damage, whether or not the words are spoken of the plaintiff in the way of his office, profession, calling, trade or business.

### 3. Slander of title, etc.

(1)  In an action for slander of title, slander of goods or other malicious falsehood, it shall not be necessary to allege or prove special damage—

    (a)  if the words upon which the action is founded are calculated to cause pecuniary damage to the plaintiff and are published in writing or other permanent form; or

    (b)  if the said words are calculated to cause pecuniary damage to the plaintiff in respect of any office, profession, calling, trade or business held or carried on by him at the time of the publication.

(2)  Section one of this Act shall apply for the purposes of this section as it applies for the purposes of the law of libel and slander.

### 4. Unintentional defamation.

(1)  A person who has published words alleged to be defamatory of another person may, if he claims that the words were published by him innocently in relation to that other person, make an offer of amends under this section; and in any such case—

    (a)  if the offer is accepted by the party aggrieved and is duly performed, no proceedings for libel or slander shall be taken or continued by that party against the person making the offer in respect of the publication in question (but without prejudice to any cause of action against any other person jointly responsible for that publication);

    (b)  if the offer is not accepted by the party aggrieved, then, except as otherwise provided by this section, it shall be a defence, in any proceedings by him for libel or slander against the person making the offer in respect of the publication in question, to prove that the words complained of were published by the defendant innocently in relation to the plaintiff and that the offer was made as soon as practicable after the defendant received notice that they were or might be defamatory of the plaintiff, and has not been withdrawn.

(2)  An offer of amends under this section must be expressed to be made for the purposes of this section, and must be accompanied by an affidavit specifying the facts relied upon by the person making it to show that the words in question were published by him innocently in relation to the party aggrieved; and for the purposes of a defence under paragraph (b) of subsection (1) of this section no evidence, other than evidence of facts

specified in the affidavit, shall be admissible on behalf of that person to prove that the words were so published.

(3)   An offer of amends under this section shall be understood to mean an offer—

(a)   in any case, to publish or join in the publication of a suitable correction of the words complained of, and a sufficient apology to the party aggrieved in respect of those words;

(b)   where copies of a document or record containing the said words have been distributed by or with the knowledge of the person making the offer, to take such steps as are reasonably practicable on his part for notifying persons to whom copies have been so distributed that the words are alleged to be defamatory of the party aggrieved.

(4)   Where an offer of amends under this section is accepted by the party aggrieved—

(a)   any question as to the steps to be taken in fulfilment of the offer as so accepted shall in default of agreement between the parties by referred to and determined by the High Court, whose decision thereon shall be final;

(b)   the power of the court to make orders as to costs in proceedings by the party aggrieved against the person making the offer in respect of the publication in question, or in proceedings in respect of the offer under paragraph (a) of this subsection, shall include power to order the payment by the person making the offer to the party aggrieved of costs on an indemnity basis and any expenses reasonably incurred or to be incurred by that party in consequence of the publication in question;

and if no such proceedings as aforesaid are taken, the High Court may, upon application made by the party aggrieved, make any such order for the payment of such costs and expenses as aforesaid as could be made in such proceedings.

(5)   For the purposes of this section words shall be treated as published by one person (in this subsection referred to as the publisher) innocently in relation to another person if and only if the following conditions are satisfied, that is to say—

(a)   that the publisher did not intend to publish them of and concerning that other person, and did not know of circumstances by virtue of which they might be understood to refer to him; or

(b)   that the words were not defamatory on the face of them, and the publisher did not know of circumstances by virtue of which they might be understood to be defamatory of that other person.

and in either case that the publisher exercised all reasonable care in relation to the publication; and any reference in this subsection to the publisher shall be construed as including a reference to any servant or agent of his who was concerned with the contents of the publication.

(6)   Paragraph (b) of subsection (1) of this section shall not apply in relation to the publication by any person of words of which he is not the author unless he proves that the words were written by the author without malice.

## 5.   Justification.

In an action for libel or slander in respect of words containing two or more distinct charges against the plaintiff, a defence of justification shall not fail by reason only that the truth of every charge is not proved if the words not proved to be true do not materially injure the plaintiff's reputation having regard to the truth of the remaining charges.

## 6.   Fair comment.

In an action for libel or slander in respect of words consisting partly of allegations of fact and partly of expression of opinion, a defence of fair comment shall not fail by reason only that the truth of every allegation or fact is not proved if the expression of opinion is fair comment having regard to such of the facts alleged or referred to in the words complained of as are proved.

**7.    Qualified privilege of newspapers.**

(1)    Subject to the provisions of this section, the publication in a newspaper of any such report or other matter as is mentioned in the Schedule to this Act shall be privileged unless the publication is proved to be made with malice.

(2)    In an action for libel in respect of the publication of any such report or matter as is mentioned in Part II of the Schedule to this Act, the provisions of this section shall not be a defence if it is proved that the defendant has been requested by the plaintiff to publish in the newspaper in which the original publication was made a reasonable letter or statement by way of explanation or contradiction, and has refused or neglected to do so, or has done so in a manner not adequate or not reasonable having regard to all the circumstances.

(3)    Nothing in this section shall be construed as protecting the publication of any matter the publication of which is prohibited by law, or of any matter which is not of public concern and the publication of which is not for the public benefit.

(4)    Nothing in this section shall be construed as limiting or abridging any privilege subsisting (otherwise than by virtue of section four of the Law of Libel Amendment Act, 1888) immediately before the commencement of this Act.

(5)    In this section the expression "newspaper" means any paper containing public news or observations thereon, or consisting wholly or mainly of advertisements, which is printed for sale and is published in the United Kingdom either periodically or in parts or numbers at intervals not exceeding thirty-six days.

**8.    Extent of Law of Libel Amendment Act 1888, s. 3.**

Section three of the Law of Libel Amendment Act, 1888 (which relates to contemporary reports of proceedings before courts exercising judicial authority) shall apply and apply only to courts exercising judicial authority within the United Kingdom.

**9.    Extension of certain defences to broadcasting.**

(1)    Section three of the Parliamentary Papers Act, 1840 (which confers protection in respect of proceedings for printing extracts from or abstracts of parliamentary papers) shall have effect as if the reference to printing included a reference to broadcasting by means of wireless telegraphy.

(2)    Section seven of this Act and section three of the Law of Libel Amendment Act, 1888, as amended by this Act shall apply in relation to reports or matters broadcast by means of wireless telegraphy as part of any programme or service provided by means of a broadcasting station within the United Kingdom, and in relation to any broadcasting by means of wireless telegraphy of any such report or matter, as they apply in relation to reports and matters published in a newspaper and to publication in a newspaper; and subsection (2) of the said section seven shall have effect, in relation to any such broadcasting, as if for the words "in the newspaper in which" there were substituted the words "in the manner in which".

(3)    In this section "broadcasting station" means any station in respect of which a licence granted by the Postmaster General under the enactments relating to wireless telegraphy is in force, being a licence which (by whatever form of words) authorises the use of the station for the purpose of providing broadcasting services for general reception.

**10.    Limitation on privilege at elections.**

A defamatory statement published by or on behalf of a candidate in any election to local government authority or to Parliament shall not be deemed to be published on a privileged occasion on the ground that it is material to a question in issue in the election, whether or not the person by whom it is published is qualified to vote at the election.

**11.    Agreements for indemnity.**

An agreement for indemnifying any person against civil liability for libel in respect of the publication of any matter shall not be unlawful unless at the time of the publication that person knows that the matter is defamatory, and does not reasonably believe that there is a good defence to any action brought upon it.

### 12. Evidence of other damages recovered by plaintiff.

In any action for libel or slander the defendant may give evidence in mitigation of damages that the plaintiff has recovered damages, or has brought actions for damages, for libel or slander in respect of the publication of words to the same effect as the words on which the action is founded, or has received or agreed to receive compensation in respect of any such publication.

### 13. Consolidation of actions for slander etc.

Section five of the Law of Libel Amendment Act 1888 (which provides for the consolidation, on the application of the defendants, of two or more actions for libel by the same plaintiff) shall apply to actions for slander of title, slander of goods or other malicious falsehood as it applies to actions for libel; and references in that section to the same, or substantially the same, libel shall be construed accordingly.

### 16. Interpretation.

(1)   Any reference in this Act to words shall be construed as including a reference to pictures, visual images, gestures and other methods of signifying meaning.

### 17. Proceedings affected and savings.

(2)   Nothing in this Act affects the law relating to criminal libel.

SCHEDULE
NEWSPAPER STATEMENTS HAVING QUALIFIED PRIVILEGE
PART I
STATEMENTS PRIVILEGED WITHOUT EXPLANATION
OR CONTRADICTION

1. A fair and accurate report of any proceedings in public of the legislature of any part of Her Majesty's dominions outside Great Britain.

2. A fair and accurate report of any proceedings in public of an international organisation in which the United Kingdom or Her Majesty's Government in the United Kingdom is a member, or of any international conference to which that government sends a representative.

3. A fair and accurate report of any proceedings in public of an international court.

4. A fair and accurate report of any proceedings before a court exercising jurisdiction throughout any part of Her Majesty's dominions outside the United Kingdom, or of any proceedings before a court-martial held outside the United Kingdom under the Naval Discipline Act, [the Army Act 1955 or the Air Force Act 1955].

5. A fair and accurate report of any proceedings in public of a body or person appointed to hold a public inquiry by the government or legislature of any part of Her Majesty's dominions outside the United Kingdom.

6. A fair and accurate copy of or extract from any register kept in pursuance of any Act of Parliament which is open to inspection by the public, or of any other document which is required by the law of any part of the United Kingdom to be open inspection by the public.

7. A notice or advertisement published by or on the authority of any court within the United Kingdom or any judge or officer of such a court.

PART II
STATEMENTS PRIVILEGED SUBJECT TO EXPLANATION OR
CONTRADICTION

8. A fair and accurate report of the findings or decision of any of the following associations, or of any committee or governing body thereof, that is to say—

(a)    an association formed in the United Kingdom for the purpose of promoting or encouraging the exercise of or interest in any art, science, religion or learning, and empowered by its constitution to exercise control over to adjudicate upon matters of interest or concern to the association, or the actions or conduct of any persons subject to such control or adjudication:

(b)    an association formed in the United Kingdom for the purpose of promoting or safeguarding the interests of any trade, business, industry or profession, or of the persons carrying on or engaged in any trade, business, industry or profession, and empowered by its constitution to exercise control over or adjudicate upon matters connected with the trade, business, industry or profession, or the actions or conduct of those persons:

(c)    an association formed in the United Kingdom for the purpose of promoting or safeguarding the interests of any game, sport or pastime to the playing or exercise of which members of the public are invited or admitted, and empowered by its constitution to exercise control over or adjudicate upon, persons connected with or taking part in the game, sport or pastime,

being a finding or decision relating to a person who is a member of or is subject by virtue of any contract to the control of the association.

9. A fair and accurate report of the proceedings at any public meeting held in the United Kingdom, that is to say, a meeting bona fide and lawfully held for a lawful purpose and for the furtherance or discussion of any matter of public concern, whether the admission to the meeting is general or restricted.

10. A fair and accurate report of the proceedings at any meeting or sitting in any part of the United Kingdom of—

(a)    any local authority or committee of a local authority or local authorities;

(b)    any justice or justices of the peace acting otherwise than as a court exercising judicial authority;

(c)    any commission, tribunal, committee or person appointed for the purposes of any inquiry by Act of Parliament, by Her Majesty or by a Minister of the Crown;

(d)    any person appointed by a local authority to hold a local inquiry in pursuance of any Act of Parliament;

(e)    any other tribunal, board, committee or body constituted by or under, and exercising functions under, an Act of Parliament,

not being a meeting or sitting admission to which is denied to representatives of newspapers and other members of the public.

11. A fair and accurate report of the proceedings at a general meeting of any company or association constituted, registered or certified by or under any Act of Parliament or incorporated by Royal Charter, not being a private company within the meaning of the Companies Act, 1948.

12. A copy or fair and accurate report or summary of any notice or other matter issued for the information of the public by or on behalf of any government department, officer of state, local authority or chief officer of police.

## THE OCCUPIERS' LIABILITY ACT 1957
### (5 & 6 Eliz. II, c. 31)

**1.    Preliminary.**

(1)    The rules enacted by the two next following sections shall have effect, in place of the rules of the common law, to regulate the duty which an occupier of premises owes to his visitors in respect of dangers due to the state of the premises or to things done or omitted to be done on them.

(2)    The rules so enacted shall regulate the nature of the duty imposed by law in consequence of a person's occupation or control of premises and of any invitation or permission he gives (or is to be treated as giving) to another to enter or use the premises, but

they shall not alter the rules of the common law as to the persons on whom a duty is so imposed or to whom it is owed; and accordingly for the purpose of the rules so enacted the persons who are to be treated as an occupier and as his visitors are the same (subject to subsection (4) of this section) as the persons who would at common law be treated as an occupier and as his invitees or licensees.

(3)    The rules so enacted in relation to an occupier of premises and his visitors shall also apply, in like manner and to the like extent as the principles applicable at common law to an occupier of premises and his invitees or licensees would apply, to regulate—

(a)    the obligations of a person occupying or having control over any fixed or moveable structure, including any vessel, vehicle or aircraft; and

(b)    the obligations of a person occupying or having control over any premises or structure in respect of damage to property, including the property of persons who are not themselves his visitors.

(4)    A person entering any premises in exercise of rights conferred by virtue of an access agreement or order under the National Parks and Access to the Countryside Act, 1949, is not, for the purposes of this Act, a visitor of the occupier of those premises.

## 2.    Extent of occupier's ordinary duty.

(1)    An occupier of premises owes the same duty, the 'common duty of care', to all his visitors, except in so far as he is free to and does extend, restrict, modify or exclude his duty to any visitor or visitors by agreement or otherwise.

(2)    The common duty of care is a duty to take such care as in all the circumstances of the case is reasonable to see that the visitor will be reasonably safe in using the premises for the purposes for which he is invited or permitted by the occupier to be there.

(3)    The circumstances relevant for the present purposes include the degree of care, and of want of care, which would ordinarily be looked for in such a visitor, so that (for example) in proper cases—

(a)    an occupier must be prepared for children to be less careful than adults; and

(b)    an occupier may expect that a person, in the exercise of his calling, will appreciate and guard against any special risks ordinarily incident to it, so far as the occupier leaves him free to do so.

(4)    In determining whether the occupier of premises has discharged the common duty of care to a visitor, regard is to be had to all the circumstances, so that (for example)—

(a)    where damage is caused to a visitor by a danger of which he had been warned by the occupier, the warning is not to be treated without more as absolving the occupier from liability, unless in all the circumstances it was enough to enable the visitor to be reasonably safe; and

(b)    where damage is caused to a visitor by a danger due to the faulty execution of any work of construction, maintenance or repair by an independent contractor employed by the occupier, the occupier is not to be treated without more as answerable for the danger if in all the circumstances he had acted reasonably in entrusting the work to an independent contractor and had taken such steps (if any) as he reasonably ought in order to satisfy himself that the contractor was competent and that the work had been properly done.

(5)    The common duty of care does not impose on an occupier any obligation to a visitor in respect of risks willingly accepted as his by the visitor (the question whether a risk was so accepted to be decided on the same principles as in other cases in which one person owes a duty of care to another).

(6)    For the purposes of this section, persons who enter premises for any purpose in the exercise of a right conferred by law are to be treated as permitted by the occupier to be there for that purpose, whether they in fact have his permission or not.

## 3.    Effect of contract on occupier's liability to third party.

(1)    Where an occupier of premises is bound by contract to permit persons who are strangers to the contract to enter or use the premises, the duty of care which he owes to

them as his visitors cannot be restricted or excluded by that contract, but (subject to any provision of the contract to the contrary) shall include the duty to perform his obligations under the contract, whether undertaken for their protection or not, in so far as those obligations go beyond the obligations otherwise involved in that duty.

(2)    A contract shall not by virtue of this section have the effect, unless it expressly so provides, of making an occupier who has taken all reasonable care answerable to strangers to the contract for dangers due to the faulty execution of any work of construction, maintenance or repair or other like operation by persons other than himself, his servants and persons acting under his direction and control.

(3)    In this section, "stranger to the contract" means a person not for the time being entitled to the benefit of the contract as a party to it or as the successor by assignment or otherwise of a party to it, and accordingly includes a party to the contract who has ceased to be so entitled.

(4)    Where by the terms or conditions governing any tenancy (including a statutory tenancy which does not in law amount to a tenancy) either the landlord or the tenant is bound, though not by contract, to permit persons to enter or use premises of which he is the occupier, this section shall apply as if the tenancy were a contract between the landlord and the tenant.

(5)    This section, in so far as it prevents the common duty of care from being restricted or excluded, applies to contracts entered into and tenancies created before the commencement of this Act, as well as to those entered into or created after its commencement; but, in so far as it enlarges the duty owed by an occupier beyond the common duty of care, it shall have effect only in relation to obligations which are undertaken after the commencement or which are renewed by agreement (whether express or implied) after that commencement.

### 5.    Implied term in contracts.

(1)    Where persons enter or use, or bring or send goods to, any premises in exercise of a right conferred by contract with a person occupying or having control of the premises, the duty he owes them in respect of dangers due to the state of the premises or to things done or omitted to be done by them, in so far as the duty depends on a term to be implied in the contract by reason of its conferring that right, shall be the common duty of care.

(2)    The foregoing subsection shall apply to fixed and moveable structures as it applies to premises.

(3)    This section does not affect the obligations imposed on a person by or by virtue of any contract for the hire of, or for the carriage for reward of persons or goods in, any vehicle, vessel, aircraft or other means of transport, or by virtue of any contract of bailment.

(4)    This section does not apply to contracts entered into before the commencement of this Act.

## THE PUBLIC BODIES (ADMISSION TO MEETINGS) ACT 1960
### (8 & 9 Eliz. II, c. 67)

### 1.    Admission to public meetings of local authorities and other bodies.

(5)    Where a meeting of a body is required by this Act to be open to the public during the proceedings or any part of them, and there is supplied to a member of the public attending the meeting, or in pursuance of paragraph (b) of subsection (4) above there is supplied for the benefit of a newspaper, any such copy of the agenda as is mentioned in that paragraph, with or without further statements or particulars for the purpose of indicating the nature of any item included in the agenda, the publication thereby of any defamatory matter contained in the agenda or in the further statements or particulars shall be privileged, unless the publication is proved to be made with malice.

## THE FACTORIES ACT 1961
### (9 & 10 Eliz. II, c. 34)

**14.    Other machinery.**

(1)    Every dangerous part of any machinery, other than prime movers and transmission machinery, shall be securely fenced unless it is in such a position or of such construction as to be as safe to every person employed or working on the premises as it would be if securely fenced.

**28.    Floors, passages and stairs.**

(1)    All floors, steps, stairs, passages and gangways shall be of sound construction and properly maintained and shall, so far as is reasonably practicable, be kept free from any obstruction and from any substance likely to cause persons to slip.

(2)    For every staircase in a building or affording a means of exit from a building, a substantial hand-rail shall be provided and maintained, which, if the staircase has an open side, shall be on that side, and in the case of a staircase having two open sides or of a staircase which, owing to the nature of its construction or the condition of the surface of the steps or other special circumstances, is specially liable to cause accidents, such a hand-rail shall be provided and maintained on both sides.

(3)    Any open side of a staircase shall also be guarded by the provision and maintenance of a lower rail or other effective means.

(4)    All openings in floors shall be securely fenced, except in so far as the nature of the work renders such fencing impracticable.

(5)    All ladders shall be soundly constructed and properly maintained.

**29.    Safe means of access and safe place of employment.**

(1)    There shall, so far as is reasonably practicable, be provided and maintained safe means of access to every place at which any person has at any time to work, and every such place shall, so far as is reasonably practicable, be made and kept safe for any person working there.

## THE LAW REFORM (HUSBAND AND WIFE) ACT 1962
### (10 & 11 Eliz. II, c. 48)

**1.    (1)**    Subject to the provisions of this section, each of the parties to a marriage shall have the like right of action in tort against the other as if they were not married.

(2)    Where an action in tort is brought by one of the parties to a marriage against the other during the subsistence of the marriage, the court may stay the action if it appears—

(a)    that no substantial benefit would accrue to either party from the continuation of the proceedings; or

(b)    that the question or questions in issue could more conveniently be disposed of on an application made under section seventeen of the Married Women's Property Act 1882 (determination of questions between husband and wife as to the title to or possession of property);

and without prejudice to paragraph (b) of this subsection the court may, in such an action, either exercise any power which could be exercised on an application under that said section seventeen, or give such directions as it thinks fit for the disposal under that section of any question arising in the proceedings.

## THE NUCLEAR INSTALLATIONS ACT 1965
### (1965, c. 57)

**7.    Duty of licensee of licensed site.**

(1)    Where a nuclear site licence has been granted in respect of any site, it shall be the duty of the licensee to secure that—

(a)    no such occurrence involving nuclear matter as is mentioned in subsection (2) of this section causes injury to any person or damage to any property of any person other than the licensee, being injury or damage arising out of or resulting from the radioactive properties, or a combination of those and any toxic, explosive or other hazardous properties, of that nuclear matter; and

(b)    no ionising radiations emitted during the period of the licensee's responsibility—

(i)    from anything caused or suffered by the licensee to be on the site which is not nuclear matter; or

(ii)    from any waste discharged (in whatever form) on or from the site, cause injury to any person or damage to any property of any person other than the licensee.

(2)    The occurrences referred to in subsection (1)(a) of this section are—

(a)    any occurrence on the licensed site during the period of the licensee's responsibility, being an occurrence involving nuclear matter;

(b)    any occurrence elsewhere than on the licensed site involving nuclear matter which is not excepted matter and which at the time of the occurrence—

(i)    is in the course of carriage on behalf of the licensee as licensee of that site; or

(ii)    is in the course of carriage to that site with the agreement of the licensee from a place outside the relevant territories; and

(iii)    in either case, is not on any other relevant site in the United Kingdom;

(c)    any occurrence elsewhere than on the licensed site involving nuclear matter which is not excepted matter and which—

(i)    having been on the licensed site at any time during the period of the licensee's responsibility; or

(ii)    having been in the course of carriage on behalf of the licensee as licensee of that site,

has not subsequently been on any relevant site, or in the course of any relevant carriage, or (except in the course of relevant carriage) within the territorial limits of a country which is not a relevant territory.

(3)    In determining the liability by virtue of subsection (1) of this section in respect of any occurrence of the licensee of a licensed site, any property which at the time of the occurrence is on that site, being—

(a)    a nuclear installation; or

(b)    other property which is on that site—

(i)    for the purpose of use in connection with the operation, or the cessation of the operation, by the licensee of a nuclear installation which is or has been on that site; or

(ii)    for the purpose of the construction of a nuclear installation on that site, shall, notwithstanding that it is the property of some other person, be deemed to be the property of the licensee.

## 9.    Duty of Crown in respect of certain sites.

If a government department uses any site for any purpose which, if section 1 of this Act applied to the Crown, would require the authority of a nuclear site licence in respect of that site, section 7 of this Act shall apply in like manner as if—

(a)    the Crown were the licensee under a nuclear site licence in respect of that site; and

(b)    any reference to the period of the licensee's responsibility were a reference to any period during which the department occupies this site.

## 12.    Right to compensation by virtue of ss. 7 to 10.

(1)    Where any injury or damage has been caused in breach of a duty imposed by section 7, 8, 9 or 10 of this Act—

(a)    subject to sections 13(1), (3) and (4), 15 and 17(1) of this Act, compensation in respect of that injury or damage shall be payable in accordance with section 16 of this Act wherever the injury or damage was incurred;

(b)    subject to subsections (3) and (4) of this section and to section 21(2) of this Act, no other liability shall be incurred by any person in respect of that injury or damage.

(2)    Subject to subsection (3) of this section, any injury or damage which, though not caused in breach of such a duty as aforesaid, is not reasonably separable from injury or damage so caused shall be deemed for the purposes of subsection (1) of this section to have been so caused.

(3)    Where any injury or damage is caused partly in breach of such a duty as aforesaid and partly by an emission of ionising radiations which does not constitute such a breach, subsection (2) of this section shall not affect any liability of any person in respect of that emission apart from this Act, but a claimant shall not be entitled to recover compensation in respect of the same injury or damage both under this Act and otherwise than under this Act.

**13.    Exclusion, extension or reduction of compensation in certain cases.**

(1)    Subject to subsections (2) and (5) of this section, compensation shall not be payable under this Act in respect of injury or damage caused by a breach of a duty imposed by section 7, 8, 9 or 10 thereof if the injury or damage—

(a)    was caused by such an occurrence as is mentioned in section 7(2)(b) or (c) or 10(2)(b) of this Act which is shown to have taken place wholly within the territorial limits of one, and one only, of the relevant territories other than the United Kingdom; or

(b)    was incurred within the territorial limits of a country which is not a relevant territory.

(2)    In the case of a breach of a duty imposed by section 7, 8 or 9 of this Act, subsection (1)(b) of this section shall not apply to injury or damage incurred by, or by persons or property on, a ship or aircraft registered in the United Kingdom.

(4)    The duty imposed by section 7, 8, 9, 10 or 11 of this Act—

(a)    shall not impose any liability on the person subject to that duty with respect to injury or damage caused by an occurrence which constitutes a breach of that duty if the occurrence, or the causing thereby of the injury or damage, is attributable to hostile action in the course of any armed conflict, including any armed conflict within the United Kingdom; but

(b)    shall impose such a liability where the occurrence, or the causing thereby of the injury or damage, is attributable to a natural disaster, notwithstanding that the disaster is of such an exceptional character that it could not reasonably have been foreseen.

(6)    The amount of compensation payable to or in respect of any person under this Act in respect of any injury or damage caused in breach of a duty imposed by section 7, 8, 9 or 10 of this Act may be reduced by reason of the fault of that person if, but only if, and to the extent that, the causing of that injury or damage is attributable to any act of that person committed with the intention of causing harm to any person or property or with reckless disregard for the consequences of his act.

**15.    Time for bringing claims under ss. 7 to 11.**

(1)    Subject to subsection (2) of this section and to section 16(3) of this Act, but notwithstanding anything in any other enactment, a claim by virtue of any of sections 7 to 11 of this Act may be made at any time before, but shall not be entertained if made at any time after, the expiration of thirty years from the relevant date, that is to say, the date of the occurrence which gave rise to the claim or, where that occurrence was a continuing one, or was one of a succession of occurrences all attributable to a particular happening on a particular relevant site or to the carrying out from time to time on a particular relevant site of a particular operation, the date of the last event in the course of that occurrence or succession of occurrences to which the claim relates.

(2)    Notwithstanding anything in subsection (1) of this section, a claim in respect of injury or damage caused by an occurrence involving nuclear matter stolen from, or lost, jettisoned or abandoned by, the person whose breach of a duty imposed by section 7, 8, 9 or 10 of this Act gave rise to the claim shall not be entertained if the occurrence takes place after the expiration of the period of twenty years beginning with the day when the nuclear matter in question was so stolen, lost, jettisoned or abandoned.

**16.    Satisfaction of claims by virtue of ss. 7 to 10.**

(1)    The liability of any person to pay compensation under this Act by virtue of a duty imposed on that person by section 7, 8 or 9 thereof shall not require him to make in respect of any one occurrence constituting a breach of that duty payments by way of such compensation exceeding in the aggregate, apart from payments in respect of interest or costs, [£20 million or, in the case of the licensees of such sites as may be prescribed, £5 million.]

[(1A) The Secretary of State may be with the approval of the Treasury by order increase or further increase either or both of the amounts specified in subsection (1) of this section; but an order under this subsection shall not affect liability in respect of any occurrence before (or beginning before) the order comes into force.]

(3)    Any claim by virtue of a duty imposed on any person by section 7, 8, 9 or 10 of this Act—

    (a)    to the extent to which, by virtue of subsection (1) or (2) of this section, though duly established, it is not or would not be payable by that person; or

    (b)    which is made after the expiration of the relevant period; or

    (c)    which, being such a claim as is mentioned in section 15(2) of this Act, is made after the expiration of the period of twenty years so mentioned; or

    (d)    which is a claim the full satisfaction of which out of funds otherwise required to be, or to be made, available for the purpose is prevented by section 21(1) of this Act,

shall be made to the appropriate authority, that is to say—

       (i)    in the case of a claim by virtue of the said section 8, the Minister of Technology;

       (ii)    in the case of a claim by virtue of the said section 9 (other than a claim in connection with a site used by a department of the Government of Northern Ireland), the Minister in charge of the government department concerned;

       (iii)    in any other case, the Minister,

and, if established to the satisfaction of the appropriate authority, and to the extent to which it cannot be satisfied out of sums made available for the purpose under section 18 of this Act or by means of a relevant foreign contribution, shall be satisfied by the appropriate authority to such extent and out of funds provided by such means as Parliament may determine.

(4)    Where in pursuance of subsection (3) of this section a claim has been made to the appropriate authority, any question affecting the establishment of the claim or as to the amount of any compensation in satisfaction of the claim may, if the authority thinks fit, be referred for decision to the appropriate court, that is to say, to whichever of the High Court, the Court of Session and the High Court of Justice in Northern Ireland would, but for the provisions of this section, have had jurisdiction in accordance with section 17(1) and (2) of this Act to determine the claim; and the claimant may appeal to that court from any decision of the authority on any such question which is not so referred; and on any such reference or appeal—

    (a)    the authority shall be entitled to appear and be heard; and

    (b)    notwithstanding anything in any Act, the decision of the court shall be final.

(5)    In this section, the expression "the relevant period" means the period of ten years beginning with the relevant date within the meaning of section 15(1) of this Act.

**18.    General cover for compensation by virtue of ss. 7 to 10.**

(1)    In the case of any occurrence in respect of which one or more persons incur liability by virtue of section 7, 8, 9 or 10 of this Act or by virtue of any relevant foreign law made for purposes corresponding to those of any of those sections, but subject to subsections (2) [to (4B)] of this section and to sections 17(3)(b) and 21(1) of this Act, there shall be made available out of moneys provided by Parliament such sums as, when aggregated—

(a)    with any funds required by, or by any relevant foreign law made for purposes corresponding to those of, section 19(1) of this Act to be available for the purpose of satisfying claims in respect of that occurrence against any licensee or relevant foreign operator; and

(b)    in the case of a claim by virtue of any such foreign law, with any relevant foreign contributions towards the satisfaction of claims in respect of that occurrence,

may be necessary to ensure that all claims in respect of that occurrence made within the relevant period and duly established, excluding, but without prejudice to, any claim in respect of interest or costs, are satisfied up to [the aggregate amount specified in subsection (1A) of this section.]

[(1A) The aggregate amount referred to in subsection (1) of this section is the equivalent in sterling of 300 million special drawing rights on —

(a)    the day (or first day) of the occurrence in question, or

(b)    if the Secretary of State certifies that another day has been fixed in relation to the occurrence in accordance with an international agreement, that other day.]

[*Subsection (1B) provides for subsection (1A) similarly to s. 16(1A)'s provision for s. 16(1).*]

**19.    Special cover for licensee's liability.**

(1)    Subject to section 3(5) of this Act and to subsection (3) of this section, where a nuclear site licence has been granted in respect of any site, the licensee shall make such provision (either by insurance or by some other means) as the Minister may with the consent of the Treasury approve for sufficient funds to be available at all times to ensure that any claims which have been or may be duly established against the licensee as licensee of that site by virtue of section 7 of this Act or any relevant foreign law made for purposes corresponding to those of section 10 of this Act (excluding, but without prejudice to, any claim in respect of interest or costs) are satisfied up to [the required amount] in respect of each severally of the following periods, that is to say—

(a)    the current cover period, if any;

(b)    any cover period which ended less than ten years before the time in question;

(c)    any earlier cover period in respect of which a claim remains to be disposed of,

being a claim made—

(i)    within the relevant period within the meaning of section 16 of this Act; and

(ii)    in the case of a claim such as is mentioned in section 15(2) of this Act, also within the period of twenty years so mentioned;

and for the purposes of this section the cover period in respect of which any claim is to be treated as being made shall be that in which the beginning of the relevant period aforesaid fell.

[(1A) In this section "the required amount", in relation to the provision to be made by a licensee in respect of a cover period, means an aggregate amount equal to the amount applicable under section 16(1) of this Act to the licensee, as licensee of the site in question, in respect of an occurrence within that period.]

# THE CRIMINAL LAW ACT 1967
## (1967, c. 58)

**3.   Use of force in making arrest, etc.**
(1)   A person may use such force as is reasonable in the circumstances in the prevention of crime, or in effecting or assisting in the lawful arrest of offenders or suspected offenders or of persons unlawfully at large.

**14.   Civil rights in respect of maintenance and champerty.**
(1)   No person shall, under the law of England and Wales, be liable in tort for any conduct on account of its being maintenance or champerty as known to the common law, except in the case of a cause of action accruing before this section has effect.

(2)   The abolition of criminal and civil liability under the law of England and Wales for maintenance and champerty shall not affect any rule of that law as to the cases in which a contract is to be treated as contrary to public policy or otherwise illegal.

# THE MISREPRESENTATION ACT 1967
## (1967, c. 7)

**1.   Removal of certain bars to rescission for innocent misrepresentation.**
Where a person has entered into a contract after a misrepresentation has been made to him, and—
    (a)   the misrepresentation has become a term of the contract; or
    (b)   the contract has been performed;
or both, then, if otherwise he would be entitled to rescind the contract without alleging fraud, he shall be so entitled, subject to the provisions of this Act, notwithstanding the matters mentioned in paragraphs (a) and (b) of this section.

**2.   Damages for misrepresentation.**
(1)   Where a person has entered into a contract after a misrepresentation has been made to him by another party thereto and as a result thereof he has suffered loss, then, if the person making the misrepresentation would be liable to damages in respect thereof had the misrepresentation been made fraudulently, that person shall be so liable notwithstanding that the misrepresentation was not made fraudulently, unless he proves that he had reasonable ground to believe and did believe up to the time the contract was made that the facts represented were true.

(2)   Where a person has entered into a contract after a misrepresentation has been made to him otherwise than fraudulently, and he would be entitled, by reason of the misrepresentation, to rescind the contract, then, if it is claimed, in any proceedings arising out of the contract, that the contract ought to be or has been rescinded, the court or arbitrator may declare the contract subsisting and award damages in lieu of rescission, if of opinion that it would be equitable to do so, having regard to the nature of the misrepresentation and the loss that would be caused by it if the contract were upheld, as well as to the loss that rescission would cause to the other party.

(3)   Damages may be awarded against a person under subsection (2) of this section whether or not he is liable to damages under subsection (1) thereof, but where he is so liable any award under the said subsection (2) shall be taken into account in assessing his liability under the said subsection (1).

**3.   Avoidance of provision excluding liability for misrepresentation.**
[If a contract contains a term which would exclude or restrict—
    (a)   any liability to which a party to a contract may be subject by reason of any misrepresentation made by him before the contract was made; or
    (b)   any remedy available to another party to the contract by reason of such a misrepresentation,

that term shall be of no effect except in so far as it satisfies the requirement of reasonableness as stated in section 11(1) of the Unfair Contract Terms Act 1977; and it is for those claiming that the term satisfies that requirement to show that it does.]

## 4. Amendments of Sale of Goods Act 1893

. . .

## 5. Saving for past transactions.

Nothing in this Act shall apply in relation to any misrepresentation or contract of sale which is made before the commencement of this Act.

## THE PARLIAMENTARY COMMISSIONER ACT 1967
## (1967, c. 13)

### 10. Reports by Commissioner.

(5) For the purposes of the law of defamation, any such publication as is hereinafter mentioned shall be absolutely privileged, that is to say—

(a) the publication of any matter by the Commissioner in making a report to either House of Parliament for the purposes of this Act;

(b) the publication of any matter by a member of the House of Commons in communicating with the Commissioner or his officers for those purposes or by the Commissioner or his officers in communicating with such a member for those purposes;

(c) the publication by such a member to the person by whom a complaint was made under this Act of a report or statement sent to the member in respect of the complaint in pursuance of subsection (1) of this section;

(d) the publication by the Commissioner to such a person as is mentioned in subsection (2) of this section of a report sent to that person in pursuance of that subsection.

## THE CIVIL EVIDENCE ACT 1968
## (1968, c. 64)

### 11. Convictions as evidence in civil proceedings.

(1) In any civil proceedings the fact that a person has been convicted of an offence by or before any court in the United Kingdom or by a court-martial there or elsewhere shall (subject to subsection (3) below) be admissible in evidence for the purpose of proving where to do so is relevant to any issue in those proceedings, that he committed that offence, whether he was so convicted upon a plea of guilty or otherwise and whether or not he is a party to the civil proceedings; but no conviction other than a subsisting one shall be admissible in evidence by virtue of this section.

(2) In any civil proceedings in which by virtue of this section a person is proved to have been convicted of an offence by or before any court in the United Kingdom or by a court-martial there or elsewhere—

(a) he shall be taken to have committed that offence unless the contrary is proved; and

(b) without prejudice to the reception of any other admissible evidence for the purpose of identifying the facts on which the conviction was based, the contents of any documents which is admissible as evidence of the conviction, and the contents of the information, complaint, indictment or charge-sheet on which the person in question was convicted, shall be admissible in evidence for that purpose.

(3) Nothing in this section shall prejudice the operation of section 13 of this Act or any other enactment whereby a conviction or a finding of fact in any criminal proceedings is for the purposes of any other proceedings made conclusive evidence of any fact.

(4) Where in any civil proceedings the contents of any document are admissible in

evidence by virtue of subsection (2) above, a copy of that document, or of the material part thereof, purporting to be certified or otherwise authenticated by or on behalf of the court or authority having custody of that document shall be admissible in evidence and shall be taken to be a true copy of that document or part unless the contrary is shown.

### 13.    Conclusiveness of convictions for purposes of defamation actions.

(1)    In an action for libel or slander in which the question whether a person did or did not commit a criminal offence is relevant to an issue arising in the action, proof that at the time when that issue falls to be determined, that person stands convicted of that offence shall be conclusive evidence that he committed that offence; and his conviction thereof shall be admissible in evidence accordingly.

(2)    In any such action as aforesaid in which by virtue of this section a person is proved to have been convicted of an offence, the contents of any document which is admissible as evidence of the conviction, and the contents of the information, complaint, indictment or charge-sheet on which that person was convicted, shall, without prejudice to the reception of any other admissible evidence for the purpose of identifying the facts on which the conviction was based, be admissible in evidence for the purpose of identifying those facts.

(3)    For the purposes of this section a person shall be taken to stand convicted of an offence if but only if there subsists against him a conviction of that offence by or before a court in the United Kingdom or by a court-martial there or elsewhere.

(4)    Subsections (4) to (6) of section 11 of this Act shall apply for the purposes of this section as they apply for the purposes of that section, but as if in the said subsection (4) the reference to subsection (2) were a reference to subsection (2) of this section.

### THE THEATRES ACT 1968
### (1968, c. 54)

### 4.    Amendment of law of defamation.

(1)    For the purposes of the law of libel and slander (including the law of criminal libel so far as it relates to the publication of defamatory matter) the publication of words in the course of a performance of a play shall, subject to section 7 of this Act, be treated as publication in permanent form.

(2)    The foregoing subsection shall apply for the purposes of section 3 (slander of title, etc.) of the Defamation Act 1952 as it applies for the purposes of the law of libel and slander.

(3)    In this section "words" includes pictures, visual images, gestures and other methods of signifying meaning.

### 7.    Exceptions for performances given in certain circumstances.

(1)    Nothing in sections 2 to 4 of this Act shall apply in relation to a performance of a play given on a domestic occasion in a private dwelling.

### THE TRADE DESCRIPTIONS ACT 1968
### (1968, c. 29)

### 1.    Prohibition of false trade descriptions.

(1)    Any person who, in the course of a trade or business,—

(a)    applies a false trade description to any goods; or

(b)    supplies or offers to supply any goods to which a false trade description is applied;

shall, subject to the provisions of this Act, be guilty of an offence.

### 35.    Saving for civil rights.

A contract for the supply of any goods shall not be void or unenforceable by reason only of a contravention of any provision of this Act.

# THE EMPLOYER'S LIABILITY (DEFECTIVE EQUIPMENT) ACT 1969
### (1969, c. 37)

**1. Extension of employer's liability for defective equipment.**

(1)    Where after the commencement of this Act—

(a)    an employee suffers personal injury in the course of his employment in consequence of a defect in equipment provided by his employer for the purposes of the employer's business; and

(b)    the defect is attributable wholly or partly to the fault of a third party (whether identified or not),

the injury shall be deemed to be also attributable to negligence on the part of the employer (whether or not he is liable in respect of the injury apart from this subsection), but without prejudice to the law relating to contributory negligence and to any remedy by way of contribution or in contract or otherwise which is available to the employer in respect of the injury.

(2)    In so far as any agreement purports to exclude or limit any liability of an employer arising under subsection (1) of this section, the agreement shall be void.

(3)    In this section—

"business" includes the activities carried on by any public body;

"employee" means a person who is employed by another person under a contract of service or apprenticeship and is so employed for the purposes of a business carried on by that other person, and "employer" shall be construed accordingly;

"equipment" includes any plant and machinery, vehicle, aircraft and clothing;

"fault" means negligence, breach of statutory duty or other act or omission which gives rise to liability in England and Wales or which is wrongful and gives rise to liability in damages in Scotland; and

"personal injury" includes loss of life, any impairment of a person's physical or mental condition and any disease.

(4)    This section binds the Crown, and persons in the service of the Crown shall accordingly be treated for the purposes of this section as employees of the Crown if they would not be so treated apart from this subsection.

# THE EMPLOYERS' LIABILITY (COMPULSORY INSURANCE) ACT 1969
### (1969, c. 57)

**1. Insurance against liability for employees.**

(1)    Except as otherwise provided by this Act, every employer carrying on any business in Great Britain shall insure, and maintain insurance, under one or more approved policies with an authorised insurer or insurers against liability for bodily injury or disease sustained by his employees, and arising out of and in the course of their employment in Great Britain in that business, but except in so far as regulations otherwise provide not including injury or disease suffered or contracted outside Great Britain.

(2)    Regulations may provide that the amount for which an employer is required by this Act to insure and maintain insurance shall, either generally or in such cases or classes of case as may be prescribed by the regulations, be limited in such manner as may be so prescribed.

**2. Employees to be covered.**

(1)    For the purposes of this Act the term "employee" means an individual who has entered into or works under a contract of service or apprenticeship with an employer whether by way of manual labour, clerical work or otherwise, whether such contract is expressed or implied, oral or in writing.

(2)    This Act shall not require an employer to insure —
    (a)    in respect of an employee of whom the employer is the husband, wife, father, mother, grandfather, grandmother, step-father, step-mother, son, daughter, grandson, granddaughter, stepson, stepdaughter, brother, sister, half-brother, half-sister; or
    (b)    except as otherwise provided by regulations, in respect of employees not ordinarily resident in Great Britain.

## THE EQUAL PAY ACT 1970
## (1970, c. 41)

**1.    Requirement of equal treatment for men and women in same employment.**
    [(1)    If the terms of a contract under which a woman is employed at an establishment in Great Britain do not include (directly or by reference to a collective agreement or otherwise) an equality clause they shall be deemed to include one.
    (2)    An equality clause is a provision which relates to terms (whether concerned with pay or not) of a contract under which a woman is employed (the "woman's contract"), and has the effect that—
    (a)    where the woman is employed on like work with a man in the same employment—
        (i)    (apart from the equality clause) any term of the woman's contract is or becomes less favourable to the woman than a term of a similar kind in the contract under which that man is employed, that term of the woman's contract shall be treated as so modified as not to be less favourable, and
        (ii)    if (apart from the equality clause) at any time the woman's contract does not include a term corresponding to a term benefiting that man included in the contract under which he is employed, the woman's contract shall be treated as including such a term; . . .]
*[Paragraphs (a), (b) and (c) contain similar provisions.]*

## THE ANIMALS ACT 1971
## (1971, c. 22)

**1.    New provisions as to strict liability for damage done by animals.**
    (1)    The provisions of sections 2 to 5 of this Act replace—
    (a)    the rules of the common law imposing a strict liability in tort for damage done by an animal on the ground that the animal is regarded as ferae naturae or that its vicious or mischievous propensities are known or presumed to be known;
    (b)    subsections (1) and (2) of section 1 of the Dogs Act 1906 as amended by the Dogs (Amendment) Act 1928 (injury to cattle or poultry); and
    (c)    the rules of the common law imposing a liability for cattle trespass.
    (2)    Expressions used in those sections shall be interpreted in accordance with the provisions of section 6 (as well as those of section 11) of this Act.

**2.    Liability for damage done by dangerous animals.**
    (1)    Where any damage is caused by an animal which belongs to a dangerous species, any person who is a keeper of the animal is liable for the damage, except as otherwise provided by this Act.
    (2)    Where damage is caused by an animal which does not belong to a dangerous species, a keeper of the animal is liable for the damage, except as otherwise provided by this Act, if—
    (a)    the damage is of a kind which the animal, unless restrained, was likely to cause or which, if caused by the animal, was likely to be severe; and

(b)    the likelihood of the damage or of its being severe was due to characteristics of the animal which are not normally so found in animals of the same species or are not normally found except at particular times or in particular circumstances.

(c)    those characteristics were known to that keeper or were at any time known to a person who at that time had charge of the animal as that keeper's servant or, where that keeper is the head of a household, were known to another keeper of the animal who is a member of that household and under the age of sixteen.

## 3.    Liability for injury done by dogs to livestock.

Where a dog causes damage by killing or injuring livestock, any person who is a keeper of the dog is liable for the damage, except as otherwise provided by this Act.

## 4.    Liability for damage and expenses due to trespassing livestock.

(1)    Where livestock belonging to any person strays on to land in the ownership or occupation of another and—

(a)    damage is done by the livestock to the land or to any property on it which is in the ownership or possession of the other person; or

(b)    any expenses are reasonably incurred by that other person in keeping the livestock while it cannot be restored to the person to whom it belongs or while it is detained in pursuance of section 7 of this Act, or in ascertaining to whom it belongs;

the person to whom the livestock belongs is liable for the damage or expenses, except as otherwise provided by this Act.

(2)    For the purposes of this section any livestock belongs to the person in whose possession it is.

## 5.    Exceptions from liability under sections 2 to 4.

(1)    A person is not liable under sections 2 to 4 of this Act for any damage which is due wholly to the fault of the person suffering it.

(2)    A person is not liable under section 2 of this Act for any damage suffered by a person who has voluntarily accepted the risk thereof.

(3)    A person is not liable under section 2 of this Act for any damage caused by an animal kept on any premises or structure to a person trespassing there, if it is proved either—

(a)    that the animal was not kept there for the protection of persons or property; or

(b)    (if the animal was kept there for the protection of persons or property) that keeping it there for that purpose was not unreasonable.

(4)    A person is not liable under section 3 of this Act if the livestock was killed or injured on land on to which it had strayed and either the dog belonged to the occupier or its presence on the land was authorised by the occupier.

(5)    A person is not liable under section 4 of this Act where the livestock strayed from a highway and its presence there was a lawful use of the highway.

(6)    In determining whether any liability for damage under section 4 of this Act is excluded by subsection (1) of this section the damage shall not be treated as due to the fault of the person suffering it by reason only that he could have prevented it by fencing; but a person is not liable under that section where it is proved that the straying of the livestock on to the land would not have occurred but for a breach by any other person, being a person having an interest in the land, of a duty to fence.

## 6.    Interpretation of certain expressions used in sections 2 to 5.

(1)    The following provisions apply to the interpretation of sections 2 to 5 of this Act.

(2)    A dangerous species is a species—

(a)    which is not commonly domesticated in the British Islands; and

(b)    whose fully grown animals normally have such characteristics that they are likely, unless restrained, to cause severe damage or that any damage they may cause is likely to be severe.

(3)    Subject to subsection (4) of this section, a person is a keeper of an animal if—

    (a)    he owns the animal or has it in his possession; or

    (b)    he is the head of a household of which a member under the age of sixteen owns the animal or has it in his possession;

and if at any time an animal ceases to be owned by or to be in the possession of a person, any person who immediately before that time was a keeper thereof by virtue of the preceding provisions of this subsection continues to be a keeper of the animal until another person becomes a keeper thereof by virtue of those provisions.

(4)    Where an animal is taken into and kept in possession for the purpose of preventing it from causing damage or of restoring it to its owner, a person is not a keeper of it by virtue only of that possession.

(5)    Where a person employed as a servant by a keeper of an animal incurs a risk incidental to his employment he shall not be treated as accepting it voluntarily.

## 7.    Detention and sale of trespassing livestock.

(1)    The right to seize and detain any animal by way of distress damage feasant is hereby abolished.

(2)    Where any livestock strays on to any land and is not then under the control of any person the occupier of the land may detain it, subject to subsection (3) of this section, unless ordered to return it by a court.

(3)    Where any livestock is detained in pursuance of this section the right to detain it ceases—

    (a)    at the end of a period of forty-eight hours, unless within that period notice of the detention has been given to the officer in charge of a police station and also, if the person detaining the livestock knows to whom it belongs, to that person; or

    (b)    when such amount is tendered to the person detaining the livestock as is sufficient to satisfy any claim he may have under section 4 of this Act in respect of the livestock; or,

    (c)    if he has no such claim, when the livestock is claimed by a person entitled to its possession.

(4)    Where livestock has been detained in pursuance of this section for a period of not less than fourteen days the person detaining it may sell it at a market or by public auction, unless proceedings are then pending for the return of the livestock or for any claim under section 4 of this Act in respect of it.

(5)    Where any livestock is sold in the exercise of the right conferred by this section and the proceeds of the sale, less the costs thereof and any costs incurred in connection with it, exceed the amount of any claim under section 4 of this Act which the vendor had in respect of the livestock, the excess shall be recoverable from him by the person who would be entitled to the possession of the livestock but for the sale.

(6)    A person detaining any livestock in pursuance of this section is liable for any damage caused to it by a failure to treat it with reasonable care and supply it with adequate food and water while it is so detained.

(7)    References in this section to a claim under section 4 of this Act in respect of any livestock do not include any claim under that section for damage done by or expenses incurred in respect of the livestock before the straying in connection with which it is detained under this section.

## 8.    Duty to take care to prevent damage from animals straying on to the highway.

(1)    So much of the rules of the common law relating to liability for negligence as excludes or restricts the duty which a person might owe to others to take such care as is reasonable to see that damage is not caused by animals straying on to a highway is hereby abolished.

(2)    Where damage is caused by animals straying from unfenced land to a highway a person who placed them on the land shall not be regarded as having committed a breach of the duty to take care by reason only of placing them there if—

    (a)    the land is common land, or is land situated in an area where fencing is not customary, or is a town or village green; and

    (b)    he had a right to place the animals on that land.

## 9.   Killing of or injury to dogs worrying livestock.

(1)   In any civil proceedings against a person (in this section referred to as the defendant) for killing or causing injury to a dog it shall be a defence to prove—

    (a)    that the defendant acted for the protection of any livestock and was a person entitled to act for the protection of that livestock; and

    (b)    that within forty-eight hours of the killing or injury notice thereof was given by the defendant to the officer in charge of a police station.

(2)   For the purposes of this section a person is entitled to act for the protection of any livestock if, and only if—

    (a)    the livestock or the land on which it is belongs to him or to any person under whose express or implied authority he is acting; and

    (b)    the circumstances are not such that liability for killing or causing injury to the livestock would be excluded by section 5(4) of this Act.

(3)   Subject to subsection (4) of this section, a person killing or causing injury to a dog shall be deemed for the purposes of this section to act for the protection of any livestock if, and only if, either—

    (a)    the dog is worrying or is about to worry the livestock and there are no other reasonable means of ending or preventing the worrying; or

    (b)    the dog has been worrying livestock, has not left the vicinity and is not under the control of any person and there are no practicable means of ascertaining to whom it belongs.

(4)   For the purposes of this section the condition stated in either of the paragraphs of the preceding subsection shall be deemed to have been satisfied if the defendant believed that it was satisfied and had reasonable ground for that belief.

(5)   For the purposes of this section—

    (a)    an animal belongs to any person if he owns it or has it in his possession; and

    (b)    land belongs to any person if he is the occupier thereof.

## 10.   Application of certain enactments to liability under sections 2 to 4.

For the purposes of [the Fatal Accidents Act 1976], the Law Reform (Contributory Negligence) Act 1945 and [the Limitation Act 1980] any damage for which a person is liable under sections 2 to 4 of this Act shall be treated as due to his fault.

## 11.   General interpretation.

In this Act—

    "common land", and "town or village green" have the same meanings as in the Commons Regulation Act 1965;

    "damage" includes the death of, or injury to, any person (including any disease and any impairment of physical or mental condition);

    "fault" has the same meaning as in the Law Reform (Contributory Negligence) Act 1945;

    "fencing" includes the construction of any obstacle designed to prevent animals from straying;

    "livestock" means cattle, horses, asses, mules, hinnies, sheep, pigs, goats and poultry, and also deer not in the wild state and, in section 3 and 9 also, while in captivity, pheasants, partridges and grouse;

    "poultry" means the domestic varieties of the following, that is to say, fowls, turkeys, geese, ducks, guinea-fowls, pigeons, peacocks and quails; and

    "species" includes sub-species and variety.

**12.    Application to Crown.**
(1)    This Act binds the Crown, but nothing in this section shall authorise proceedings to be brought against Her Majesty in her private capacity.
(2)    Section 38(3) of the Crown Proceedings Act 1947 (interpretation of references to Her Majesty in her private capacity) shall apply as if this section were contained in that Act.

## THE CARRIAGE OF GOODS BY SEA ACT 1971
### (1971, c. 19)

**1.    Application of Hague Rules as amended.**
(1)    In this Act, "the Rules" means the International Convention for the unification of certain rules of law relating to bills of lading signed at Brussels on 25 August 1924, as amended by the Protocol signed at Brussels on 23 February 1968 [and by the Protocol signed at Brussels on 21 December 1979].
(2)    The provisions of the Rules, as set out in the Schedule to this Act, shall have the force of law.

**3.    Absolute warranty of seaworthiness not to be implied in contracts to which Rules apply.**
There shall not be implied in any contract for the carriage of goods by sea to which the Rules apply by virtue of this Act any absolute undertaking by the carrier of the goods to provide a seaworthy ship.

## SCHEDULE
## THE HAGUE RULES AS AMENDED BY THE
## BRUSSELS PROTOCOL 1968

### ARTICLE III

1. The carrier shall be bound before and at the beginning of the voyage to exercise due diligence to—
(a)    Make the ship seaworthy . . .

6. . . .
subject to paragraph 6 *bis* the carrier and the ship shall in any event be discharged from all liability whatsoever in respect of the goods, unless suit is brought within one year of their delivery or of the date when they should have been delivered. This period may, however, be extended if the parties so agree after the cause of action has arisen . . .

8. Any clause, covenant, or agreement in a contract of carriage relieving the carrier or the ship from liability for loss or damage to, or in connection with, goods arising from negligence, fault, or failure in the duties and obligations provided in this article or lessening such liability otherwise than as provided in these Rules, shall be null and void and of no effect. A benefit of insurance in favour of the carrier or similar clause shall be deemed to be a clause relieving the carrier from liability.

### ARTICLE IV BIS

1. The defences and limits of liability provided for in these Rules shall apply in any action against the carrier in respect of loss or damage to goods covered by a contract of carriage whether the action be founded in contract or in tort.
2. If such an action is brought against a servant or agent of the carrier (such servant or agent not being an independent contractor), such servant or agent shall be entitled to avail himself of the defences and limits of liability which the carrier is entitled to invoke under these Rules.
3. The aggregate of the amounts recoverable from the carrier, and such servants and agents, shall in no case exceed the limit provided for in these Rules.

4. Nevertheless, a servant or agent of the carrier shall not be entitled to avail himself of the provisions of this article, if it is proved that the damage resulted from an act or omission of the servant or agent done with intent to cause damage or recklessly and with knowledge that damage would probably result.

## THE MINERAL WORKINGS (OFFSHORE INSTALLATIONS) ACT 1971
### (1971, c. 61)

**6.    Safety regulations.**
   (1)    The Secretary of State may make regulations for the safety, health and welfare of persons on offshore installations in waters to which this Act applies, and generally, and whether or not by way of supplementing the preceding sections of this Act, for the safety of such installations and the prevention of accidents on or near them.

**11.    Civil liability for breach of statutory duty.**
   (1)    This section has effect as respects—
      (a)    a duty imposed on any person by any provision of this Act, or
      (b)    a duty imposed on any person by any provision of regulations made under this Act which expressly applies the provisions of this section.
   (2)    Breach of any such duty shall be actionable so far, and only so far, as it causes personal injury, and references in section 1 of [the Fatal Accidents Act 1976], as it applies in England and Wales, and [in Article 3(1) of the Fatal Accidents (Northern Ireland) Order 1977], to a wrongful act, neglect or default shall include references to any breach of a duty which is so actionable.
   (3)    Subsection (2) above is without prejudice to any action which lies apart from the provisions of this Act.
   (4)    Neither section 9(3) of this Act, nor any defences afforded by regulations made in pursuance of section 7(2)(b) of this Act, shall afford a defence in any civil proceedings, whether brought by virtue of this section or not.
   (7)    In this section "personal injury" includes any disease and any impairment of a person's physical or mental condition and includes any fatal injury.

## THE UNSOLICITED GOODS AND SERVICES ACT 1971
### (1971, c. 30)

**1.    Rights of recipient of unsolicited goods.**
   (1)    In the circumstances specified in the following subsection, a person who after the commencement of this Act receives unsolicited goods, may as between himself and the sender, use, deal with or dispose of them as if they were an unconditional gift to him, and any right of the sender to the goods shall be extinguished.
   (2)    The circumstances referred to in the preceding subsection are that the goods were sent to the recipient with a view to his acquiring them, that the recipient has no reasonable cause to believe that they were sent with a view to their being acquired for the purposes of a trade or business and has neither agreed to acquire nor agreed to return them, and either—
      (a)    that during the period of six months beginning with the day on which the recipient received the goods the sender did not take possession of them and the recipient did not unreasonably refuse to permit the sender to do so; or
      (b)    that not less than thirty days before the expiration of the period aforesaid the recipient gave notice to the sender in accordance with the following subsection, and that during the period of thirty days beginning with the day on which the notice was given the sender did not take possession of the goods and the recipient did not unreasonably refuse to permit the sender to do so.
   (3)    A notice in pursuance of the preceding subsection shall be in writing and shall—

(a)    state the recipient's name and address and, if possession of the goods in question may not be taken by the sender at this address, the address at which it may be so taken;

(b)    contain a statement, however expressed, that the goods are unsolicited, and may be sent by post.

(4)    In this section "sender", in relation to any goods, includes any person on whose behalf or with whose consent the goods are sent, and any other person claiming through or under the sender or any such person.

## 2.    Demands and threats regarding payment.

(1)    A person who, not having reasonable cause to believe there is a right to payment, in the course of any trade or business makes a demand for payment, or asserts a present or prospective right to payment, for what he knows are unsolicited goods sent (after the commencement of this Act) to another person with a view to his acquiring them, shall be guilty of an offence and on summary conviction shall be liable to a fine not exceeding £200.

(2)    A person who, not having reasonable cause to believe there is a right to payment in the course of any trade or business and with a view to obtaining any payment for what he knows are unsolicited goods sent as aforesaid—

(a)    threatens to bring any legal proceedings; or

(b)    places or causes to be placed the name of any person on a list of defaulters or debtors or threatens to do so; or

(c)    invokes or causes to be invoked any other collection procedure or threatens to do so,

shall be guilty of an offence and shall be liable on summary conviction to a fine not exceeding £400.

## 3.    Directory entries.

(1)    A person shall not be liable to make any payment, and shall be entitled to recover the payment made by him, by way of charge for including or arranging for the inclusion in a directory of an entry relating to that person or his trade or business, unless there has been signed by him or on his behalf an order complying with this section or a note complying with this section of his agreement to the charge and, in the case of a note of agreement to the charge, before the note was signed, a copy of it was supplied, for retention by him, to him or to a person acting on his behalf.

(2)    A person shall be guilty of an offence punishable on summary conviction with a fine not exceeding £400 if, in a case where a payment in respect of a charge would, in the absence of an order or note of agreement to the charge complying with this section, be recoverable from him in accordance with the terms of subsection (1) above, he demands payment, or asserts a present or prospective right to payment, of the charge or any part of it, without knowing or having reasonable cause to believe that the entry to which the charge relates was ordered in accordance with this section or a proper note of agreement has been duly signed.

(3)    For the purposes of subsection (1) above, an order for an entry in a directory must be made by means of an order form or other stationery belonging to the person to whom, or to whose trade or business, the entry is to relate and bearing, in print, the name and address (or one or more of the addresses) of that person; and the note required by this section of a person's agreement to a charge must state the amount of the charge immediately above the place for signature, and—

(a)    must identify the directory or proposed directory, and give the following particulars of it—

(i)    the proposed date of publication of the directory or of the issue in which the entry is to be included and the name and address of the person producing it;

(ii)    if the directory or that issue is to be put on sale, the price at which it is to be offered for sale and the minimum number of copies which are to be available for sale;

(iii)       if the directory or that issue is to be distributed free of charge (whether or not it is also to be put on sale), the minimum number of copies which are to be so distributed; and

(b)      must set out or give reasonable particulars of the entry in respect of which the charge would be payable.

(4)     Nothing in this section shall apply to a payment due under a contract entered into before the commencement of this Act, or entered into by the acceptance of an offer made before that commencement.

**[3A.     Contents and form of notes of agreement, invoices and similar documents.**

(1)     For the purposes of this Act, the Secretary of State may make regulations as to the contents and form of notes of agreement, invoices and similar documents; and, without prejudice to the generality of the foregoing, any such regulations may—

(a)      require specified information to be included,

(b)      prescribe the manner in which specified information is to be included,

(c)      prescribe such other requirements (whether as to presentation, type, size, colour or disposition of lettering, quality or colour of paper or otherwise) as the Secretary of State may consider appropriate for securing that specified information is clearly brought to the attention of the recipient of any note of agreement, invoice or similar document.

(d)      make different provision for different classes or descriptions of notes of agreement, invoices and similar documents or for the same class or description in different circumstances,

(e)      contain such supplementary and incidental provisions as the Secretary of State may consider appropriate.

(2)     Any reference in this section to a note of agreement includes any such copy as is mentioned in section 3(1) of this Act.

(3)     Regulations under this section shall be made by statutory instrument and shall be subject to annulment in pursuance of a resolution of either House of Parliament.]

**4.     Unsolicited publications.**

(1)     A person shall be guilty of an offence if he sends or causes to be sent to another person any book, magazine or leaflet (or advertising material for any such publication) which he knows or ought reasonably to know is unsolicited and which describes or illustrates human sexual techniques.

(2)     A person found guilty of an offence under this section shall be liable on summary conviction to a fine not exceeding £100 for a first offence and to a fine not exceeding £400 for any subsequent offence.

(3)     A prosecution for an offence under this section shall not in England and Wales be instituted except by, or with the consent of, the Director of Public Prosecutions.

**5.     Offences by corporations.**

(1)     Where an offence under this Act which has been committed by a body corporate is proved to have been committed with the consent or connivance of, or to be attributable to any neglect on the part of, any director, manager, secretary, or other similar officer of the body corporate, or of any person who was purporting to act in any such capacity, he as well as the body corporate shall be guilty of that offence and shall be liable to be proceeded against and punished accordingly.

(2)     Where the affairs of a body corporate are managed by its members, this section shall apply in relation to the acts or defaults of a member in connection with his functions of management as if he were a director of the body corporate.

**6.     Interpretation.**

(1)     In this Act, unless the context or subject matter otherwise requires,—

"acquire" includes hire;

"send" includes deliver, and "sender" shall be construed accordingly;

"unsolicited" means, in relation to goods sent to any person, that they are sent without any prior request made by him or on his behalf.

[(2)    For the purposes of this Act any invoice or similar document stating the amount of any payment and not complying with the requirements of regulations under section 3A of this Act applicable thereto shall be regarded as asserting a right to the payment.]

## THE DEFECTIVE PREMISES ACT 1972
### (1972, c. 35)

**1.    Duty to build dwellings properly.**

(1)    A person taking on work for or in connection with the provision of a dwelling (whether the dwelling is provided by the erection or by the conversion or enlargement of a building) owes a duty—

(a)    if the dwelling is provided to the order of any person, to that person; and

(b)    without prejudice to paragraph (a) above, to every person who acquires an interest (whether legal or equitable) in the dwelling;

to see that the work which he takes on is done in a workmanlike or, as the case may be, professional manner, with proper materials and so that as regards that work the dwelling will be fit for habitation when completed.

(2)    A person who takes on any such work for another on terms that he is to do it in accordance with instructions given by or on behalf of that other shall, to the extent to which he does it properly in accordance with those instructions, be treated for the purposes of this section as discharging the duty imposed on him by subsection (1) above except where he owes a duty to that other to warn him of any defects in the instructions and fails to discharge that duty.

(3)    A person shall not be treated for the purposes of subsection (2) above as having given instructions for the doing of work merely because he has agreed to the work being done in a specified manner, with specified materials or to a specified design.

(4)    A person who—

(a)    in the course of a business which consists of or includes providing or arranging for the provision of dwellings or installations in dwellings; or

(b)    in the exercise of a power of making such provision or arrangements conferred by or by virtue of any enactment;

arranges for another to take on work for or in connection with the provision of a dwelling shall be treated for the purposes of this section as included among the persons who have taken on the work.

(5)    Any cause of action in respect of a breach of the duty imposed by this section shall be deemed, for the purposes of the Limitation Act 1939, the Law Reform (Limitation of Actions, etc.) Act 1954 and the Limitation Act 1963, to have accrued at the time when the dwelling was completed, but if after that time a person who has done work for or in connection with the provision of the dwelling does further work to rectify the work he has already done, any such cause of action in respect of that further work shall be deemed for those purposes to have accrued at the time when the further work was finished.

[*The references in s. 1(5) should now be read as to the Limitation Act 1980. See the Limitation Act, s. 40(2); the Interpretation Act 1978, s. 17(2).*]

**2.    Cases excluded from the remedy under section 1.**

(1)    Where—

(a)    in connection with the provision of a dwelling or its first sale or letting for habitation any rights in respect of defects in the state of the dwelling are conferred by an approved scheme to which this section applies on a person having or acquiring an interest in the dwelling; and

(b)   it is stated in a document of a type approved for the purposes of this section that the requirements as to design or construction imposed by or under the scheme have, or appear to have, been substantially complied with in relation to the dwelling;
no action shall be brought by any person having or acquiring an interest in the dwelling for breach of the duty imposed by section 1 above in relation to the dwelling.

(2)   A scheme to which this section applies—

(a)   may consist of any number of documents and any number of agreements or other transactions between any number of persons; but

(b)   must confer, by virtue of agreements entered into with persons having or acquiring an interest in the dwellings to which the scheme applies, rights on such persons in respect of defects in the state of the dwellings.

(3)   In this section "approved" means approved by the Secretary of State, and the power of the Secretary of State to approve a scheme or document for the purposes of this section shall be exercisable by order, except that any requirements as to construction or design imposed under a scheme to which this section applies may be approved by him without making any order or, if he thinks fit, by order.

(4)   The Secretary of State—

(a)   may approve a scheme or document for the purposes of this section with or without limiting the duration of his approval; and

(b)   may by order revoke or vary a previous order under this section or, without such an order, revoke or vary a previous approval under this section given otherwise than by order.

(5)   The production of a document purporting to be a copy of an approval given by the Secretary of State otherwise than by order and certified by an officer of the Secretary of State to be a true copy of the approval shall be conclusive evidence of the approval, and without proof of the handwriting or official position of the person purporting to sign the certificate.

(6)   The power to make an order under this section shall be exercisable by statutory instrument which shall be subject to annulment in pursuance of a resolution by either House of Parliament.

(7)   Where an interest in a dwelling is compulsorily acquired—

(a)   no action shall be brought by the acquiring authority for breach of the duty imposed by section 1 above in respect of the dwelling; and

(b)   if any work for or in connection with the provision of the dwelling was done otherwise than in the course of a business by the person in occupation of the dwelling at the time of the compulsory acquisition, the acquiring authority and not that person shall be treated as the person who took on the work and accordingly as owing that duty.

## 3.   Duty of care with respect to work done on premises not abated by disposal of premises.

(1)   Where work of construction, repair, maintenance or demolition or any other work is done on or in relation to premises, any duty of care owed, because of the doing of the work, to persons who might reasonably be expected to be affected by defects in the state of the premises created by the doing of the work shall not be abated by the subsequent disposal of the premises by the person who owed the duty.

(2)   This section does not apply—

(a)   in the case of premises which are let, where the relevant tenancy of the premises commenced, or the relevant tenancy agreement of the premises was entered into, before the commencement of this Act;

(b)   in the case of premises disposed of in any other way, when the disposal of the premises was completed, or a contract for their disposal was entered into, before the commencement of this Act; or

(c)    in either case, where the relevant transaction disposing of the premises is entered into in pursuance of an enforceable option by which the consideration for the disposal was fixed before the commencement of this Act.

**4.    Landlord's duty of care in virtue of obligation or right to repair premises demised.**

(1)    Where premises are let under a tenancy which puts on the landlord an obligation to the tenant for the maintenance or repair of the premises the landlord owes to all persons who might reasonably be expected to be affected by defects in the state of the premises a duty to take such care as is reasonable in all the circumstances to see that they are reasonably safe from personal injury or from damage to their property caused by a relevant defect.

(2)    The said duty is owed if the landlord knows (whether as the result of being notified by the tenant or otherwise) or if he ought in all the circumstances to have known of the relevant defect.

(3)    In this section "relevant defect" means a defect in the state of the premises existing at or after the material time and arising from, or continuing because of, an act or omission by the landlord which constituted or would if he had had notice of the defect, have constituted a failure by him to carry out his obligation to the tenant for the maintenance or repair of the premises; and for the purposes of the foregoing provision "the material time" means—

(a)    where the tenancy commenced before this Act, the commencement of this Act; and

(b)    in all other cases, the earliest following times, that is to say—

(i)     the time when the tenancy commences;

(ii)    the time when the tenancy agreement is entered into;

(iii)   the time when possession is taken of the premises in contemplation of the letting.

(4)    Where premises are let under a tenancy which expressly or impliedly gives the landlord the right to enter the premises to carry out any description of maintenance or repair of the premises, then, as from the time when he first is, or by notice or otherwise can put himself, in a position to exercise the right and so long as he is or can put himself in that position, he shall be treated for the purposes of subsections (1) to (3) above (but for no other purpose) as if he were under an obligation to the tenant for that description of maintenance or repair of the premises; but the landlord shall not owe the tenant any duty by virtue of this subsection in respect of any defect in the state of the premises arising from, or continuing because of, a failure to carry out an obligation expressly imposed on the tenant by the tenancy.

(5)    For the purposes of this section obligations imposed or rights given by any enactment in virtue of a tenancy shall be treated as imposed or given by the tenancy.

(6)    This section applies to a right of occupation given by contract or any enactment and not amounting to a tenancy as if the right were a tenancy, and "tenancy" and cognate expressions shall be construed accordingly.

**5.    Application to Crown.**

This Act shall bind the Crown, but as regards the Crown's liability in tort shall not bind the Crown further than the Crown is made liable in tort by the Crown Proceedings Act 1947.

**6.    Supplemental.**

(1)    In this Act: "disposal", in relation to premises, includes a letting, and an assignment or surrender of a tenancy, of the premises and the creation by contract of any other right to occupy the premises, and "dispose" shall be construed accordingly; "personal injury" includes any disease and any impairment of a person's physical or mental condition . . .

(2)    Any duty imposed by or enforceable by virtue of any provision of this Act is in addition to any duty a person may owe apart from that provision.

(3)    Any term of an agreement which purports to exclude or restrict, or has the effect of excluding or restricting, the operation of any of the provisions of this Act, or any liability arising by virtue of any such provision, shall be void.

## THE GUARDIANSHIP ACT 1973
### (1973, c. 29)

**1.    Equality of parental rights.**
[(2)    Notwithstanding anything in section 85(2) of the Children Act 1975, an agreement may be made between the father and mother of a child as to the exercise by either of them, during any period when they are not living with each other in the same household, of any of the parental rights and duties with respect to the child; but no such agreement shall be enforced by any court if the court is of opinion that it will not be for the benefit of the child to give effect to it.]

## THE POWERS OF CRIMINAL COURTS ACT 1973
### (1973, c. 62)

**35.    Compensation orders against convicted persons.**
[(1)    Subject to the provisions of this Part of this Act and to section 40 of the Magistrates' Courts Act 1980 (which imposes a monetary limit on the powers of a magistrates' court under this section), a court by or before which a person is convicted of an offence, instead of or in addition to dealing with him in any other way, may, on application or otherwise, make an order (in this Act referred to as "a compensation order") requiring him to pay compensation for any personal injury, loss or damage resulting from that offence or any other offence which is taken into consideration by the court in determining sentence [or to make payments for funeral expenses or bereavement in respect of a death resulting from any such offence, other than a death due to an accident arising out of the presence of a motor vehicle on a road; and a court shall give reasons, on passing sentence, if it does not make such an order in a case where this section empowers it to do so].

[(1A) Compensation under subsection (1) above shall be of such amount as the court considers appropriate having regard to any evidence and to any representations that are made by or on behalf of the accused or the prosecutor.]

(2)    In the case of an offence under the Theft Act 1968, where the property in question is recovered, any damage to the property occurring while it was out of the owner's possession shall be treated for the purposes of subsection (1) above as having resulted from the offence, however and by whomsoever the damage was caused.

[(3)    A compensation order may only be made in respect of injury, loss or damage (other than loss suffered by a person's dependants in consequence of his death) which was due to an accident arising out of the presence of a motor vehicle on a road, if—

(a)    it is in respect of damage which is treated by subsection (2) above as resulting from an offence under the Theft Act 1968; or

(b)    it is in respect of injury, loss or damage as respects which—

(i)    the offender is uninsured in relation to the use of the vehicle; and

(ii)    compensation is not payable under any arrangements to which the Secretary of State is a party;

and, where a compensation order is made in respect of injury, loss or damage due to such an accident, the amount to be paid may include an amount representing the whole or part of any loss of or reduction in preferential rates of insurance attributable to the accident.

(3A)    A vehicle the use of which is exempted from insurance by section 144 of the Road Traffic Act 1972 is not uninsured for the purposes of subsection (3) above.

(3B)    A compensation order in respect of funeral expenses may be made for the benefit of anyone who incurred the expenses.

(3C) A compensation order in respect of bereavement may only be made for the benefit of a person for whose benefit a claim for damages for bereavement could be made under section 1A of the Fatal Accidents Act 1976.

(3D) The amount of compensation in respect of bereavement shall not exceed the amount for the time being specified in section 1A(3) of the Fatal Accidents Act 1976.]

(4)    In determining whether to make a compensation order against any person, and in determining the amount to be paid by any person under such an order, the court shall have regard to his means so far as they appear or are known to the court.

[(4A) Where the court considers:

(a)    that it would be appropriate both to impose a fine and to make a compensation order; but

(b)    that the offender has insufficient means to pay both an appropriate fine and appropriate compensation, the court shall give preference to compensation (though it may impose a fine as well).]

**[38.    Effect of compensation order on subsequent award of damages in civil proceedings.**

(1)    This section shall have effect where a compensation order has been made in favour of any person in respect of any injury, loss or damage and a claim by him in civil proceedings for damages in respect the injury, loss or damage subsequently falls to be determined.

(2)    The damages in the civil proceedings shall be assessed without regard to the order; but the plaintiff may only recover an amount equal to the aggregate of the following—

(a)    any amount by which they exceed the compensation; and

(b)    a sum equal to any portion of the compensation which he fails to recover, and may not enforce the judgment, so far as it relates to a sum such as is mentioned in paragraph (b) above, without the leave of the court.]

## THE SUPPLY OF GOODS (IMPLIED TERMS) ACT 1973
### (1973, c. 13)

**8.    Implied terms as title.**

[(1)    In every hire-purchase agreement, other than one to which subsection (2) below applies, there is—

(a)    an implied condition on the part of the creditor that he will have a right to sell the goods at the time when the property is to pass; and

(b)    an implied warranty that—

(i)      the goods are free, and will remain free until the time when the property is to pass, from any charge or encumbrance not disclosed or known to the person to whom the goods are bailed or (in Scotland) hired before the agreement is made, and

(ii)     that person will enjoy quiet possession of the goods except so far as it may be disturbed by any person entitled to the benefit of any charge or encumbrance so disclosed or known.

(2)    In a hire-purchase agreement, in the case of which there appears from the agreement or is to be inferred from the circumstances of the agreement an intention that the creditor should transfer only such title as he or a third person may have, there is—

(a)    an implied warranty that all charges or encumbrances known to the creditor and not known to the person to whom the goods are bailed or hired have been disclosed to that person before the agreement is made; and

(b)    an implied warranty that neither—

(i)      the creditor; nor

(ii)     in a case where the parties to the agreement intend that any title which may be transferred shall be only such title as a third person may have, that person; nor

(iii)    anyone claiming through or under the creditor or that third person otherwise than under a charge or encumbrance disclosed or known to the person to whom the goods are bailed or hired, before the agreement is made;
will disturb the quiet possession of the person to whom the goods are bailed or hired.]

## 9.    Bailing or hiring by description.

[(1)    Where under a hire-purchase agreement goods are bailed or (in Scotland) hired by description, there is an implied condition that the goods will correspond with the description, and if under the agreement the goods are bailed or hired by reference to a sample as well as a description, it is not sufficient that the bulk of the goods corresponds with the sample if the goods do not also correspond with the description.

(2)    Goods shall not be prevented from being bailed or hired by description by reason only that, being exposed for sale, bailment or hire, they are selected by the person to whom they are bailed or hired.]

## 10.    Implied undertakings as to quality or fitness.

[(1)    Except as provided by this section and section 11 below and subject to the provisions of any other enactment, including any enactment of the Parliament of Northern Ireland or the Northern Ireland Assembly, there is no implied condition or warranty as to the quality or fitness for any particular purpose of goods bailed or (in Scotland) hired under a hire-purchase agreement.

(2)    Where the creditor bails or hires goods under a hire-purchase agreement in the course of a business, there is an implied condition that the goods [supplied under the agreement] are of merchantable quality, except that there is no such condition—
    (a)    as regards defects specifically drawn to the attention of the person to whom the goods are bailed or hired before the agreement is made; or
    (b)    if that person examines the goods before the agreement is made, as regards defects which that examination ought to reveal.

(3)    Where the creditor bails or hires goods under a hire-purchase agreement in the course of a business and the person to whom the goods are bailed or hired, expressly or by implication, makes known—
    (a)    to the creditor in the course of negotiations conducted by the creditor in relation to the making of the hire-purchase agreement, or
    (b)    to a credit-broker in the course of negotiations conducted by that broker in relation to goods sold by him to the creditor before forming the subject matter of the hire-purchase agreement,
any particular purpose for which the goods are being bailed or hired, there is an implied condition that the goods supplied under the agreement are reasonably fit for that purpose, whether or not that is a purpose for which such goods are commonly supplied, except where the circumstances show that the person to whom the goods are bailed or hired does not rely, or that it is unreasonable for him to rely, on the skill or judgment of the creditor or credit-broker.

(4)    An implied condition or warranty as to quality or fitness for a particular purpose may be annexed to a hire-purchase agreement by usage.

(5)    The preceding provisions of this section apply to a hire-purchase agreement made by a person who in the course of a business is acting as agent for the creditor as they apply to an agreement made by the creditor in the course of a business, except where the creditor is not bailing or hiring in the course of a business and either the person to whom the goods are bailed or hired knows that fact or reasonable steps are taken to bring it to the notice of that person before the agreement is made.

(6)    In subsection (3) above and this subsection—
    (a)    "credit-broker" means a person acting in the course of a business of credit brokerage;

    (b)    "credit brokerage" means the effecting of introductions of individuals desiring to obtain credit—

        (i)        to persons carrying on any business so far as it relates to the provision of credit, or

        (ii)       to other persons engaged in credit brokerage.]

## 11.    Samples.

[Where under a hire-purchase agreement goods are bailed or (in Scotland) hired by reference to a sample, there is an implied condition—

    (a)    that the bulk will correspond with the sample in quality; and

    (b)    that the person to whom the goods are bailed or hired will have a reasonable opportunity of comparing the bulk with the sample; and

    (c)    that the goods will be free from any defect, rendering them unmerchantable, which would not be apparent on reasonable examination of the sample.]

## 12.    Exclusion of implied terms and conditions.

[(1)    An express condition or warranty does not negative a condition or warranty implied by this Act unless inconsistent with it.]

## 14.    Special provisions as to conditional sale agreements.

[(1)    Section 11(4) of the Sale of Goods Act 1979 (whereby in certain circumstances a breach of a condition in a contract of sale is treated only as a breach of warranty) shall not apply to [a conditional sale agreement where the buyer deals as consumer within Part I of the Unfair Contract Terms Act 1977 . . .]

    (2)    In England and Wales and Northern Ireland a breach of a condition (whether express or implied) to be fulfilled by the seller under any such agreement shall be treated as a breach of warranty, and not as grounds for rejecting the goods and treating the agreement as repudiated, if (but only if) it would have fallen to be so treated had the condition been contained or implied in a corresponding hire-purchase agreement as a condition to be fulfilled by the creditor.

## 15.    Supplementary.

[(1)    In sections 8 to 14 above and this section—

"business" includes a profession and the activities of any government department (including a Northern Ireland department), [or local or public authority];

"buyer" and "seller" includes a person to whom rights and duties under a conditional sale agreement have passed by assignment or operation of law;

"condition" and "warranty" in relation to Scotland, mean stipulation, and any stipulation referred to in sections 8(1)(a), 9, 10 and 11 above shall be deemed to be material to the agreement.

"conditional sale agreement" means an agreement for the sale of goods under which the purchase price or part of it is payable by instalments, and the property in the goods is to remain in the seller (notwithstanding that the buyer is to be in possession of the goods) until such conditions as to the payment of instalments or otherwise as may be specified in the agreement are fulfilled;

["consumer sale" has the same meaning as in section 55 of the Sale of Goods Act 1979 (as set out in paragraph 11 of Schedule 1 to that Act)];

"creditor" means the person by whom the goods are bailed or (in Scotland) hired under a hire-purchase agreement or the person to whom his rights and duties under the agreement have passed by assignment or operation of law; and

"hire-purchase agreement" means an agreement, other than conditional sale agreement, under which—

    (a)    goods are bailed or (in Scotland) hired in return for periodical payments by the person to whom they are bailed or hired, and

(b)    the property in the goods will pass to that person if the terms of the agreement are complied with and one or more of the following occurs—
     (i)        the exercise of an option to purchase by that person,
     (ii)       the doing of any other specified act by any party to the agreement,
     (iii)      the happening of any other specified event.

(2)    Goods of any kind are merchantable quality within the meaning of section 10(2) above if they are as fit for the purpose or purposes for which goods of that kind are commonly bought as it is reasonable to expect having regard to any description applied to them, the price (if relevant) and all the other relevant circumstances; and in section 11 above "unmerchantable" shall be construed accordingly.

(3)    In section 14(2) above "corresponding hire-purchase agreement" means, in relation to a conditional sale agreement, a hire-purchase agreement relating to the same goods as the conditional sale agreement and made between the same parties and at the same time and in the same circumstances and, as nearly as may be, in the same terms as the conditional sale agreement.

(4)    Nothing in sections 8 to 13 above shall prejudice the operation of any other enactment including any enactment of the Parliament of Northern Ireland or the Northern Ireland Assembly or any rule of law whereby any condition or warranty, other than one relating to quality or fitness, is to be implied in any hire-purchase agreement.]

## THE CONSUMER CREDIT ACT 1974
### (1974, c. 39)
### PART IV

**46.    False or misleading advertisements.**

(1)    If an advertisement to which this Part applies conveys information which in a material respect is false or misleading the advertiser commits an offence.

(2)    Information stating or implying an intention on the advertiser's part which he has not got is false.

### PART V

**55.    Disclosure of information.**

(1)    Regulations may require specified information to be disclosed in the prescribed manner to the debtor or hirer before a regulated agreement is made.

(2)    A regulated agreement is not properly executed unless regulations under subsection (1) were complied with before the making of the agreement.

**56.    Antecedent negotiations.**

(1)    In this Act "antecedent negotiations" means any negotiations with the debtor or hirer—
(a)    conducted by the creditor or owner in relation to the making of any regulated agreement, or
(b)    conducted by a credit-broker in relation to goods sold or proposed to be sold by the credit-broker to the creditor before forming the subject-matter of a debtor-creditor-supplier agreement within section 12(a), or
(c)    conducted by the supplier in relation to a transaction financed or proposed to be financed by a debtor-creditor-supplier agreement within section 12(b) or (c),
and "negotiator" means the person by whom negotiations are so conducted with the debtor or hirer.

(2)    Negotiations with the debtor in a case falling within subsection (1)(b) or (c) shall be deemed to be conducted by the negotiator in the capacity of agent of the creditor as well as in his actual capacity.

(3)    An agreement is void if, and to the extent that, it purports in relation to an actual or prospective regulated agreement—

(a)    to provide that a person acting as, or on behalf of, a negotiator is to be treated as the agent of the debtor or hirer, or

(b)    to relieve a person from liability for acts or omissions of any person acting as, or on behalf of, a negotiator.

(4)    For the purposes of this Act, antecedent negotiations shall be taken to begin when the negotiator and the debtor or hirer first enter into communication (including communication by advertisement), and to include any representations made by the negotiator to the debtor or hirer and any other dealings between them.

## 57.    Withdrawal from prospective agreement.

(1)    The withdrawal of a party from a prospective regulated agreement shall operate to apply this Part to the agreement, any linked transaction and any other thing done in anticipation of the making of the agreement as it would apply if the agreement were made and then cancelled under section 69.

## 60.    Form and content of agreements.

(1)    The Secretary of State shall make regulations as to the form and content of documents embodying regulated agreements, and the regulations shall contain such provisions as appear to him appropriate with a view to ensuring that the debtor or hirer is made aware of—

(a)    the rights and duties conferred or imposed on him by the agreement,

(b)    the amount and rate of the total charge for credit (in the case of a consumer credit agreement),

(c)    the protection and remedies available to him under this Act, and

(d)    any other matters which, in the opinion of the Secretary of State, it is desirable for him to know about in connection with the agreement.

## 65.    Consequences of improper execution.

(1)    An improperly-executed regulated agreement is enforceable against the debtor or hirer on an order of the court only.

## 67.    Cancellable agreements.

A regulated agreement may be cancelled by the debtor or hirer in accordance with this Part if the antecedent negotiations included oral representations made when in the presence of the debtor or hirer by an individual acting as, or on behalf of, the negotiator, unless—

(a)    the agreement is secured on land, or is a restricted-use credit agreement to finance the purchase of land or is an agreement for a bridging loan in connection with the purchase of land, or

(b)    the unexecuted agreement is signed by the debtor or hirer at premises at which any of the following is carrying on any business (whether on a permanent or temporary basis)—

(i)    the creditor or owner;

(ii)    any party to a linked transaction (other than the debtor or hirer or a relative of his);

(iii)    the negotiator in any antecedent negotiations.

## 68.    Cooling-off period.

The debtor or hirer may serve notice of cancellation of a cancellable agreement between his signing of the unexecuted agreement and—

(a)    the end of the fifth day following the day on which he received a copy under section 63(2) or a notice under section 64(1)(b), or

(b)    if (by virtue of regulations made under section 64(4)) section 64(1)(b) does not apply, the end of the fourteenth day following the day on which he signed the unexecuted agreement.

**69.   Notice of cancellation.**

(1)   If within the period specified in section 68 the debtor or hirer under a cancellable agreement serves on—

   (a)   the creditor or owner, or

   (b)   the person specified in the notice under section 64(1), or

   (c)   a person who (whether by virtue of subsection (6) or otherwise) is the agent of the creditor or owner,

a notice (a "notice of cancellation") which, however expressed and whether or not conforming to the notice given under section 64(1), indicates the intention of the debtor or hirer to withdraw from the agreement, the notice shall operate—

   (i)       to cancel the agreement, and any linked transaction, and

   (ii)      to withdraw any offer by the debtor or hirer, or his relative, to enter into a linked transaction.

(4)   Except as otherwise provided by or under this Act, an agreement or transaction cancelled under subsection (1) shall be treated as if it had never been entered into.

**70.   Cancellation: recovery of money paid by debtor or hirer.**

(1)   On the cancellation of a regulated agreement, and of any linked transaction,—

   (a)   any sum paid by the debtor or hirer, or his relative, under or in contemplation of the agreement or transaction, including any item in the total charge for credit, shall become repayable, and

   (b)   any sum, including any item in the total charge for credit, which but for the cancellation is, or would or might become, payable by the debtor or hirer, or his relative, under the agreement or transaction shall cease to be, or shall not become, so payable, and

   (c)   in the case of a debtor-creditor-supplier agreement falling within section 12(b), any sum paid on the debtor's behalf by the creditor to the supplier shall become repayable to the creditor.

(3)   A sum repayable under subsection (1) is repayable by the person to whom it was originally paid, but in the case of a debtor-creditor-supplier agreement falling within section 12(b) the creditor and the supplier shall be under a joint and several liability to repay sums paid by the debtor, or his relative, under the agreement or under a linked transaction falling within section 19(1)(b) and accordingly, in such a case, the creditor shall be entitled, in accordance with rules of court, to have the supplier made a party to any proceedings brought against the creditor to recover any such sums.

(4)   Subject to any agreement between them, the creditor shall be entitled to be indemnified by the supplier for loss suffered by the creditor in satisfying his liability under subsection (3), including costs reasonably incurred by him in defending proceedings instituted by the debtor.

**71.   Cancellation: repayment of credit.**

(1)   Notwithstanding the cancellation of a regulated consumer credit agreement, other than a debtor-creditor-supplier agreement for restricted-use credit, the agreement shall continue in force so far as it relates to repayment of credit and payment of interest.

## PART VI

**75.   Liability of creditor for breaches by supplier.**

(1)   If the debtor under a debtor-creditor-supplier agreement falling within section 12(b) or (c) has, in relation to a transaction financed by the agreement, any claim against the supplier in respect of a misrepresentation or breach of contract, he shall have a like claim against the creditor, who, with the supplier, shall accordingly be jointly and severally liable to the debtor.

(2)   Subject to any agreement between them, the creditor shall be entitled to be indemnified by the supplier for loss suffered by the creditor in satisfying his liability under

subsection (1), including costs reasonably incurred by him in defending proceedings instituted by the debtor.

(3)    Subsection (1) does not apply to a claim—

(a)    under a non-commercial agreement, or

(b)    so far as the claim relates to any single item to which the supplier has attached a cash price not exceeding £30 or more than £10,000.

(4)    This section applies notwithstanding that the debtor, in entering into the transaction, exceeded the credit limit or otherwise contravened any term of the agreement.

(5)    In an action brought against the creditor under subsection (1) he shall be entitled, in accordance with rules of court, to have the supplier made a party to the proceedings.

### 76.    Duty to give notice before taking certain action.

(1)    The creditor or owner is not entitled to enforce a term of a regulated agreement by—

(a)    demanding earlier payment of any sum, or

(b)    recovering possession of any goods or land, or

(c)    treating any right conferred on the debtor or hirer by the agreement as terminated, restricted or deferred,

except by or after giving the debtor or hirer not less than seven days' notice of his intention to do so.

(2)    Subsection (1) applies only where—

(a)    a period for the duration of the agreement is specified in the agreement, and

(b)    that period has not ended when the creditor or owner does an act mentioned in subsection (1),

but so applies notwithstanding that, under the agreement, any party is entitled to terminate it before the end of the period so specified.

(6)    Subsection (1) does not apply to a right of enforcement arising by reason of any breach by the debtor or hirer of the regulated agreement.

## PART VII

### 87.    Need for default notice.

(1)    Service of a notice on the debtor or hirer in accordance with section 88 (a "default notice") is necessary before the creditor or owner can become entitled, by reason of any breach by the debtor or hirer of a regulated agreement,—

(a)    to terminate the agreement, or

(b)    to demand earlier payment of any sum, or

(c)    to recover possession of any goods or land, or

(d)    to treat any right conferred on the debtor or hirer by the agreement as terminated, restricted or deferred, or

(e)    to enforce any security.

(2)    Subsection (1) does not prevent the creditor from treating the right to draw upon any credit as restricted or deferred, and taking such steps as may be necessary to make the restriction or deferment effective.

(4)    Regulations may provide that subsection (1) is not to apply to agreements described by the regulations.

### 88.    Contents and effect of default notice.

(1)    The default notice must be in the prescribed form and specify—

(a)    the nature of the alleged breach;

(b)    if the breach is capable of remedy, what action is required to remedy it and the date before which that action is to be taken;

(c)    if the breach is not capable of remedy, the sum (if any) required to be paid as compensation for the breach, and the date before which it is to be paid.

**94.    Right to complete payments ahead of time.**

(1)    The debtor under a regulated consumer credit agreement is entitled at any time, by notice to the creditor and the payment to the creditor of all amounts payable by the debtor to him under the agreement (less any rebate allowable under section 95), to discharge the debtor's indebtedness under the agreement.

**96.    Effect on linked transactions.**

(1)    Where for any reason the indebtedness of the debtor under a regulated consumer credit agreement is discharged before the time fixed by the agreement, he, and any relative of his, shall at the same time be discharged from any liability under a linked transaction, other than a debt which has already become payable.

**99.    Right to terminate hire-purchase etc., agreements.**

(1)    At any time before the final payment by the debtor under a regulated hire-purchase or regulated conditional sale agreement falls due, the debtor shall be entitled to terminate the agreement by giving notice to any person entitled or authorised to receive the sums payable under the agreement.

(2)    Termination of an agreement under subsection (1) does not affect any liability under the agreement which has accrued before the termination.

(4)    In the case of a conditional sale agreement relating to goods, where the property in the goods, having become vested in the debtor, is transferred to a person who does not become the debtor under the agreement, the debtor shall not thereafter be entitled to terminate the agreement under subsection (1).

**100.    Liability of debtor on termination of hire-purchase etc., agreement.**

(1)    Where a regulated hire-purchase or regulated conditional sale agreement is terminated under section 99 the debtor shall be liable, unless the agreement provides for a smaller payment, or does not provide for any payment, to pay to the creditor the amount (if any) by which one-half of the total price exceeds the aggregate of the sums paid and the sums due in respect of the total price immediately before the termination.

(3)    If in any action the court is satisfied that a sum less than the amount specified in subsection (1) would be equal to the loss sustained by the creditor in consequence of the termination of the agreement by the debtor, the court may make an order for the payment of that sum in lieu of the amount specified in subsection (1).

## PART VIII

**113.    Act not to be evaded by use of security.**

(1)    Where a security is provided in relation to an actual or prospective regulated agreement, the security shall not be enforced so as to benefit the creditor or owner, directly or indirectly, to an extent greater (whether as respects the amount of any payment or the time or manner of its being made) than would be the case if the security were not provided and any obligations of the debtor or hirer, or his relative, under or in relation to the agreement were carried out to the extent (if any) to which they would be enforced under this Act.

(2)    In accordance with subsection (1), where a regulated agreement is enforceable on an order of the court or the Director only, any security provided in relation to the agreement is enforceable (so far as provided in relation to the agreement) where such an order has been made in relation to the agreement, but not otherwise.

(7)    Where an indemnity [or guarantee] is given in a case where the debtor or hirer is a minor, or [an indemnity is given in a case where he] is otherwise not of full capacity, the reference in subsection (1) to the extent to which his obligations would be enforced shall be read in relation to the indemnity [or guarantee] as a reference to the extent to which [those obligations] would be enforced if he were of full capacity.

PART IX

## 127.    Enforcement orders in cases of infringement.

(1)    In the case of an application for an enforcement order under—

(a)    section 65(1) (improperly executed agreements), . . . the court shall dismiss the application if, but (subject to subsections (3) and (4)) only if, it considers it just to do so having regard to—

(i)    prejudice caused to any person by the contravention in question, and the degree of culpability for it; and

(ii)    the powers conferred on the court by subsection (2) and sections 135 and 136.

(2)    If it appears to the court just to do so, it may in an enforcement order reduce or discharge any sum payable by the debtor or hirer, or any surety, so as to compensate him for prejudice suffered as a result of the contravention in question.

## 129.    Time orders.

(1)    If it appears to the court just to do so—

(a)    on an application for an enforcement order; or

(b)    on an application made by a debtor or hirer under this paragraph after service on him of—

(i)    a default notice, or

(ii)    a notice under section 76(1) or 98(1); or

(c)    in an action brought by a creditor or owner to enforce a regulated agreement or any security, or recover possession of any goods or land to which a regulated agreement relates,

the court may make an order under this section (a "time order").

(2)    A time order shall provide for one or both of the following, as the court considers just—

(a)    the payment by the debtor or hirer or any surety of any sum owed under a regulated agreement or a security by such instalments, payable at such times, as the court, having regard to the means of the debtor or hirer and any surety, considers reasonable;

(b)    the remedying by the debtor or hirer of any breach of a regulated agreement (other than non-payment of money) within such period as the court may specify.

## 132.    Financial relief for hirer.

(1)    Where the owner under a regulated consumer hire agreement recovers possession of goods to which the agreement relates otherwise than by action, the hirer may apply to the court for an order that—

(a)    the whole or part of any sum paid by the hirer to the owner in respect of the goods shall be repaid, and

(b)    the obligation to pay the whole or part of any sum owed by the hirer to the owner in respect of the goods shall cease,

and if it appears to the court just to do so, having regard to the extent of the enjoyment of the goods by the hirer, the court shall grant the application in full or in part.

## 137.    Extortionate credit bargains.

(1)    If the court finds a credit bargain extortionate it may reopen the credit agreement so as to do justice between the parties.

## 138.    When bargains are extortionate.

(1)    A credit bargain is extortionate if it—

(a)    requires the debtor or a relative of his to make payments (whether unconditionally, or on certain contingencies) which are grossly exorbitant, or

(b)    otherwise grossly contravenes ordinary principles of fair dealing.

(2)    In determining whether a credit bargain is extortionate, regard shall be had to such evidence as is adduced concerning—

    (a)    interest rates prevailing at the time it was made,

    (b)    the factors mentioned in subsection (3) to (5), and

    (c)    any other relevant considerations.

  (3)    Factors applicable under subsection (2) in relation to the debtor include—

    (a)    his age, experience, business capacity and state of health; and

    (b)    the degree to which, at the time of making the credit bargain, he was under financial pressure, and the nature of that pressure.

  (4)    Factors applicable under subsection (2) in relation to the creditor include—

    (a)    the degree of risk accepted by him, having regard to the value of any security provided;

    (b)    his relationship to the debtor; and

    (c)    whether or not a colourable cash price was quoted for any goods or services included in the credit bargain.

  (5)    Factors applicable under subsection (2) in relation to a linked transaction include the question how far the transaction was reasonably required for the protection of debtor or creditor, or was in the interest of the debtor.

### 139. Reopening of extortionate agreements.

  (2)    In reopening the agreement, the court may, for the purpose of relieving the debtor or a surety from payment of any sum in excess of that fairly due and reasonable, by order—

    (a)    direct accounts to be taken, or (in Scotland) an accounting to be made, between any persons,

    (b)    set aside the whole or part of any obligation imposed on the debtor or a surety by the credit bargain or any related agreement,

    (c)    require the creditor to repay the whole or part of any sum paid under the credit bargain or any related agreement by the debtor or a surety, whether paid to the creditor or any other person,

    (d)    direct the return to the surety of any property provided for the purposes of the security, or

    (e)    alter the terms of the credit agreement or any security instrument.

  (3)    An order may be made under subsection (2) notwithstanding that its effect is to place a burden on the creditor in respect of an advantage unfairly enjoyed by another person who is a party to a linked transaction.

## PART XI

### 162. Powers of entry and inspection.

  (1)    A duly authorised officer of an enforcement authority, at all reasonable hours and on production, if required, of his credentials, may—

    (a)    in order to ascertain whether a breach of any provision of or under this Act has been committed, inspect any goods and enter any premises (other than premises used only as a dwelling); . . .

    (c)    if he has reasonable cause to believe that a breach of any provision of or under this Act has been committed, seize and detain any goods in order to ascertain (by testing or otherwise) whether such a breach has been committed;

    (d)    seize and detain any goods, books or documents which he has reason to believe may be required as evidence in proceedings for an offence under this Act;

    (e)    for the purpose of exercising his powers under this subsection to seize goods, books or documents, but only if and to the extent that it is reasonably necessary for securing that the provisions of this Act and of any regulations made under it are duly observed, require any person having authority to do so to break open any container and, if that person does not comply, break it open himself.

  (2)    An officer seizing goods, books or documents in exercise of his powers under this section shall not do so without informing the person he seizes them from.

(4)    An officer entering premises by virtue of this section may take such other persons and equipment with him as he thinks necessary; and on leaving premises entered by virtue of a warrant under subsection (3) shall, if they are unoccupied or the occupier is temporarily absent, leave them as effectively secured against trespassers as he found them.

(6)    A person who is not a duly authorised officer of an enforcement authority, but purports to act as such under this section, commits an offence.

### 163.    Compensation for loss.

(1)    Where, in exercising his powers under section 162, an officer of an enforcement authority seizes and detains goods and their owner suffers loss by reason of—
    (a)    that seizure, or
    (b)    the loss, damage or deterioration of the goods during detention,
then, unless the owner is convicted of an offence under this Act committed in relation to the goods, the authority shall compensate him for the loss so suffered.

### 165.    Obstruction of authorised officers.

(1)    Any person who—
    (a)    wilfully obstructs an officer of an enforcement authority acting in pursuance of this Act; or
    (b)    wilfully fails to comply with any requirement properly made to him by such an officer under section 162; or
    (c)    without reasonable cause fails to give such an officer (so acting) other assistance or information he may reasonably require in performing his functions under this Act,
commits an offence.

### 170.    No further sanctions for breach of Act.

(1)    A breach of any requirement made (otherwise than by any court) by or under this Act shall incur no civil or criminal sanction as being such a breach, except to the extent (if any) expressly provided by or under this Act.

### 173.    Contracting-out forbidden.

(1)    A term contained in a regulated agreement or linked transaction, or in any other agreement relating to an actual or prospective regulated agreement or linked transaction, is void if, and to the extent that, it is inconsistent with a provision for the protection of the debtor or hirer or his relative or any surety contained in this Act or in any regulation made under this Act.

(2)    Where a provision specifies the duty or liability of the debtor or hirer or his relative or any surety in certain circumstances, a term is inconsistent with that provision if it purports to impose, directly or indirectly, an additional duty or liability on him in those circumstances.

(3)    Notwithstanding subsection (1), a provision of this Act under which a thing may be done in relation to any person on an order of the court or the Director only shall not be taken to prevent its being done at any time with that person's consent given at that time, but the refusal of such consent shall not give rise to any liability.

### 175.    Duty of persons deemed to be agents.

Where under this Act a person is deemed to receive a notice or payment as agent of the creditor or owner under a regulated agreement, he shall be deemed to be under a contractual duty to the creditor or owner to transmit the notice, or remit the payment, to him forthwith.

### 181.    Power to alter monetary limits etc.

(1)    The Secretary of State may by order made by statutory instrument amend, or further amend, any of the following provisions of this Act so as to reduce or increase a sum mentioned in that provision, namely, sections . . . 75(3)(b) . . .

**189.  Definitions.**
(1)    In this Act, unless the context otherwise requires—
"representation" includes any condition or warranty, and any other statement or undertaking, whether oral or in writing;

## THE CONTROL OF POLLUTION ACT 1974
### (1974, c. 40)

**3.    Prohibition of unlicensed disposal of waste.**
(1)    Except in prescribed cases, a person shall not—
(a)    deposit controlled waste on any land or cause or knowingly permit controlled waste to be deposited on any land; or
(b)    use any plant or equipment, or cause or knowingly permit any plant or equipment to be used, for the purpose of disposing of controlled waste or of dealing in a prescribed manner with controlled waste,
unless the land on which the waste is deposited or, as the case may be, which forms the site of the plant or equipment is occupied by the holder of a licence issued in pursuance of section 5 of this Act (in this Part of this Act referred to as a "disposal licence") which authorises the deposit or use in question and the deposit or use is in accordance with the conditions, if any, specified in the licence.
(2)    Except in a case falling within the following subsection, a person who contravenes any of the provisions of the preceding subsection shall, subject to subsection (4) of this section, be guilty of an offence and liable on summary conviction to a fine of an amount not exceeding £400 or on conviction on indictment to imprisonment for a term not exceeding two years or a fine or both.
(3)    A person who contravenes paragraph (a) of subsection (1) of this section in a case where—
(a)    the waste in question is of a kind which is poisonous, noxious or polluting; and
(b)    its presence on the land is likely to give rise to an environmental hazard; and
(c)    it is deposited on the land in such circumstances or for such a period that whoever deposited it there may reasonably be assumed to have abandoned it there or to have brought it there for the purpose of its being disposed of (whether by himself or others) as waste,
shall, subject to the following subsection, be guilty of an offence and liable on summary conviction to imprisonment for a term not exceeding six months or a fine not exceeding £400 or both or, on conviction or indictment, to imprisonment for a term not exceeding five years or a fine or both.
(4)    It shall be a defence for a person charged with an offence under this section to prove—
(a)    that he—
(i)    took care to inform himself, from persons who were in a position to provide the information, as to whether the deposit or use to which the charge relates would be in contravention of subsection (1) of this section, and
(ii)    did not know and had no reason to suppose that the information given to him was false or misleading and that the deposit or use might be in contravention of that subsection; or
(b)    that he acted under instructions from his employer and neither knew nor had reason to suppose that the deposit or use was in contravention of the said subsection (1); or
(c)    in the case of an offence of making, causing or permitting a deposit or use otherwise than in accordance with conditions specified in a disposal licence, that he took all such steps as were reasonably open to him to ensure that the conditions were complied with; or

(d)    that the acts specified in the charge were done in an emergency in order to avoid danger to the public and that, as soon as reasonably practicable after they were done, particulars of them were furnished to the disposal authority in whose area the acts were done.

## 18.    Application of preceding provisions to other waste.

(1)    The Secretary of State may, after consultation with such bodies as he considers appropriate, make regulations providing that prescribed provisions of section 1 to 11 and 14 to 17 of this Act shall have effect in a prescribed area—

(a)    as if references in those provisions to controlled waste or controlled waste of a kind specified in the regulations included references to such waste as is mentioned in section 30(3)(c)(ii) of this Act which is of a kind so specified; and

(b)    with such other modifications as are prescribed;

and regulations made in pursuance of this subsection may make such modifications of any enactment other than the sections aforesaid as the Secretary of State considers appropriate in connection with the regulations.

(2)    A person who—

(a)    deposits on any land any waste other than controlled waste; or

(b)    causes or knowingly permits the deposit on any land of any waste other than controlled waste,

in a case where, if the waste were controlled waste and any disposal licence relating to the land were not in force, he would be guilty of an offence under section 3(3) of this Act shall be guilty of such an offence and punishable accordingly unless the act charged was done in pursuance of and in accordance with the terms of any consent, licence, approval or authority granted under any enactment (excluding any planning permission under the enactments relating to town and country planning); and in this subsection 'land' includes such water as is mentioned in section 4(4) of this Act.

## 88.    Civil liability for contravention of s. 3(3).

(1)    Where any damage is caused by poisonous, noxious or polluting waste which has been deposited on land any person who deposited it or caused or knowingly permitted it to be deposited, in either case so as to commit an offence under section 3(3) or by virtue of section 18(2) of this Act, is liable for the damage except where the damage—

(a)    was due wholly to the fault of the person who suffered it; or

(b)    was suffered by a person who voluntarily accepted the risk thereof.

(2)    The matters which under paragraphs (a) to (c) of subsection (4) of section 3 of this Act may be proved by way of defence to a charge of committing an offence under subsection (3) of that section may be proved also by way of defence to an action brought by virtue of the preceding subsection (the reference in the said paragraph (a) to the charge being construed as a reference to the act alleged to give rise to the liability).

(3)    In this section—

"damage" includes the death of, or injury to, any person (including any disease and any impairment of physical or mental condition);

"fault" has the same meaning as in the Law Reform (Contributory Negligence) Act 1945 and

"land" includes such water as is mentioned in section 4(4) of this Act.

(4)    For the purposes of the following enactments, namely—

(a)    [the Fatal Accidents Act 1976];

(b)    the Law Reform (Contributory Negligence) Act 1945; and

(c)    [the Limitation Act 1980],

and for the purposes of any action of damages in Scotland arising out of the death of or personal injury to, any person, any damage for which a person is liable under subsection (1) of this section shall be treated as due to his fault.

(5)    Subsection (1) of this section is without prejudice to any liability which arises from the provisions of this section.

## THE HEALTH AND SAFETY AT WORK ACT 1974
### (1974, c. 37)

**2. General duties of employers to their employees.**

(1) It shall be the duty of every employer to ensure, so far as is reasonably practicable, the health, safety and welfare of work of all his employees.

**3. General duties of employers and self-employed to persons other than their employees.**

(1) It shall be the duty of every employer to conduct his undertaking in such a way as to ensure, so far as is reasonably practicable, that persons not in his employment who may be affected thereby are not thereby exposed to risks to their health or safety.

(2) It shall be the duty of every self-employed person to conduct his undertaking in such a way as to ensure, so far as is reasonably practicable, that he and other persons (not being his employees) who may be affected thereby are not thereby exposed to risks to their health or safety.

(3) In such cases as may be prescribed, it shall be the duty of every employer and every self-employed person, in the prescribed circumstances and in the prescribed manner, to give to persons (not being his employees) who may be affected by the way in which he conducts his undertaking the prescribed information about such aspects of the way in which he conducts his undertaking as might affect their health or safety.

**4. General duties of persons concerned with premises to persons other than their employees.**

(1) This section has effect for imposing on persons duties in relation to those who—
    (a) are not their employees; but
    (b) use non-domestic premises made available to them as a place of work or as a place where they may use plant or substances provided for their use there,
and applies to premises so made available and other non-domestic premises used in connection with them.

(2) It shall be the duty of each person who has, to any extent, control of premises to which this section applies or of the means of access thereto or egress therefrom or of any plant or substance in such premises to take such measures as it is reasonable for a person in his position to take to ensure, so far as is reasonably practicable, that the premises, all means of access thereto or egress therefrom available for use by persons using the premises, and any plant or substance in the premises or, as the case may be, provided for use there, is or are safe and without risks to health.

(3) Where a person has, by virtue of any contract or tenancy, an obligation of any extent in relation to—
    (a) the maintenance or repair of any premises to which this section applies or any means of access thereto or egress therefrom; or
    (b) the safety of or the absence of risks to health arising from plant or substances in any such premises;
that person shall be treated, for the purposes of subsection (2) above, as being a person who has control of the matters to which his obligation extends.

(4) Any reference in this section to a person having control of any premises or matter is a reference to a person having control of the premises or matter in connection with the carrying on by him of a trade, business or other undertaking (whether for profit or not).

**10. Establishment of the Commission and the Executive.**

(1) There shall be two bodies corporate to be called the Health and Safety Commission and the Health and Safety Executive . . .

## 15. Health and safety regulations.

[(1)    Subject to the provisions of section 50, the Secretary of State, the Minister of Agriculture, Fisheries and Food or the Secretary of State and the Minister acting jointly shall have power to make regulations under this section for any of the general purposes of this Part (and regulations so made are in this Part referred to as "health and safety regulations").]

(2)    Without prejudice to the generality of the preceding subsection, health and safety regulations may for any of the general purposes of this Part make provision for any of the purposes mentioned in Schedule 3.

(3)    Health and safety regulations—
    (a)    may repeal or modify any of the existing statutory provisions;
    (b)    may exclude or modify in relation to any specified class of case any of the provisions of sections 2 to 9 or any of the existing statutory provisions;
    (c)    may make a specified authority or class of authorities responsible, to such extent as may be specified, for the enforcement of any of the relevant statutory provisions.

(4)    Health and safety regulations—
    (a)    may impose requirements by reference to the approval of the Commission or any other specified body or person;
    (b)    may provide for references in the regulations to any specified document to operate as references to that document as revised or re-issued from time to time.

(5)    Health and safety regulations—
    (a)    may provide (either unconditionally or subject to conditions, and with or without limit of time) for exemptions from any requirement or prohibition imposed by or under any of the relevant statutory provisions;
    (b)    may enable exemptions from any requirement or prohibition imposed by or under any of the relevant statutory provisions to be granted (either unconditionally or subject to conditions, and with or without limit of time) by any specified person or by any person authorised in that behalf by a specified authority.

(6)    Health and safety regulations—
    (a)    may specify the persons or classes of persons who, in the event of a contravention of a requirement or prohibition imposed by or under the regulations, are to be guilty of an offence, whether in addition to or to the exclusion of other persons or classes of persons;
    (b)    may provide for any specified defence to be available in proceedings for any offence under the relevant statutory provisions either generally or in specified circumstances;
    (c)    may exclude proceedings on indictment in relation to offences consisting of a contravention of a requirement or prohibition imposed by or under any of the existing statutory provisions, sections 2 to 9 or health and safety regulations;
    (d)    may restrict the punishments [(other than the maximum fine on conviction on indictment)] which can be imposed in respect of any such offence as is mentioned in paragraph (c) above.

(7)    Without prejudice to section 35, health and safety regulations may make provision for enabling offences under any of the relevant statutory provisions to be treated as having been committed at any specified place for the purpose of bringing any such offence within the field of responsibility of any enforcing authority or conferring jurisdiction on any court to entertain proceedings for any such offence.

(8)    Health and safety regulations may take the form of regulations applying to particular circumstances only or to a particular case only (for example, regulations applying to particular premises only).

(9)    If an Order in Council is made under section 84(3) providing that this section shall apply to or in relation to persons, premises or work outside Great Britain then, notwithstanding the Order, health and safety regulations shall not apply to or in relation to

aircraft in flight, vessels, hovercraft or offshore installations outside Great Britain or persons at work outside Great Britain in connection with submarine cables or submarine pipelines except in so far as the regulations expressly so provide.

(10) In this section "specified" means specified in health and safety regulations.

### 17. Use of approved codes of practice in criminal proceedings.

A failure on the part of any person to observe any provision of an approved code of practice shall not of itself render him liable to any civil or criminal proceedings; but where in any criminal proceedings a party is alleged to have committed an offence by reason of a contravention of any requirement or prohibition imposed by or under any such provision as is mentioned in section 16(1) being a provision for which there was an approved code of practice at the time of the alleged contravention, the following subsection shall have effect with respect to that code in relation to those proceedings.

### 47. Civil liability.

(1) Nothing in this Part shall be construed—

(a) as conferring a right of action in any civil proceedings in respect of any failure to comply with any duty imposed by sections 2 to 7 or any contravention of section 8; or

(b) as affecting the extent (if any) to which breach of a duty imposed by any of the existing statutory provisions is actionable; or

(c) as affecting the operation of section 12 of the Nuclear Installations Act 1965 (right to compensation by virtue of certain provisions of that Act).

(2) Breach of a duty imposed by health and safety regulations [. . .] shall, so far as it causes damages, be actionable except in so far as the regulations provide otherwise.

(3) No provision made by virtue of section 15(6)(b) shall afford a defence in any civil proceedings, whether brought by virtue of subsection (2) above or not; but as regards any duty imposed as mentioned in subsection (2) above health and safety regulations [. . .] may provide for any defence specified in the regulations to be available in any action for breach of that duty.

(4) Subsections (1)(a) and (2) above are without prejudice to any right of action which exists apart from the provisions of this Act, and subsection (3) above is without prejudice to any defence which may be available apart from the provisions of the regulations there mentioned.

(5) Any term of an agreement which purports to exclude or restrict the operation of subsection (2) above, or any liability arising by virtue of that subsection, shall be void, except in so far as health and safety regulations [. . .] provide otherwise.

(6) In this section "damage" includes the death of, or injury to, any person (including any disease and any impairment of a person's physical or mental condition).

## THE REHABILITATION OF OFFENDERS ACT 1974
### (1974, c. 53)

### 4. Effect of rehabilitation.

(1) Subject to sections 7 and 8 below, a person who has become a rehabilitated person for the purposes of this Act in respect of a conviction shall be treated for all purposes in law as a person who has not committed or been charged with or prosecuted for or convicted of or sentenced for the offence or offences which were the subject of that conviction; and, notwithstanding the provisions of any other enactment or rule of law to the contrary, but subject as aforesaid—

(a) no evidence shall be admissible in any proceedings before a judicial authority exercising its jurisdiction or functions in Great Britain to prove that any such person has committed or been charged with or prosecuted for or convicted of or sentenced for any offence which was the subject of a spent conviction; and

(b)    a person shall not, in any such proceedings, be asked, and, if asked, shall not be required to answer, any question relating to his past which cannot be answered without acknowledging or referring to a spent conviction or spent convictions or any circumstances ancillary thereto.

## 8.    Defamation actions.

(1)    This section applies to any action for libel or slander begun after the commencement of this Act by a rehabilitated person and founded upon the publication of any matter imputing that the plaintiff has committed or been charged with or prosecuted for or convicted of or sentenced for an offence which was the subject of a spent conviction.

(2)    Nothing in section 4(1) above shall affect an action to which this section applies where the publication complained of took place before the conviction in question became spent, and the following provisions of this section shall not apply in any such case.

(3)    Subject to subsections (5) and (6) below, nothing in section 4(1) above shall prevent the defendant in an action to which this section applies from relying on any defence of justification or fair comment or of absolute or qualified privilege which is available to him, or restrict the matters he may establish in support of any such defence.

(4)    Without prejudice to the generality of subsection (3) above, where in any such action malice is alleged against a defendant who is relying on a defence of qualified privilege, nothing in section 4(1) above shall restrict the matters he may establish in rebuttal of the allegation.

(5)    A defendant in any such action shall not by virtue of subsection (3) above be entitled to rely upon the defence of justification if the publication is proved to have been made with malice.

(6)    Subject to subsection (7) below a defendant in any such action shall not, by virtue of subsection (3) above, be entitled to rely on any matter or adduce or require any evidence for the purpose of establishing (whether under section 3 of the Law of Libel Amendment Act 1888 or otherwise) the defence that the matter published constituted a fair and accurate report of judicial proceedings if it is proved that the publication contained a reference to evidence which was ruled to be inadmissible in the proceedings by virtue of section 4(1) above.

(7)    Subsection (3) above shall apply without the qualifications imposed by subsection (6) above in relation to—

(a)    any report of judicial proceedings contained in any bona fide series of law reports which does not form part of any other publication and consists solely of reports of proceedings in courts of law, and

(b)    any report or account of judicial proceedings published for bona fide educational, scientific or professional purposes or given in the course of any lecture, class or discussion given or held for any of those purposes.

## THE SOLICITORS ACT 1974
### (1974, c. 47)

## 37.    Professional indemnity.

(1)    The Council, with the concurrence of the Master of the Rolls, may make rules (in this Act referred to as "indemnity rules") concerning indemnity against loss arising from claims in respect of any description of civil liability incurred—

(a)    by a solicitor or former solicitor in connection with his practice or with any trust of which he is or formerly was a trustee;

(b)    by an employee or former employee of a solicitor or former solicitor in connection with that solicitor's practice or with any trust of which that solicitor or the employee is or formerly was a trustee.

(2)    For the purpose of providing such indemnity, indemnity rules—

(a)    may authorise or require the Society to establish and maintain a fund or funds;

(b)    may authorise or require the Society to take out and maintain insurance with authorised insurers;

(c)    may require solicitors or any specified class of solicitors to take out and maintain insurance with authorised insurers.

# THE TRADE UNION AND LABOUR RELATIONS ACT 1974
## (1974, c. 52)

**2.    Status of trade unions.**

(5)    The purposes of any trade union which is not a special register body and, in so far as they relate to the regulation of relations between employers and employers' associations and workers, the purposes of any trade union which is such a body, shall not, by reason only that they are in restraint of trade, be unlawful so as—

(a)    to make any member of the trade union liable to criminal proceedings for conspiracy or otherwise, or

(b)    to make any agreement or trust void or voidable;

nor shall any rule of a trade union which is not a special register body or, in so far as it so relates, any rule of any other trade union be unlawful or unenforceable by reason only that it is in restraint of trade.

**3.    Status of employers' associations.**

[*Section 3(5) is similar to s. 2(5).*]

**13.    Acts in contemplation or furtherance of trade disputes.**

[(1)    An act done by a person in contemplation or furtherance of a trade dispute shall not be actionable in tort on the ground only—

(a)    that it induces another person to break a contract or interferes or induces any other person to interfere with its performance; or

(b)    that it consists in his threatening that a contract (whether one to which he is a party or not) will be broken or its performance interfered with, or that he will induce another person to break a contract or to interfere with its performance.]

(4)    An agreement or combination by two or more persons to do or procure the doing of any act in contemplation or furtherance of a trade dispute shall not be actionable in tort if the act is one which, if done without any such agreement or combination, would not be actionable in tort.

**15.    Peaceful picketing.**

[(1)    It shall be lawful for a person in contemplation or furtherance of a trade dispute to attend—

(a)    at or near his own place of work, or

(b)    if he is an official of a trade union, at or near the place of work of a member of that union whom he is accompanying and whom he represents,

for the purpose only of peacefully obtaining or communicating information, or peacefully persuading any person to work or abstain from working.]

**16.    No compulsion to work.**

No court shall, whether by way of—

(a)    an order for specific performance or specific implement of a contract of employment, or

(b)    an injunction or interdict restraining a breach or threatened breach of such a contract,

compel an employee to do any work or attend at any place for the doing of any work.

**18.    Enforceability of collective agreements.**

(1)    Subject to subsection (3) below, any collective agreement made before 1st December 1971 or after the commencement of this section shall be conclusively presumed not to have been intended by the parties to be a legally enforceable contract unless the agreement—

(a)    is in writing, and

(b)    contains a provision which (however expressed) states that the parties intend that the agreement shall be a legally enforceable contract.

(2)    Any such agreement which satisfies the conditions in subsection (1)(a) and (b) above shall be conclusively presumed to have been intended by the parties to be a legally enforceable contract.

(4)    Notwithstanding anything in subsections (2) and (3) above, any terms of a collective agreement (whether made before or after the commencement of this section) which prohibit or restrict the right of workers to engage in a strike or other industrial action, or have the effect of prohibiting or restricting that right, shall not form part of any contract between any worker and the person for whom he works unless the collective agreement—

(a)    is in writing; and

(b)    that those terms shall or may be incorporated in such a contract; and

(c)    is reasonably accessible at his place of work to the worker to whom it applies and is available for him to consult during working hours; and

(d)    is one where each trade union which is a party to the agreement is an independent trade union;

and unless the contract with that worker expressly or impliedly incorporates those terms in the contract.

(5)    Subsection (4) above shall have effect notwithstanding any provision to the contrary in any agreement (including a collective agreement or a contract with any worker).

**29.    Meaning of trade dispute.**

(1)    In this Act "trade dispute" means a dispute [between workers and their employer] . . . which [relates wholly or mainly to] one or more of the following, that is to say—

(a)    terms and conditions of employment, or the physical conditions in which any workers are required to work;

(b)    engagement or non-engagement, or termination or suspension of employment or the duties of employment, of one or more workers;

(c)    allocation of work or the duties of employment as between workers or groups of workers;

(d)    matters of discipline;

(e)    the membership or non-membership of a trade union on the part of a worker;

(f)    facilities for officials of trade unions; and

(g)    machinery for negotiation or consultation, and other procedures, relating to any of the foregoing matters, including the recognition by employers or employers' associations of the right of a trade union to represent workers in any such negotiation or consultation or in the carrying out of such procedures.

## THE AIR TRAVEL RESERVE FUND ACT 1975
### (1975, c. 36)

**2.    Limits on the application of the Air Travel Reserve Fund.**

(1)    Subject to the following provisions of this section and any rules made by the Authority under section 3 below, the Fund may be applied in making payments to or for the benefit of customers of air travel organisers in respect of losses or liabilities incurred by

them in connection with overseas air travel contracts to which this section applies or overseas surface travel contracts.

(2) A person is a customer of an air travel organiser within the meaning of this section if he has made any payment to an air travel organiser under or with a view to entering into a contract with him; and for the purposes of this section a loss or liability incurred by a customer of an air travel organiser is a loss or liability incurred in connection with a contract of any description mentioned in subsection (1) above if—

(a) it is a loss incurred in respect of any payment made by the customer to the air travel organiser under or in contemplation of a contract of that description; or

(b) it is a loss or (as the case may be) a liability incurred in consequence of a breach by the air travel organiser of any of his obligations towards the customer under a contract of that description.

(3) Subsection (1) above does not apply to losses or liabilities incurred in connection with a contract of any description mentioned in that subsection unless—

(a) the losses or liabilities were incurred in consequence of the inability of the air travel organiser to meet his financial commitments under or in respect of contracts of that description . . .

## THE GUARD DOGS ACT 1975
### (1975, c. 50)

**1. Control of guard dogs.**

(1) A person shall not use or permit the use of a guard dog at any premises unless a person ("the handler") who is capable of controlling the dog is present on the premises and the dog is under the control of the handler at all times while it is being so used except while it is secured so that it is not at liberty to go free about the premises.

(3) A person shall not use or permit the use of a guard dog at any premises unless a notice containing a warning that a guard dog is present is clearly exhibited at each entrance to the premises.

**2. Restriction on keeping guard dogs without a licence.**

(1) A person shall not keep a dog at guard dog kennels unless he holds a licence under section 3 of this Act in respect of the kennels.

(2) A person shall not use or permit the use at any premises of a guard dog if he knows or has reasonable cause to suspect that the dog (when not being used as a guard dog) is normally kept at guard dog kennels in breach of subsection (1) of this section.

**5. Offences, penalties and civil liability.**

(1) A person who contravenes section 1 or 2 of this Act shall be guilty of an offence and liable on summary conviction to a fine not exceeding £400.

(2) The provisions of this Act shall not be construed as—

(a) conferring a right of action in any civil proceedings (other than proceedings for the recovery of a fine or any prescribed fee) in respect of any contravention of this Act or of any regulations made under this Act or of any of the terms or conditions of a licence granted under section 3 of this Act; or

(b) derogating from any right of action or other remedy (whether civil or criminal) in proceedings instituted otherwise than by virtue of this Act.

## THE PETROLEUM AND SUBMARINE PIPE-LINES ACT 1975
### (1975, c. 74)

**30. Civil liability for breach of statutory duty.**

(1) Breach of a duty imposed on any person by a provision of regulations which are made in pursuance of this Part of this Act and which state that this subsection applies to

such a breach shall be actionable so far, and only so far, as the breach causes personal injury; and references in section 1 of [the Fatal Accidents Act 1976], as it applies in England, Wales [and in Article 3(1) of the Fatal Accidents (Northern Ireland) Order 1977], to a wrongful act, neglect or default shall include references to any such breach which is so actionable.

(2)    Nothing in the preceding subsection prejudices any action which lies apart from the provisions of that subsection.

(3)    A defence to a charge which is available by virtue of section 32(3)(c) of this Act shall not be a defence in any civil proceedings which are brought either in pursuance of this section or otherwise.

(5)    In subsection (1) of this section "personal injury" includes any disease, any impairment of a person's physical or mental condition and any fatal injury.

## THE SEX DISCRIMINATION ACT 1975
### (1975, c. 65)

### 1.    Sex discrimination against women.

(1)    A person discriminates against a woman in any circumstances relevant for the purposes of any provision of this Act if—

(a)    on the ground of her sex he treats her less favourably than he treats or would treat a man, or

(b)    he applies to her a requirement or condition which applies or would apply equally to a man but—

(i)    which is such that the proportion of women who can comply with it is considerably smaller than the proportion of men who can comply with it, and

(ii)    which he cannot show to be justifiable irrespective of the sex of the person to whom it is applied, and

(iii)    which is to her detriment because she cannot comply with it.

(2)    If a person treats or would treat a man differently according to the man's marital status, his treatment of a woman is for the purposes of subsection (1)(a) to be compared to his treatment of a man having the like marital status.

### 2.    Sex discrimination against men.

(1)    Section 1, and the provisions of Parts II and III relating to sex discrimination against women, are to be read as applying equally to the treatment of men, and for that purpose shall have effect with such modifications as are requisite.

(2)    In the application of subsection (1) no account shall be taken of special treatment afforded to women in connection with pregnancy or childbirth.

### 29.    Discrimination in provision of goods, facilities or services.

(1)    It is unlawful for any person concerned with the provision (for payment or not) of goods, facilities or services to the public or a section of the public to discriminate against a woman who seeks to obtain or use those goods, facilities or services—

(a)    by refusing or deliberately omitting to provide her with any of them, or

(b)    by refusing or deliberately omitting to provide her with goods, facilities or services of the like quality, in the like manner and on the like terms as are normal in his case in relation to male members of the public or (where she belongs to a section of the public) to male members of that section.

### 41.    Liability of employers and principals.

(1)    Anything done by a person in the course of his employment shall be treated for the purposes of this Act as done by his employer as well as by him, whether or not it was done with the employer's knowledge or approval.

(2)    Anything done by a person as agent for another person with the authority (whether express or implied, and whether precedent or subsequent) of that other person shall be treated for the purposes of this Act as done by that other person as well as by him.

(3)    In proceedings brought under this Act against any person in respect of an act alleged to have been done by an employee of his it shall be a defence for that person to prove that he took such steps as were reasonably practicable to prevent the employee from doing that act, or from doing in the course of his employment acts of that description.

## 66.    Claims under Part III [ss. 22-36].

(1)    A claim by any person ("the claimant") that another person ("the respondent")—

(a)    has committed an act of discrimination against the claimant which is unlawful by virtue of Part III,  . . . may be made the subject of civil proceedings in like manner as any other claim in tort or (in Scotland) in reparation for breach of statutory duty.

(3)    As respects an unlawful act of discrimination falling within section 1(1)(b) (or, where this section is applied by section 65(1)(b), section 3(1)(b)) no award of damages shall be made if the respondent proves that the requirement or condition in question was not applied with the intention of treating the claimant unfavourably on the ground of his sex or marital status as the case may be.

(4)    For the avoidance of doubt it is hereby declared that damages in respect of an unlawful act of discrimination may include compensation for injury to feelings whether or not they include compensation under any other head.

## 71.    Persistent discrimination.

(1)    If, during the period of five years beginning on the date on which either of the following became final in the case of any person, namely,—

(a)    a non-discrimination notice served on him,

(b)    a finding by a court or tribunal under section 63 or 66, or section 2 of the Equal Pay Act 1970, that he has done an unlawful discriminatory act or an act in breach of a term modified or included by virtue of an equality clause,

it appears to the Commission that unless restrained he is likely to do one or more acts falling within paragraph (b), or contravening section 37, the Commission may apply to a county court for an injunction, or to the sheriff court for an order, restraining him from doing so; and the court, if satisfied that the application is well-founded, may grant the injunction or order in the terms applied for or in more limited terms.

## 77.    Validity and revision of contracts.

(1)    A term of a contract is void where—

(a)    its inclusion renders the making of the contract unlawful by virtue of this Act, or

(b)    it is included in furtherance of an act rendered unlawful by this Act, or

(c)    it provides for the doing of an act which would be rendered unlawful by this Act.

(2)    Subsection (1) does not apply to a term the inclusion of which constitutes or is in furtherance of, or provides for, unlawful discrimination against a party to the contract, but the term shall be unenforceable against that party.

(3)    A term in a contract which purports to exclude or limit any provision of this Act or the Equal Pay Act 1970 is unenforceable by any person in whose favour the term would operate apart from this subsection.

(4)    Subsection (3) does not apply—

(a)    to a contract settling a complaint to which section 63(1) of this Act or section 2 of the Equal Pay Act 1970 applies where the contract is made with the assistance of a conciliation officer;

(b)    to a contract settling a claim to which section 66 applies.

(5)    On the application of any person interested in a contract to which subsection (2) applies, a county court or sheriff court may make such order as it thinks just for removing

or modifying any term made unenforceable by that subsection; but such an order shall not be made unless all persons affected have been given notice of the application (except where under rules of court notice may be dispensed with) and have been afforded an opportunity to make representations to the court.

(6) An order under subsection (5) may include provision as respects any period before the making of the order.

## THE SOCIAL SECURITY ACT 1975
### (1975, c. 14)

**87. Benefit to be inalienable.**

(1) Subject to the provisions of this Act, every assignment of, or charge on, benefit and every agreement to assign or charge benefit shall be void; and, on the bankruptcy of a beneficiary, the benefit shall not pass to any trustee or other person acting on behalf of his creditors.

## THE UNSOLICITED GOODS AND SERVICES (AMENDMENT) ACT 1975
### (1975, c. 13)

**2. Amendments consequential on section 1.**

(1) In section 3(3) of the Act of 1971 for the words from "must state" to the end there shall be substituted the words "shall comply with the requirements of regulations under section 3A of this Act applicable thereto".

**3. Provision for offence under section 3(2) of the Act of 1971 to be prosecuted on indictment.**

(1) An offence under section 3(2) of the Act of 1971 may be prosecuted on indictment; and a person convicted on indictment of an offence under that section shall be liable to a fine.

(2) This section applies only to offences committed after the coming into operation of this section.

**4. Short title, citation, commencement, transitional provisions and extent.**

(2) Sections 1 and 3 of this Act and this section shall come into operation on the passing of this Act but any regulations made by virtue of the said section 1 shall not come into operation before the date appointed by order under subsection (3) below for the coming into operation of section 2 of this Act.

(3) Section 2 of this Act shall come into operation on such date as the Secretary of State may by order made by statutory instrument appoint; and different dates may be appointed by order under this subsection for different provisions of that section.

## THE CONGENITAL DISABILITIES (CIVIL LIABILITY) ACT 1976
### (1976, c. 28)

**1. Civil liability to child born disabled.**

(1) If a child is born disabled as the result of such an occurrence before its birth as is mentioned in subsection (2) below, and a person (other than the child's own mother) is under this section answerable to the child in respect of the occurrence, the child's disabilities are to be regarded as damage resulting from the wrongful act of that person and actionable accordingly at the suit of the child.

(2) An occurrence to which this section applies is one which—

(a) affected either parent of the child in his or her ability to have a normal, healthy child; or (b)　affected the mother during her pregnancy, or affected her or the child in the course of its birth, so that the child is born with disabilities which would not otherwise have been present.

(3)　Subject to the following subsections, a person (here referred to as 'the defendant') is answerable to the child if he was liable in tort to the parent or would, if sued in due time, have been so; and it is no answer that there could not have been such liability because the parent suffered no actionable injury, if there was a breach of legal duty which, accompanied by injury, would have given rise to the liability.

(4)　In the case of an occurrence preceding the time of conception, the defendant is not answerable to the child if at that time either or both of the parents knew the risk of their child being born disabled (that is to say, the particular risk created by the occurrence); but should it be the child's father who is the defendant, this subsection does not apply if he knew of the risk and the mother did not.

(5)　The defendant is not answerable to the child, for anything he did or omitted to do when responsible in a professional capacity for treating or advising the parent, if he took reasonable care having due regard to then received professional opinion applicable to the particular class of case; but this does not mean that he is answerable only because he departed from received opinion.

(6)　Liability to the child under this section may be treated as having been excluded or limited by contract made with the parent affected, to the same extent and subject to the same restrictions as liability in the parent's own case; and a contract term which could have been set up by the defendant in an action by the parent, so as to exclude or limit his liability to him or her, operates in the defendant's favour to the same, but no greater, extent in an action under this section by the child.

(7)　If in the child's action under this section it is shown that the parent affected shared the responsibility for the child being born disabled, the damages are to be reduced to such extent as the court thinks just and equitable having regard to the extent of the parent's responsibility.

**2.　Liability of woman driving while pregnant.**

A woman driving a motor vehicle when she knows (or ought reasonably to know) herself to be pregnant is to be regarded as being under the same duty to take care for the safety of her unborn child as the law imposes on her with respect to the safety of other people; and if in consequence of her breach of that duty her child is born with disabilities which would not otherwise have been present, those disabilities are to be regarded as damage resulting from her wrongful act and actionable accordingly at the suit of the child.

**3.　Disabled birth due to radiation.**

(1)　Section 1 of this Act does not affect the operation of the Nuclear Installations Act 1965 as to liability for, and compensation in respect of, injury or damage caused by occurrences involving nuclear matter or the emission of ionising radiations.

(2)　For the avoidance of doubt anything which—
(a)　affects a man in his ability to have a normal, healthy child; or
(b)　affects a woman in that ability, or so affects her when she is pregnant that her child is born with disabilities which would not otherwise have been present,
is an injury for the purposes of that Act.

(3)　If a child is born disabled as the result of an injury to either of its parents caused in breach of a duty imposed by any of sections 7 to 11 of that Act (nuclear site licensees and others to secure that nuclear incidents do not cause injury to persons, etc.), the child's disabilities are to be regarded under the subsequent provisions of that Act (compensation and other matters) as injuries caused on the same occasion, and by the same breach of duty, as was the injury to the parent.

(4)　As respects compensation to the child, section 13(6) of that Act (contributory fault of person injured by radiation) is to be applied as if the reference there to fault were to the fault of the parent.

(5)   Compensation is not payable in the child's case if the injury to the parent preceded the time of the child's conception and at that time either or both of the parents knew the risk of their child being born disabled (that is to say, the particular risk created by the injury).

### 4.   Interpretation and other supplementary provisions.

(1)   References in this Act to a child being born disabled or with disabilities are to its being born with any deformity, disease or abnormality, including predisposition (whether or not susceptible or immediate prognosis) to physical or mental defect in the future.

(2)   In this Act—

(a)   "born" means born alive (the moment of a child's birth being when it first has a life separate from its mother), and "birth" has a corresponding meaning; and

(b)   "motor vehicle" means a mechanically propelled vehicle intended or adapted for use on roads.

(3)   Liability to a child under section 1 or 2 of this Act is to be regarded—

(a)   as respects all its incidents and any matters arising or to arise out of it; and

(b)   subject to any contrary context or intention, for the purpose of construing references in enactments and documents to personal or bodily injuries and cognate matters,

as liability for personal injuries sustained by the child immediately after its birth.

(4)   No damages shall be recoverable under either of those sections in respect of any loss of expectation of life, nor shall any such loss be taken into account in the compensation payable in respect of a child under the Nuclear Installations Act 1965 as extended by section 3, unless (in either case) the child lives for at least 48 hours.

(5)   This Act applies in respect of births after (but not before) its passing, and in respect of any such birth it replaces any law in force before its passing, whereby a person could be liable to a child in respect of disabilities with which it might be born; but in section 1(3) of this Act the expression "liable in tort" does not include any reference to liability by virtue of this Act or to liability by virtue of any such law.

### 5.   Crown application.

This Act binds the Crown.

## THE DANGEROUS WILD ANIMALS ACT 1976
### (1976, c. 38)

### 1.   Licences.

(1)   Subject to section 5 of this Act, no person shall keep any dangerous wild animal except under the authority of a licence granted in accordance with the provisions of this Act by a local authority.

(3)   A local authority shall not grant a licence under this Act unless it is satisfied that—

(a)   it is not contrary to the public interest on the grounds of safety, nuisance or otherwise to grant the licence; . . .

(e)   all reasonable precautions will be taken at all such times to prevent and control the spread of infectious diseases; . . .

### 4.   Power to seize and to dispose of animals without compensation.

(1)   Where—

(a)   an animal is being kept contrary to section 1(1) of the Act, or

(b)   any condition of a licence under this Act is contravened or not complied with,

the local authority in whose area any animal concerned is for the time being may seize the animal, and either retain it in the authority's possession or destroy or otherwise dispose of it, and shall not be liable to pay compensation to any person in respect of the exercise of its powers under this subsection.

(2)    A local authority which incurs any expenditure in exercising its powers under subsection (1)(a) of this section shall be entitled to recover the amount of the expenditure summarily as a civil debt from any person who was at the time of the seizure a keeper of the animal concerned.

(3)    A local authority which incurs any expenditure in exercising its powers under subsection (1)(b) of this section shall be entitled to recover the amount of the expenditure summarily as a civil debt from the person to whom the licence concerned was granted.

## THE FATAL ACCIDENTS ACT 1976
### (1976, c. 30)

**1.    Right of action for wrongful act causing death.**

[(1)    If death is caused by any wrongful act, neglect or default which is such as would (if death had not ensued) have entitled the person injured to maintain an action and recover damages in respect thereof, the person who would have been liable if death had not ensued shall be liable to an action for damages, notwithstanding the death of the person injured.

(2)    Subject to section 1A(2) below, every such action shall be for the benefit of the dependants of the person ("the deceased") whose death has been so caused.

(3)    In this Act "dependant" means—

(a)    the wife or husband or former wife or husband of the deceased;

(b)    any person who—

(i)    was living with the deceased in the same household immediately before the date of the death; and

(ii)    had been living with the deceased in the same household for at least two years before that date; and

(iii)    was living during the whole of that period as the husband or wife of the deceased;

(c)    any parent or other ascendant of the deceased;

(d)    any person who was treated by the deceased as his parent;

(e)    any child or other descendant of the deceased;

(f)    any person (not being a child of the deceased) who, in the case of any marriage to which the deceased was at any time a party, was treated by the deceased as a child of the family in relation to that marriage;

(g)    any person who is, or is the issue of, a brother, sister, uncle or aunt of the deceased.

(4)    The reference to the former wife or husband of the deceased in subsection (3)(a) above includes a reference to a person whose marriage to the deceased has been annulled or declared void as well as a person whose marriage to the deceased has been dissolved.

(5)    In deducing any relationship for the purposes of subsection (3) above—

(a)    any relationship by affinity shall be treated as a relationship of consanguinity, any relationship of the half blood as a relationship of the whole blood, and the stepchild of any person as his child, and

(b)    an illegitimate person shall be treated as the legitimate child of his mother and reputed father.

(6)    Any reference in this Act to injury includes any disease and any impairment of a person's physical or mental condition.]

**[1A.    Bereavement.**

(1)    An action under this Act may consist of or include a claim for damages for bereavement.

(2)    A claim for damages for bereavement shall only be for the benefit—

(a)    of the wife or husband of the deceased; and

(b)    where the deceased was a minor who was never married—

    (i)     of his parents, if he was legitimate; and

    (ii)    of his mother, if he was illegitimate.

(3)    Subject to subsection (5) below, the sum to be awarded as damages under this section shall be £3,500.

(4)    Where there is a claim for damages under this section for the benefit of both the parents of the deceased, the sum awarded shall be divided equally between them (subject to any deduction falling to be made in respect of costs not recovered from the defendant).

(5)    The Lord Chancellor may by order made by statutory instrument, subject to annulment in pursuance of a resolution of either House of Parliament, amend this section by varying the sum for the time being specified in subsection (3) above.]

## 2.   Persons entitled to bring the action.

[(1)    The action shall be brought by and in the name of the executor or administrator of the deceased.

(2)    If—

    (a)    there is no executor or administrator of the deceased, or

    (b)    no action is brought within six months after the death by and in the name of an executor or administrator of the deceased,

the action may be brought by and in the name of all or any of the persons for whose benefit an executor or administrator could have brought it.

(3)    Not more than one action shall lie for and in respect of the same subject matter of complaint.

(4)    The plaintiff in the action shall be required to deliver to the defendant or his solicitor full particulars of the persons for whom and on whose behalf the action is brought and of the nature of the claim in respect of which damages are sought to be recovered.]

## 3.   Assessment of damages.

[(1)    In the action such damages, other than damages for bereavement, may be awarded as are proportioned to the injury resulting from the death to the dependants respectively.

(2)    After deducting the costs not recovered from the defendant any amount recovered otherwise than as damages for bereavement shall be divided among the dependants in such shares as may be directed.

(3)    In an action under this Act where there fall to be assessed damages payable to a widow in respect of the death of her husband there shall not be taken into account the re-marriage of the widow or her prospects of re-marriage.

(4)    In an action under this Act where there fall to be assessed damages payable to a person who is a dependant by virtue of section 1(3)(b) above in respect of the death of the person with whom the dependant was living as husband or wife there shall be taken into account (together with any other matter that appears to the court to be relevant to the action) the fact that the dependant had no enforceable right to financial support by the deceased as a result of their living together.

(5)    If the dependants have incurred funeral expenses in respect of the deceased, damages may be awarded in respect of those expenses.

(6)    Money paid into court in satisfaction of a cause of action under this Act may be in one sum without specifying any person's share.]

## 4.   Assessment of damages; disregard of benefits.

[In assessing damages in respect of a person's death in an action under this Act, benefits which have accrued or will or may accrue to any person from his estate or otherwise as a result of his death shall be disregarded.]

## 5.   Contributory negligence.

Where any person dies as the result partly of his own fault and partly of the fault of any other person or persons, and accordingly if an action were brought for the benefit of the estate under the Law Reform (Miscellaneous Provisions) Act 1934 the damages recoverable would be reduced under section 1(1) of the Law Reform (Contributory Negligence) Act 1945, any damages recoverable in an action [. . .] under this Act shall be reduced to a proportionate extent.

## THE RACE RELATIONS ACT 1976
### (1976, c. 74)

*[The following sections of this Act are similar to the corresponding provisions of the Sex Discrimination Act 1975 (ante) in brackets: RRA, ss. 1 (SDA, ss. 1, 2), 20 (SDA 29), 32 (SDA 41), 57 (SDA 66), 62 (SDA 71), 72 (SDA 77).]*

## THE RESALE PRICES ACT 1976
### (1976, c. 53)

**1.   Collective agreement by suppliers.**

(1)   It is unlawful for any two or more persons carrying on business in the United Kingdom as suppliers of any goods to make or carry out any agreement or arrangement by which they undertake—

(a)   to withhold supplies of goods for delivery in the United Kingdom from dealers (whether party to the agreement or arrangement or not) who resell or have resold goods in breach of any condition as to the price at which those goods may be resold;

(b)   to refuse to supply goods for delivery in the United Kingdom to such dealers except on terms and conditions which are less favourable than those applicable in the case of other dealers carrying on business in similar circumstances; or

(c)   to supply goods only to persons who undertake or have undertaken—

(i)     to withhold supplies of goods as described in paragraph (a) above; or

(ii)    to refuse to supply goods as described in paragraph (b) above.

(2)   It is unlawful for any two or more such persons to make or carry out any agreement or arrangement authorising—

(a)   the recovery of penalties (however described) by or on behalf of the parties to the agreement or arrangement from dealers who resell or have resold goods in breach of any such condition as is described in paragraph (a) of subsection (1) above; or

(b)   the conduct of any domestic proceedings in connection therewith.

**5.   Exclusive dealing.**

A contract for the sale of goods to which not more than two persons are party is not unlawful under this part of this Act by reason only of undertakings by the purchaser in relation to the goods sold and by the vendor in relation to other goods of the same description.

**25.   Contravention of and compliance with the Act.**

(1)   No criminal proceedings lie against any person on the ground that he has committed, or aided, abetted, counselled or procured the commission of, or conspired or attempted to commit, or incited others to commit, any contravention of sections 1 and 2 and sections 9 and 11 above.

(2)   Without prejudice to the right of any person to bring civil proceedings by virtue of subsection (3) below, compliance with those sections shall be enforceable by civil proceedings on behalf of the Crown for an injunction or other appropriate relief.

(3)   The obligation to comply with those sections is a duty owed to any person who may be affected by a contravention of them, and any breach of that duty is actionable accordingly (subject to the defences and other incidents applying to actions for breach of statutory duty).

# THE PROTECTION FROM EVICTION ACT 1977
## (1977, c. 43)

**1.　Unlawful eviction and harassment of occupier.**

　　(1)　In this section "residential occupier", in relation to any premises, means a person occupying the premises as a residence, whether under a contract or by virtue of any enactment or rule of law giving him the right to remain in occupation or restricting the right of any other person to recover possession of the premises.

　　(2)　If any person unlawfully deprives the residential occupier of any premises of his occupation of the premises or any part thereof, or attempts to do so, he shall be guilty of an offence unless he proves that he believed, and had reasonable cause to believe, that the residential occupier had ceased to reside in the premises.

　　(3)　If any person with intent to cause the residential occupier of any premises—

　　　　(a)　to give up the occupation of the premises or any part thereof; or

　　　　(b)　to refrain from exercising any right or pursuing any remedy in respect of the premises or part thereof;

does acts [likely] to interfere with the peace or comfort of the residential occupier or members of his household, or persistently withdraws or withholds services reasonably required for the occupation of the premises as a residence, he shall be guilty of an offence.

　　[(3A) Subject to subsection (3B) below, the landlord of a residential occupier or an agent of the landlord shall be guilty of an offence if—

　　　　(a)　he does acts likely to interfere with the peace or comfort of the residential occupier or members of his household, or

　　　　(b)　he persistently withdraws or withholds services reasonably required for the occupation of the premises in question as a residence,

and (in either case) he knows, or has reasonable cause to believe, that that conduct is likely to cause the residential occupier to give up the occupation of the whole or part of the premises or to refrain from exercising any right or pursuing any remedy in respect of the whole or part of the premises.

　　(3B)　A person shall not be guilty of an offence under subsection (3A) above if he proves that he had reasonable grounds for doing the acts or withdrawing or withholding the services in question.]

　　(5)　Nothing in this section shall be taken to prejudice any liability or remedy to which a person guilty of an offence thereunder may be subject in civil proceedings.

**2.　Restriction on re-entry without due process of law.**

Where any premises are let as a dwelling on a lease which is subject to a right of re-entry or forfeiture it shall not be lawful to enforce that right otherwise than by proceedings in the court while any person is lawfully residing in the premises or part of them.

**3.　Prohibition of eviction without due process of law.**

　　(1)　Where any premises have been let as a dwelling under a tenancy which is not a statutorily protected tenancy and—

　　　　(a)　the tenancy (in this section referred to as the former tenancy) has come to an end, but

　　　　(b)　the occupier continues to reside in the premises or part of them,

it shall not be lawful for the owner to enforce against the occupier, otherwise than by proceedings in the court, his right to recover possession of the premises.

　　(2)　In this section "the occupier", in relation to any premises, means any person lawfully residing in the premises or part of them at the termination of the former tenancy.

## THE TORTS (INTERFERENCE WITH GOODS) ACT 1977
## (1977, c. 32)

**1.   Definition of "wrongful interference with goods".**
In this Act "wrongful interference", or "wrongful interference with goods", means—
    (a)    conversion of goods (also called trover),
    (b)    trespass to goods,
    (c)    negligence so far as it results in damage to goods or to an interest in goods,
    (d)    subject to section 2, any other tort so far as it results in damage to goods or to an interest in goods.
[and references in this Act (however worded) to proceedings for wrongful interference or to a claim or right to claim for wrongful interference shall include references to proceedings by virtue of Part I of the Consumer Protection Act 1987 (product liability) in respect of any damage to goods or to an interest in goods or, as the case may be, to a claim or right to claim by virtue of that Part in respect of any such damage.]

**2.   Abolition of detinue.**
    (1)    Detinue is abolished.
    (2)    An action lies in conversion for loss or destruction of goods which a bailee has allowed to happen in breach of his duty to his bailor (that is to say it lies in a case which is not otherwise conversion, but would have been detinue before detinue was abolished).

**3.   Forms of judgment where goods are detained.**
    (1)    In proceedings for wrongful interference against a person who is in possession or in control of the goods relief may be given in accordance with this section, so far as appropriate.
    (2)    The relief is—
    (a)    an order for delivery of the goods, and for payment of any consequential damages, or
    (b)    an order for delivery of the goods, but giving the defendant the alternative of paying damages by reference to the value of the goods, together in either alternative with payment of any consequential damages, or
    (c)    damages.
    (3)    Subject to rules of court—
    (a)    relief shall be given under only one of paragraphs (a), (b) and (c) of subsection (2),
    (b)    relief under paragraph (a) of subsection (2) is at the discretion of the court, and the claimant may choose between the others.
    (4)    If it is shown to the satisfaction of the court that an order under subsection (2)(a) had not been complied with, the court may—
    (a)    revoke the order, or the relevant part of it, and
    (b)    make an order for payment of damages by reference to the value of the goods.
    (5)    Where an order is made under subsection (2)(b) the defendant may satisfy the order by returning the goods at any time before execution of judgment, but without prejudice to liability to pay any consequential damages.
    (6)    An order for delivery of the goods under subsection (2)(a) or (b) may impose such conditions as may be determined by the court, or pursuant to rules of court, and in particular, where damages by reference to the value of the goods would not be the whole of the value of the goods, may require an allowance to be made by the claimant to reflect the difference.
    For example, a bailor's action against the bailee may be one in which the measure of damages is not the full value of the goods, and then the court may order delivery of the goods, but require the bailor to pay the bailee a sum reflecting the difference.

(7)    Where under subsection (1) or subsection (2) of section 6 an allowance is to be made in respect of an improvement of the goods, and an order is made under subsection (2)(a) or (b), the court may assess the allowance to be made in respect of the improvement, and by the order require, as a condition for delivery of the goods, that allowance to be made by the claimant.

(8)    This section is without prejudice—

    (a)    to the remedies afforded by section 133 of the Consumer Credit Act, or . . .

    (c)    to any jurisdiction to afford ancillary or incidental relief.

**4.    Interlocutory relief where goods are detained.**

(1)    In this section "proceedings" means proceedings for wrongful interference.

(2)    On the application of any person in accordance with rules of court, the High Court shall, in such circumstances as may be specified in the rules, have power to make an order providing for the delivery up of any goods which are or may become the subject matter of subsequent proceedings in the court, or as to which any question may arise in proceedings.

(3)    Delivery shall be, as the order may provide, to the claimant or to a person appointed by the court for the purpose, and shall be on such terms and conditions as may be specified in the order.

**5.    Extinction of title on satisfaction of claim for damages.**

(1)    Where damages for wrongful interference are, or would fall to be, assessed on the footing that the claimant is being compensated—

    (a)    for the whole of his interest in the goods, or

    (b)    for the whole of his interest in the goods subject to a reduction for contributory negligence,

payment of the assessed damages (under all heads), or as the case may be settlement of a claim for damages for the wrong (under all heads), extinguishes the claimant's title to that interest.

(2)    In subsection (1) the reference to the settlement of the claim includes—

    (a)    where the claim is made in court proceedings, and the defendant has paid a sum into court to meet the whole claim, the taking of that sum by the claimant, and

    (b)    where the claim is made in court proceedings, and the proceedings are settled or compromised, the payment of what is due in accordance with the settlement or compromise, and

    (c)    where the claim is made out of court and is settled or compromised, the payment of what is due in accordance with the settlement or compromise.

(3)    It is hereby declared that subsection (1) does not apply where damages are assessed on the footing that the claimant is being compensated for the whole of his interest in the goods, but the damages paid are limited to some lesser amount by virtue of any enactment or rule of law.

(4)    Where under section 7(3) the claimant accounts over to another person (the "third party") so as to compensate (under all heads) the third party for the whole of his interest in the goods, the third party's title to that interest is extinguished.

(5)    This section has effect subject to any agreement varying the respective rights of the parties to the agreement, and where the claim is made in court proceedings has effect subject to any order of the court.

**6.    Allowance for improvement of the goods.**

(1)    If in proceedings for wrongful interference against a person (the "improver") who has improved the goods, it is shown that the improver acted in the mistaken but honest belief that he had a good title to them, an allowance shall be made for the extent to which, at the time as at which the goods fall to be valued in assessing damages, the value of the goods is attributable to the improvement.

(2)     If, in proceedings for wrongful interference against a person ("the purchaser") who has purported to purchase the goods—

    (a)     from the improver, or

    (b)     where after such a purported sale the goods passed by a further purported sale on one or more occasions, on any such occasion,

it is shown that the purchaser acted in good faith, an allowance shall be made on the principle set out in subsection (1).

For example, where a person in good faith buys a stolen car from the improver and is sued in conversion by the true owner the damages may be reduced to reflect the improvement, but if the person who bought the stolen car from the improver sues the improver for failure of consideration, and the improver acted in good faith, subsection (3) below will ordinarily make a comparable reduction in the damages he recovers from the improver.

(3)     If in a case within subsection (2) the person purporting to sell the goods acted in good faith, then in proceedings by the purchaser for recovery of the purchase price because of failure of consideration, or in any other proceedings founded on that failure of consideration, an allowance shall, where appropriate, be made on the principle set out in subsection (1).

(4)     This section applies, with the necessary modifications, to a purported bailment or other disposition of goods as it applies to a purported sale of goods.

## 7.     Double liability.

(1)     In this section "double liability" means the double liability of the wrongdoer which can arise—

    (a)     where one of two or more rights of action for wrongful interference is founded on a possessory title, or

    (b)     where the measure of damages in an action for wrongful interference founded on a proprietary title is or includes the entire value of the goods, although the interest is one of two or more interests in the goods.

(2)     In proceedings to which any two or more claimants are parties, the relief shall be such as to avoid double liability of the wrongdoer as between those claimants.

(3)     On satisfaction, in whole or in part, of any claim for an amount exceeding that recoverable if subsection (2) applied, the claimant is liable to account over to the other person having a right to claim to such extent as will avoid double liability.

(4)     Where, as the result of enforcement of a double liability, any claimant is unjustly enriched to an extent, he shall be liable to reimburse the wrongdoer to that extent.

For example, if a converter of goods pays damages first to a finder of the goods, and then to the true owner, the finder is unjustly enriched unless he accounts over to the true owner under subsection (3); and then the true owner is unjustly enriched and becomes liable to reimburse the converter of the goods.

## 8.     Competing rights to the goods.

(1)     The defendant in an action for wrongful interference shall be entitled to show, in accordance with rules of court, that a third party has a better right than the plaintiff as respects all or any part of the interest claimed by the plaintiff, or in right of which he sues, and any rule of law (sometimes called jus tertii) to the contrary is abolished.

(2)     Rules of court relating to proceedings for wrongful interference may—

    (a)     require the plaintiff to give particulars of his title,

    (b)     require the plaintiff to identify any person who, to his knowledge, has or claims any interest in the goods,

    (c)     authorise the defendant to apply for directions as to whether any person should be joined with a view to establishing whether he has a better right than the plaintiff, or has a claim as a result of which the defendant might be doubly liable,

(d)    where a party fails to appear on an application within paragraph (c), or to comply with any direction given by the court on such an application, authorise the court to deprive him of any right of action against the defendant for the wrong either unconditionally, or subject to such terms or conditions as may be specified.

(3)    Subsection (2) is without prejudice to any other power of making rules of court.

## 10.   Co-owners.

(1)    Co-ownership is no defence to an action founded on conversion or trespass to goods where the defendant without the authority of the other co-owner—

(a)    destroys the goods, or disposes of the goods in a way giving a good title to the entire property in the goods, or otherwise does anything equivalent to the destruction of the other's interest in the goods, or

(b)    purports to dispose of the goods in a way which would give a good title to the entire property in the goods if he was acting with the authority of all co-owners of the goods.

(2)    Subsection (1) shall not affect the law concerning execution or enforcement of judgments, or concerning any form of distress.

(3)    Subsection (1)(a) is by way of restatement of existing law so far as it relates to conversion.

## 11.   Minor amendments.

(1)    Contributory negligence is no defence in proceedings founded on conversion, or on intentional trespass to goods.

(2)    Receipt of goods by way of pledge is conversion if the delivery of the goods is conversion.

(3)    Denial of title is not of itself conversion.

## 12.   Bailee's power of sale.

(1)    This section applies to goods in the possession or under the control of a bailee where—

(a)    the bailor is in breach of an obligation to take delivery of the goods or, if the terms of the bailment so provide, to give directions as to their delivery, or

(b)    the bailee could impose such an obligation by giving notice to the bailor, but is unable to trace or communicate with the bailor, or

(c)    the bailee can reasonably expect to be relieved of any duty to safeguard the goods on giving notice to the bailor, but is unable to trace or communicate with the bailor.

(2)    In the cases of Part I of Schedule 1 to this Act a bailee may, for the purposes of subsection (1), impose an obligation on the bailor to take delivery of the goods, or as the case may be to give directions as to their delivery, and in those cases the said Part I sets out the method of notification.

(3)    If the bailee—

(a)    has in accordance with Part II of Schedule 1 to this Act given notice to the bailor of his intention to sell the goods under this subsection, or

(b)    has failed to trace or communicate with the bailor with a view to giving him such a notice, after having taken reasonable steps for the purpose,
and is reasonably satisfied that the bailor owns the goods, he shall be entitled, as against the bailor, to sell the goods.

(4)    Where subsection (3) applies but the bailor did not in fact own the goods, a sale under this section, or under section 13, shall not give a good title as against the owner, or as against a person claiming under the owner.

(5)    A bailee exercising his powers under subsection (3) shall be liable to account to the bailor for the proceeds of sale, less any cost of sale, and—

(a)    the account shall be taken on the footing that the bailee should have adopted the best method of sale reasonably available in the circumstances, and

(b)    where subsection (3)(a) applies, any sum payable in respect of the goods by the bailor to the bailee which accrued due before the bailee gave notice of intention to sell the goods shall be deductible from the proceeds of sale.

(6)    A sale duly made under this section gives a good title to the purchaser as against the bailor.

(7)    In this section, section 13, and Schedule 1 to this Act,

(a)    "bailor" and "bailee" include their respective successors in title, and

(b)    references to what is payable, paid or due to the bailee in respect of the goods include references to what would be payable by the bailor to the bailee as a condition of delivery of the goods at the relevant time.

(8)    This section, and Schedule 1 to this Act, have effect subject to the terms of the bailment.

(9)    This section shall not apply where the goods were bailed before the commencement of this Act.

**13.    Sale authorised by the court.**

(1)    If a bailee of the goods to which section 12 applies satisfies the court that he is entitled to sell the goods under section 12, or that he would be so entitled if he had given any notice required in accordance with Schedule 1 to this Act, the court—

(a)    may authorise the sale of the goods subject to such terms and conditions, if any, as may be specified in the order, and

(b)    may authorise the bailee to deduct from the proceeds of sale any costs of sale and any amount due from the bailor to the bailee in respect of the goods, and

(c)    may direct the payment into court of the net proceeds of sale, less any amount deducted under paragraph (b), to be held to the credit of the bailor.

(2)    A decision of the court authorising a sale under this section shall, subject to any right of appeal, be conclusive, as against the bailor, of the bailee's entitlement to sell the goods, and gives a good title to the purchaser as against the bailor.

(3)    In this section "the court" means the High Court or a county court, and a county court shall have jurisdiction in the proceedings if the value of the goods does not exceed the county court limit.

**14.    Interpretation.**

(1)    In this Act, unless the context otherwise requires—

. . .

"goods" includes all chattels personal other than things in action and money. . . .

**16.    Extent and application to the Crown.**

(3)    This Act shall bind the Crown, but as regards the Crown's liability in tort shall not bind the Crown further than the Crown is made liable in tort by the Crown Proceedings Act 1947.

**Section 12.**

## SCHEDULES

### SCHEDULE 1
### UNCOLLECTED GOODS

#### PART I
#### POWER TO IMPOSE OBLIGATION TO COLLECT GOODS

1.    (1)    For the purposes of section 12(1) a bailee may, in the circumstances specified in this Part of this Schedule, by notice given to the bailor impose on him an obligation to take delivery of the goods.

(2)    The notice shall be in writing, and may be given either—

(a)    by delivering it to the bailor, or

(b)    by leaving it at his proper address, or

(c)    by post.

(3)    The notice shall—

(a)    specify the name and address of the bailee, and give sufficient particulars of the goods and the address or place where they are held, and

(b)    state that the goods are ready for delivery to the bailor, or where combined with a notice terminating the contract of bailment, will be ready for delivery when the contract is terminated, and

(c)    specify the amount, if any, which is payable by the bailor to the bailee in respect of the goods and which became due before the giving of the notice.

(4)    Where the notice is sent by post it may be combined with a notice under Part II of this Schedule if the notice is sent by post in a way complying with paragraph 6(4).

(5)    References in this Part of this Schedule to taking delivery of the goods include, where the terms of the bailment admit, references to giving directions as to their delivery.

(6)    This Part of this Schedule is without prejudice to the provisions of any contract requiring the bailor to take delivery of the goods.

### Goods accepted for repair or other treatment

**2.**    If a bailee has accepted goods for repair or other treatment on the terms (expressed or implied) that they will be re-delivered to the bailor when the repair or other treatment has been carried out, the notice may be given at any time after the repair or other treatment has been carried out.

### Goods accepted for valuation or appraisal

**3.**    If a bailee has accepted goods in order to value or appraise them, the notice may be given at any time after the bailee has carried out the valuation or appraisal.

### Storage, warehousing, etc.

**4.**    (1)    If a bailee is in possession of goods which he has held as custodian, and his obligation as custodian has come to an end, the notice may be given at any time after the ending of the obligation, or may be combined with any notice terminating his obligation as custodian.

(2)    This paragraph shall not apply to goods held by a person as mercantile agent, that is to say by a person having in the customary course of his business as a mercantile agent authority either to sell goods or to consign goods for the purpose of sale, or to buy goods, or to raise money on the security of goods.

### Supplemental

**5.**    Paragraphs 2, 3 and 4 apply whether or not the bailor has paid any amount due to the bailee in respect of the goods, and whether or not the bailment is for reward, or in the course of business, or gratuitous.

## PART II
## NOTICE OF INTENTION TO SELL GOODS

**6.**    (1)    A notice under section 12(3) shall—

(a)    specify the name and address of the bailee, and give sufficient particulars of the goods and the address or place where they are held, and

(b)    specify the date on or after which the bailee proposes to sell the goods, and

(c)    specify the amount, if any, which is payable by the bailor to the bailee in respect of the goods, and which became due before the giving of the notice.

(2)    The period between giving of the notice and the date specified in the notice as that on or after which the bailee proposes to exercise the power of sale shall be such as will afford the bailor a reasonable opportunity of taking delivery of the goods.

(3)    If any amount is payable in respect of the goods by the bailor to the bailee, and become due before giving of the notice, the said period shall be not less than three months.

(4)    The notice shall be in writing and shall be sent by post in a registered letter, or by the recorded delivery service.

7.    (1)    The bailee shall not give a notice under section 12(3), or exercise his right to sell the goods pursuant to such a notice, at a time when he has notice that, because of a dispute concerning the goods, the bailor is questioning or refusing to pay all or any part of what the bailee claims to be due to him in respect of the goods.

(2)    This paragraph shall be left out of account in determining under section 13(1) whether a bailee of goods is entitled to sell the goods under section 12, or would be so entitled if he had given any notice required in accordance with this Schedule.

## THE UNFAIR CONTRACT TERMS ACT 1977
### (1977, c. 50)
### PART I

### 1.    Scope of Part I.

(1)    For the purposes of this Part of this Act, "negligence" means the breach—

(a)    of any obligation, arising from the express or implied terms of a contract, to take reasonable care or exercise reasonable skill in the performance of the contract;

(b)    of any common law duty to take reasonable care or exercise reasonable skill (but not any stricter duty);

(c)    of the common duty of care imposed by the Occupiers' Liability Act 1957 or the Occupier's Liability Act (Northern Ireland) 1957.

(2)    This Part of this Act is subject to Part III; and in relation to contracts, the operation of sections 2 to 4 and 7 is subject to the exceptions made by Schedule I.

(3)    In the case of both contract and tort, sections 2 to 7 apply (except where the contrary is stated in section 6(4)) only to business liability, that is liability for breach of obligations or duties arising—

(a)    from things done or to be done by a person in the course of a business (whether his own business or another's); or

(b)    from the occupation of premises used for business purposes of the occupier; and references to liability are to be read accordingly [but liability of an occupier of premises for breach of an obligation or duty towards a person obtaining access to the premises for recreational or educational purposes, being liability for loss or damage suffered by reason of the dangerous state of the premises, is not a business liability of the occupier unless granting that person such access for the purposes concerned falls within the business purposes of the occupier].

(4)    In relation to any breach of duty or obligation, it is immaterial for any purpose of this Part of this Act whether the breach was inadvertent or intentional, or whether liability for it arises directly or vicariously.

### 2.    Negligence liability.

(1)    A person cannot by reference to any contract term or to a notice given to persons generally or to particular persons exclude or restrict his liability for death or personal injury resulting from negligence.

(2)    In the case of other loss or damage, a person cannot so exclude or restrict his liability for negligence except in so far as the term or notice satisfies the requirement of reasonableness.

(3)    Where a contract term or notice purports to exclude or restrict liability for negligence a person's agreement to or awareness of it is not of itself to be taken as indicating his voluntary acceptance of any risk.

### 3.    Liability arising in contract.

(1)    This section applies as between contracting parties where one of them deals as consumer or on the other's written standard terms of business.

(2)    As against that party, the other cannot by reference to any contract term—

(a)    when himself in breach of contract, exclude or restrict any liability of his in respect of the breach; or

(b)    claim to be entitled—

(i)    to render a contractual performance substantially different from that which was reasonably expected of him, or

(ii)    in respect of the whole or any part of his contractual obligation, to render no performance at all,

except in so far as (in any of the cases mentioned above in this subsection) the contract term satisfies the requirement of reasonableness.

### 4.    Unreasonable indemnity clauses.

(1)    A person dealing as consumer cannot by reference to any contract term be made to indemnify another person (whether a party to the contract or not) in respect of liability that may be incurred by the other for negligence or breach of contract, except in so far as the contract term satisfies the requirement of reasonableness.

(2)    This section applies whether the liability in question—

(a)    is directly that of the person to be indemnified or is incurred by him vicariously;

(b)    is to the person dealing as consumer or to someone else.

### 5.    "Guarantee" of consumer goods.

(1)    In the case of goods of a type ordinarily supplied for private use or consumption, where loss or damage—

(a)    arises from the goods proving defective while in consumer use; and

(b)    results from the negligence of a person concerned in the manufacture or distribution of the goods,

liability for the loss or damage cannot be excluded or restricted by reference to any contract term or notice contained in or operating by reference to a guarantee of the goods.

(2)    For these purposes—

(a)    goods are to be regarded as "in consumer use" when a person is using them, or has them in his possession for use, otherwise than exclusively for the purposes of a business; and

(b)    anything in writing is a guarantee if it contains or purports to contain some promise or assurance (however worded or presented) that defects will be made good by complete or partial replacement, or by repair, monetary compensation or otherwise.

(3)    This section does not apply as between the parties to a contract under or in pursuance of which possession or ownership of the goods passed.

### 6.    Sale and hire-purchase.

(1)    Liability for breach of the obligations arising from—

(a)    [section 12 of the Sale of Goods Act 1979] (seller's implied undertakings as to title, etc.);

(b)    section 8 of the Supply of Goods (Implied Terms) Act 1973 (the corresponding thing in relation to hire-purchase),

cannot be excluded or restricted by reference to any contract term.

(2)    As against a person dealing as consumer, liability for breach of the obligations arising from—

(a)    [section 13, 14 or 15 of the [1979] Act] (seller's implied undertakings as to conformity of goods with description or sample, or as to their quality or fitness for a particular purpose);

(b)     section 9, 10 or 11 of the 1973 Act (the corresponding things in relation to hire-purchase),
cannot be excluded or restricted by reference to any contract term.

(3)     As against a person dealing otherwise than as consumer, the liability specified in subsection (2) above can be excluded or restricted by reference to a contract term, but only in so far as the term satisfies the requirement of reasonableness.

(4)     The liabilities referred to in this section are not only the business liabilities defined by section 1(3), but include those arising under any contract of sale of goods or hire-purchase agreement.

### 7.   Miscellaneous contracts under which goods pass.

(1)     Where the possession or ownership of goods passes under or in pursuance of a contract not governed by the law of sale of goods or hire-purchase, subsections (2) to (4) below apply as regards the effect (if any) to be given to contract terms excluding or restricting liability for breach of obligation arising by implication of law from the nature of the contract.

(2)     As against a person dealing as consumer, liability in respect of the goods' correspondence with description or sample, or their quality or fitness for any particular purpose, cannot be excluded or restricted by reference to any such term.

(3)     As against a person dealing otherwise than as consumer, that liability can be excluded or restricted by reference to such a term, but only in so far as the term satisfies the requirement of reasonableness.

[(3A) Liability for breach of the obligations arising under section 2 of the Supply of Goods and Services Act 1982 (implied terms about title etc. in certain contracts for the transfer of the property in goods) cannot be excluded or restricted by reference to any such term.]

(4)     Liability in respect of—
(a)     the right to transfer ownership of the goods, or give possession; or
(b)     the assurance of quiet possession to a person taking goods in pursuance of the contract,
cannot [(in a case to which subsection (3A) above does not apply)] be excluded or restricted by reference to any such term except in so far as the term satisfies the requirement of reasonableness.

(c)     This section does not apply in the case of goods passing on a redemption of trading stamps within the Trading Stamps Act 1964 or the Trading Stamps Act (Northern Ireland) 1965.

### 9.   Effect of breach.

(1)     Where for reliance upon it a contract term has to satisfy the requirement of reasonableness, it may be found to do so and be given effect accordingly notwithstanding that the contract has been terminated either by breach or by a party electing to treat it as repudiated.

(2)     Where on a breach the contract is nevertheless affirmed by a party entitled to treat it as repudiated, this does not of itself exclude the requirement of reasonableness in relation to any contract term.

### 10.   Evasion by means of secondary contract.

A person is not bound by any contract term prejudicing or taking away rights of his which arise under, or in connection with the performance of, another contract, so far as those rights extend to the enforcement of another's liability which this Part of this Act prevents that other from excluding or restricting.

### 11.   The "reasonableness" test.

(1)     In relation to a contract term, the requirement of reasonableness for the purposes of this Part of this Act, section 3 of the Misrepresentation Act 1967 and section 3 of the

Misrepresentation Act (Northern Ireland) 1967 is that the term shall have been a fair and reasonable one to be included having regard to the circumstances which were, or ought reasonably to have been, known to or in the contemplation of the parties when the contract was made.

(2)    In determining for the purposes of section 6 or 7 above whether a contract term satisfies the requirement of reasonableness, regard shall be had in particular to the matters specified in Schedule 2 to this Act; but this subsection does not prevent the court or arbitrator from holding, in accordance with any rule of law, that a term which purports to exclude or restrict any relevant liability is not a term of the contract.

(3)    In relation to a notice (not being a notice having contractual effect), the requirement of reasonableness under this Act is that it should be fair and reasonable to allow reliance on it, having regard to all the circumstances obtaining when the liability arose or (but for the notice) would have arisen.

(4)    Where by reference to a contract term or notice a person seeks to restrict liability to a specified sum of money, and the question arises (under this or any other Act) whether the term or notice satisfies the requirement of reasonableness, regard shall be had in particular (but without prejudice to subsection (2) above in the case of contract terms) to—

(a)    the resources which he could expect to be available to him for the purpose of meeting the liability should it arise; and

(b)    how far it was open to him to cover himself by insurance.

(5)    It is for those claiming that a contract term or notice satisfies the requirement of reasonableness to show that it does.

**12.    "Dealing as consumer".**

(1)    A party to a contract "deals as consumer" in relation to another party if—

(a)    he neither makes the contract in the course of a business nor holds himself out as doing so; and

(b)    the other party does make the contract in the course of a business; and

(c)    in the case of a contract governed by the law of sale of goods or hire-purchase, or by section 7 of this Act, the goods passing under or in pursuance of the contract are of a type ordinarily supplied for private use or consumption.

(2)    But on a sale by auction or by competitive tender the buyer is not in any circumstances to be regarded as dealing as consumer.

(3)    Subject to this, it is for those claiming that a party does not deal as consumer to show that he does not.

**13.    Varieties of exemption clause.**

(1)    To the extent that this Part of this Act prevents the exclusion or restriction of any liability it also prevents—

(a)    making the liability or its enforcement subject to restrictive or onerous conditions;

(b)    excluding or restricting any right or remedy in respect of the liability, or subjecting a person to any prejudice in consequence of his pursuing any such right or remedy;

(c)    excluding or restricting rules of evidence or procedure;

and (to that extent) sections 2 and 5 to 7 also prevent excluding or restricting liability by reference to terms and notices which exclude or restrict the relevant obligation or duty.

(2)    But an agreement in writing to submit present or future differences to arbitration is not to be treated under this Part of this Act as excluding or restricting any liability.

**14.    Interpretation of Part I.**

In this Part of the Act—

"business" includes a profession and the activities of any government department or local or public authority;

"goods" has the same meaning as in [the Sale of Goods Act 1979];

"hire-purchase agreement" has the same meaning as in the Consumer Credit Act 1974;

"negligence" has the meaning given by section 1(1);

"notice" includes an announcement, whether or not in writing, and any other communication or pretended communication; and

"personal injury" includes any disease and any impairment of physical or mental condition.

## PART III

### 26.   International supply contracts.

(1)   The limits imposed by this Act on the extent to which a person may exclude or restrict liability by reference to a contract term do not apply to liability arising under such a contract as is described in subsection (3) below.

(2)   The terms of such a contract are not subject to any requirement of reasonableness under section 3 or 4: and nothing in Part II of this Act shall require the incorporation of the terms of such a contract to be fair and reasonable for them to have effect.

(3)   Subject to subsection (4), that description of contract is one whose characteristics are the following—

(a)   either it is a contract of sale of goods or it is one under or in pursuance of which the possession or ownership of goods passes; and

(b)   it is made by parties whose places of business (or, if they have none, habitual residences) are in the territories of different States (the Channel Islands and the Isle of Man being treated for this purpose as different States from the United Kingdom).

(4)   A contract falls within subsection (3) above only if either—

(a)   the goods in question are, at the time of the conclusion of the contract, in the course of carriage, or will be carried, from the territory of one State to the territory of another; or

(b)   the acts constituting the offer and acceptance have been done in the territories of different States; or

(c)   the contract provides for the goods to be delivered to the territory of a State other than that within whose territory those acts were done.

### 27.   Choice of law clauses.

(1)   Where the proper law of a contract is the law of any part of the United Kingdom only by choice of the parties (and apart from that choice would be the law of some country outside the United Kingdom) sections 2 to 7 and 16 to 21 of this Act do not operate as part of the proper law.

(2)   This Act has effect notwithstanding any contract term which applies or purports to apply the law of some country outside the United Kingdom, where (either or both)—

(a)   the term appears to the court, or arbitrator or arbiter to have been imposed wholly or mainly for the purpose of enabling the party imposing it to evade the operation of this Act; or

(b)   in the making of the contract one of the parties dealt as consumer, and he was then habitually resident in the United Kingdom, and the essential steps necessary for the making of the contract were taken there, whether by him or by others on his behalf.

### 29.   Saving for other relevant legislation.

(1)   Nothing in this Act removes or restricts the effect of, or prevents reliance upon, any contractual provision which—

(a)   is authorised or required by the express terms or necessary implication of an enactment; or

(b)   being made with a view to compliance with an international agreement to which the United Kingdom is a party, does not operate more restrictively than is contemplated by the agreement.

(2)   A contract term is to be taken—

(a)    for the purposes of Part I of this Act, as satisfying the requirement of reasonableness . . .
if it is incorporated or approved by, or incorporated pursuant to a decision or ruling of, a competent authority acting in the exercise of any statutory jurisdiction or function and is not a term in a contract to which the competent authority is itself a party.

(3)    In this section—
"competent authority" means any court, arbitrator or arbiter, government department or public authority;
"enactment" means any legislation (including subordinate legislation) of the United Kingdom or Northern Ireland and any instrument having effect by virtue of such legislation; and
"statutory" means conferred by an enactment.

## SCHEDULES

**Section 1(2)**                                      **SCHEDULE 1**

### SCOPE OF SECTIONS 2 TO 4 AND 7

1.    Sections 2 to 4 of this Act do not extend to—
(a)    any contract of insurance (including a contract to pay an annuity on human life);
(b)    any contract so far as it relates to the creation or transfer of an interest in land, or to the termination of such an interest, whether by extinction, merger, surrender, forfeiture or otherwise;
(c)    any contract so far as it relates to the creation or transfer of a right or interest in any patent, trade mark, copyright, registered design, technical or commercial information or other intellectual property, or relates to the termination of any such right or interest;
(d)    any contract so far as it relates—
(i)    to the formation or dissolution of a company (which means any body corporate or unincorporated association and includes a partnership), or
(ii)    to its constitution or the rights or obligations of its corporators or members;
(e)    any contract so far as it relates to the creation or transfer of securities or of any right or interest in securities.

2.    Section 2(1) extends to—
(a)    any contract of marine salvage or towage;
(b)    any charterparty of a ship or hovercraft; and
(c)    any contract for the carriage of goods by ship or hovercraft;
but subject to this sections 2 to 4 and 7 do not extend to any such contract except in favour of a person dealing as consumer.

3.    Where goods are carried by ship or hovercraft in pursuance of a contract which either—
(a)    specifies that as the means of carriage over part of the journey to be covered, or
(b)    makes no provision as to the means of carriage and does not exclude that means,
then sections 2(2), 3 and 4 do not, except in favour of a person dealing as consumer, extend to the contract as it operates for and in relation to the carriage of the goods by that means.

4.    Section 2(1) and (2) do not extend to a contract of employment, except in favour of the employee.

5.    Section 2(1) does not affect the validity of any discharge and indemnity given by a person, on or in connection with an award to him of compensation for pneumoconiosis attributable to employment in the coal industry, in respect of any further claim arising from his contracting that disease.

**Sections 11 (2) and 24 (2)**      SCHEDULE 2

## "GUIDELINES" FOR APPLICATION OF REASONABLENESS TEST

The matters to which regard is to be had in particular for the purposes of sections 6(3), 7(3) and (4), 20 and 21 are any of the following which appear to be relevant—

(a) the strength of the bargaining positions of the parties relative to each other, taking into account (among other things) alternative means by which the customer's requirements could have been met;

(b) Whether the customer received an inducement to agree to the term, or in accepting it had an opportunity of entering into a similar contract with other persons, but without having to accept a similar term;

(c) whether the customer knew or ought reasonably to have known of the existence and extent of the term (having regard, among other things, to any custom of the trade and any previous course of dealing between the parties);

(d) where the term excludes or restricts any relevant liability if some condition is not complied with, whether it was reasonable at the time of the contract to expect that compliance with that condition would be practicable;

(e) whether the goods were manufactured, processed or adapted to the special order of the customer.

## THE CIVIL LIABILITY (CONTRIBUTION) ACT 1978
### (1978, c. 47)

**1.   Entitlement to contribution.**

(1)   Subject to the following provisions of this section, any person liable in respect of any damage suffered by another person may recover contribution from any other person liable in respect of the same damage (whether jointly with him or otherwise).

(2)   A person shall be entitled to recover contribution by virtue of subsection (1) above notwithstanding that he has ceased to be liable in respect of the damage in question since the time when the damage occurred, provided that he was so liable immediately before he made or was ordered or agreed to make the payment in respect of which the contribution is sought.

(3)   A person shall be liable to make contribution by virtue of subsection (1) above notwithstanding that he has ceased to be liable in respect of the damage in question since the time when the damage occurred, unless he ceased to be liable by virtue of the expiry of a period of limitation or prescription which extinguished the right on which the claim against him in respect of the damage was based.

(4)   A person who has made or agreed to make any payment in bona fide settlement or compromise of any claim made against him in respect of any damage (including a payment into court which has been accepted) shall be entitled to recover contribution in accordance with this section without regard to whether or not he himself is or ever was liable in respect of the damage, provided, however, that he would have been liable assuming that the factual basis of the claim against him could be established.

(5)   A judgment given in any action brought in any part of the United Kingdom by or on behalf of the person who suffered the damage in question against any person from whom contribution is sought under this section shall be conclusive in the proceedings for contribution as to any issue determined by that judgment in favour of the person from whom the contribution is sought.

(6)   References in this section to a person's liability in respect of any damage are references to any such liability which has been or could be established in an action brought against him in England and Wales by or on behalf of the person who suffered the damage; but it is immaterial whether any issue arising in any such action was or would be

determined (in accordance with the rules of private international law) by reference to the law of a country outside England and Wales.

## 2. Assessment of contribution.

(1)    Subject to subsection (3) below, in any proceedings for contribution under section 1 above the amount of the contribution recoverable from any person shall be such as may be found by the court to be just and equitable having regard to the extent of that person's responsibility for the damage in question.

(2)    Subject to subsection (3) below, the court shall have power in any such proceedings to exempt any person from liability to make contribution or to direct that the contribution to be recovered from any person shall amount to a complete indemnity.

(3)    Where the amount of the damages which have or might have been awarded in respect of the damage in question in any action brought in England and Wales by or on behalf of the person who suffered it against the person from whom the contribution is sought was or would have been subject to—

(a)    any limit imposed by or under any enactment or by any agreement made before the damage occurred;

(b)    any reduction by virtue of section 1 of the Law Reform (Contributory Negligence) Act 1945 or section 5 of the Fatal Accidents Act 1976; or

(c)    any corresponding limit or reduction under the law of a country outside England and Wales;

the person from whom the contribution is sought shall not by virtue of any contribution awarded under section 1 above be required to pay in respect of the damage a greater amount than the amount of those damages as so limited or reduced.

## 3. Proceedings against persons jointly liable for the same debt or damage.

Judgment recovered against any person liable in respect of any debt or damage shall not be a bar to an action, or to the continuance of an action, against any other person who is (apart from any such bar) jointly liable with him in respect of the same debt or damage.

## 4. Successive actions against persons liable (jointly or otherwise) for the same damage.

If more than one action is brought in respect of any damage by or on behalf of the person by whom it was suffered against persons liable in respect of the damage (whether jointly or otherwise) the plaintiff shall not be entitled to costs in any of those actions, other than that in which judgment is first given, unless the court is of the opinion that there was reasonable ground for bringing the action.

## 5. Application to the Crown.

Without prejudice to section 4(1) of the Crown Proceedings Act 1947 (indemnity and contribution), this Act shall bind the Crown, but nothing in this Act shall be construed as in any way affecting Her Majesty in Her private capacity (including in right of Her Duchy of Lancaster) or the Duchy of Cornwall.

## 6. Interpretation.

(1)    A person is liable in respect of any damage for the purposes of this Act if the person who suffered it (or anyone representing his estate or dependants) is entitled to recover compensation from him in respect of that damage (whatever the legal basis of his liability, whether tort, breach of contract, breach of trust or otherwise).

(2)    References in this Act to an action brought by or on behalf of the person who suffered any damage include references to an action brought for the benefit of his estate or dependants.

(3)    In this Act "dependants" has the same meaning as in the Fatal Accidents Act 1976.

(4)    In this Act, except in section 1(5) above, "action" means an action brought in England and Wales.

7. **Savings.**

(3) The right to recover contribution in accordance with section 1 above supersedes any right, other than an express contractual right, to recover contribution (as distinct from indemnity) otherwise than under this Act in corresponding circumstances; but nothing in this Act shall affect—

(a) any express or implied contractual or other right to indemnity; or

(b) any express contractual provision regulating or excluding contribution;

which would be enforceable apart from this Act (or render enforceable any agreement for indemnity or contribution which would not be enforceable apart from this Act).

## THE STATE IMMUNITY ACT 1978
### (1978, c. 33)

1. **General immunity from jurisdiction.**

(1) A State is immune from the jurisdiction of the courts of the United Kingdom except as provided in the following provisions of this Part of this Act.

(2) A court shall give effect to the immunity conferred by this section even though the State does not appear in the proceedings in question.

3. **Commercial transactions and contracts to be performed in United Kingdom.**

(1) A State is not immune as respects proceedings relating to—

(a) a commercial transaction entered into by the State; or

(b) an obligation of the State which by virtue of a contract (whether a commercial transaction or not) falls to be performed wholly or partly in the United Kingdom.

(2) This section does not apply if the parties to the dispute are States or have otherwise agreed in writing; and subsection (1)(b) above does not apply if the contract (not being a commercial transaction) was made in the territory of the State concerned and the obligation in question is governed by its administrative law.

5. **Personal injuries and damage to property.**

A State is not immune as respects proceedings in respect of—

(a) death or personal injury; or

(b) damage to or loss of tangible property,

caused by an act or omission in the United Kingdom.

## THE ARBITRATION ACT 1979
### (1979, c. 42)

3. **Exclusion agreements affecting rights under sections 1 and 2.**

(1) Subject to the following provisions of this section and section 4 below—

(a) the High Court shall not under section 1(3)(b) above, grant leave to appeal with respect to a question of law arising out of an award, and

(b) the High Court shall not, under section 1(5)(b) above, grant leave to make an application with respect to an award, and

(c) no application may be made under section 2(1)(a) above with respect to a question of law,

if the parties to the reference in question have entered into an agreement in writing (in this section referred to as an "exclusion agreement") which excludes the right of appeal under section 1 above in relation to that award or, in a case falling within paragraph (c) above, in relation to an award to which the determination of the question of law is material.

(4) Except as provided by subsection (1) above, sections 1 and 2 above shall have effect notwithstanding anything in any agreement purporting—

(a) to prohibit or restrict access to the High Court; or

(b) to restrict the jurisdiction of that court; or

(c)    to prohibit or restrict the making of a reasoned award.

(6)    An exclusion agreement shall be of no effect in relation to an award made on, or a question of law arising in the course of a reference under, an arbitration agreement which is a domestic arbitration agreement unless the exclusion agreement is entered into after the commencement of the arbitration in which the award is made or, as the case may be, in which the question of law arises.

## THE MERCHANT SHIPPING ACT 1979
### (1979, c. 39)

**17.    Limitation of liability.**

(1)    The provisions of the Convention on Limitation of Liability for Maritime Claims 1976 as set out in Part I of Schedule 4 to this Act (hereafter in this section and in Part II of that Schedule referred to as "the Convention") shall have the force of law in the United Kingdom.

## SCHEDULE 4
## CONVENTION ON LIMITATION OF LIABILITY FOR MARITIME CLAIMS 1976

**Art. 1.    Persons entitled to limit liability.**

**1.**    Shipowners and salvors, as hereinafter defined, may limit their liability in accordance with the rules of this Convention for claims set out in Article 2.

**4.**    If any claims set out in Article 2 are made against any person for whose act, neglect or default the shipowner or salvor is responsible, such person shall be entitled to avail himself of the limitation of liability provided for in this Convention.

**Art. 2.    Claims subject to limitation.**

**1.**    Subject to Articles 3 and 4 the following claims, whatever the basis of liability may be, shall be subject to limitation of liability:

(a)    claims in respect of loss of life or personal injury or loss of or damage to property (including damage to harbour works, basins and waterways and aids to navigation), occurring on board or in direct connexion with the operation of the ship or with salvage operations, and consequential loss resulting therefrom;

(b)    claims in respect of loss resulting from delay in the carriage by sea of cargo, passengers or their luggage;

(c)    claims in respect of other loss resulting from infringement of rights other than contractual rights, occurring in direct connexion with the operation of the ship or salvage operations; . . .

**Art. 11.    Constitution of the fund.**

**1.**    Any person alleged to be liable may constitute a fund with the Court or other competent authority in any State Party in which legal proceedings are instituted in respect of claims subject to limitation. The fund shall be constituted in the sum of such of the amounts set out in Articles 6 and 7 as are applicable to claims for which that person may be liable, together with interest thereon from the date of the occurrence giving rise to the liability until the date of the constitution of the fund. Any fund thus constituted shall be available only for the payment of claims in respect of which limitation of liability can be invoked.

**Art. 13.    Bar to other actions.**

**1.**    Where a limitation fund has been constituted in accordance with Article 11, any person having made a claim against the fund shall be barred from exercising any right in respect of such a claim against any other assets of a person by or on behalf of whom the fund has been constituted.

# THE PNEUMOCONIOSIS ETC. (WORKERS' COMPENSATION) ACT 1979
## (1979, c. 41)

**1.  Lump sum payments.**

(1)  If, on a claim by a person who is disabled by a disease to which this Act applies, the Secretary of State is satisfied that the conditions of entitlement mentioned in section 2(1) below are fulfilled, he shall in accordance with this Act make to that person a payment of such amount as may be prescribed by regulations.

(2)  If, on a claim by the dependant of a person who, immediately before he died, was disabled by a disease to which this Act applies, the Secretary of State is satisfied that the conditions of entitlement mentioned in section 2(2) below are fulfilled, he shall in accordance with this Act make to that dependant a payment of such amount as may be so prescribed.

(3)  The diseases to which this Act applies are pneumoconiosis, byssinosis and diffuse mesothelioma.

(4)  Regulations under this section may prescribe different amounts for different cases or classes of cases or for different circumstances.

**2.  Conditions of entitlement.**

(1)  In the case of a person who is disabled by a disease to which this Act applies, the conditions of entitlement are—

   (a)  that disablement benefit is payable to him in respect of the disease;

   (b)  that every relevant employer of his has ceased to carry on business; and

   (c)  that he has not brought any action, or compromised any claim, for damages in repect of the disablement.

(2)  In the case of the dependant of a person who, immediately before he died, was disabled by a disease to which this Act applies, the conditions of entitlement are—

   (a)  that no payment under this Act has been made to the deceased in respect of the disease;

   (b)  that death benefit is payable to or in respect of the dependant by reason of the deceased's death as a result of the disease, or that disablement benefit was payable to the deceased in respect of the disease immediately before he died;

   (c)  that every relevant employer of the deceased has ceased to carry on business; and

   (d)  that neither the deceased nor his personal representatives nor any relative of his has brought any action, or compromised any claim, for damages in respect of the disablement or death.

(4)  For the purposes of this section any action which has been dismissed otherwise than on the merits (as for example for want of prosecution or under any enactment relating to the limitation of actions) shall be disregarded.

**5.  Reconsideration of determinations.**

(1)  Subject to subsection (2) below, the Secretary of State may reconsider a determination that a payment should not be made under this Act on the ground—

   (a)  that there has been a material change of circumstances since the determination was made; or

   (b)  that the determination was made in ignorance of, or was based on a mistake as to, some material fact;

and the Secretary of State may, on the ground set out in paragraph (b) above, reconsider a determination that such a payment should be made.

(4)  If, whether fraudulently or otherwise, any person misrepresents or fails to disclose any material fact and in consequence of the misrepresentation or failure a payment is made under this Act, the person to whom the payment was made shall be liable to repay the amount of that payment to the Secretary of State unless he can show that the misrepresentation or failure occurred without his connivance or consent.

**9.    Financial provisions.**
(1)    There shall be paid out of moneys provided by Parliament—
(a)    any expenditure incurred by the Secretary of State in making payments under this Act . . .

## THE SALE OF GOODS ACT 1979
### (1979, c. 54)

**2.    Contract of sale.**
(1)    A contract of sale of goods is a contract by which the seller transfers or agrees to transfer the property in goods to the buyer for a money consideration, called the price.

**3.    Capacity to buy and sell.**
(1)    Capacity to buy and sell is regulated by the general law concerning capacity to contract and to transfer and acquire property.
(2)    Where necessaries are sold and delivered to a minor or to a person who by reason of mental incapacity or drunkenness is incompetent to contract, he must pay a reasonable price for them.
(3)    In subsection (2) above "necessaries" means goods suitable to the condition in life of the minor or other person concerned and to his actual requirements at the time of the sale and delivery.

**4.    How contract of sale is made.**
(1)    Subject to this and any other Act, a contract of sale may be made in writing (either with or without seal), or by word of mouth, or partly in writing and partly by word of mouth, or may be implied from the conduct of the parties.

**6.    Goods which have perished.**
Where there is a contract for the sale of specific goods, and the goods without the knowledge of the seller have perished at the time when the contract is made, the contract is void.

**7.    Goods perishing before sale but after agreement to sell.**
Where there is an agreement to sell specific goods and subsequently the goods, without any fault on the part of the seller or buyer, perish before the risk passes to the buyer, the agreement is avoided.

**8.    Ascertainment of price.**
(1)    The price in a contract of sale may be fixed by the contract, or may be left to be fixed in a manner agreed by the contract, or may be determined by the course of dealing between the parties.
(2)    Where the price is not determined as mentioned in subsection (1) above the buyer must pay a reasonable price.
(3)    What is a reasonable price is a question of fact dependent on the circumstances of each particular case.

**9.    Agreement to sell at valuation.**
(1)    Where there is an agreement to sell goods on the terms that the price is to be fixed by the valuation of a third party, and he cannot or does not make the valuation, the agreement is avoided; but if the goods or any part of them have been delivered to and appropriated by the buyer he must pay a reasonable price for them.
(2)    Where the third party is prevented from making the valuation by the fault of the seller or buyer, the party not at fault may maintain an action for damages against the party at fault.

**10.    Stipulations about time.**

(1)    Unless a different intention appears from the terms of the contract, stipulations as to time of payment are not of the essence of a contract of sale.

(2)    Whether any other stipulation as to time is or is not of the essence of the contract depends on the terms of the contract.

**11.    When condition to be treated as warranty.**

(2)    Where a contract of sale is subject to a condition to be fulfilled by the seller, the buyer may waive the condition, or may elect to treat the breach of the condition as a breach of warranty and not as a ground for treating the contract as repudiated.

(3)    Whether a stipulation in a contract of sale is a condition, the breach of which may give rise to a right to treat the contract as repudiated, or a warranty, the breach of which may give rise to a claim for damages but not to a right to reject the goods and treat the contract as repudiated, depends in each case on the construction of the contract; and a stipulation may be a condition, though called a warranty in the contract.

(4)    Where a contract of sale is not severable and the buyer has accepted the goods or part of them, the breach of a condition to be fulfilled by the seller can only be treated as a breach of warranty, and not as a ground for rejecting the goods and treating the contract as repudiated, unless there is an express or implied term of the contract to that effect.

(6)    Nothing in this section affects a condition or warranty whose fulfilment is excused by law by reason of impossibility or otherwise.

**12.    Implied terms about title, etc.**

(1)    In a contract of sale, other than one to which subsection (3) below applies, there is an implied condition on the part of the seller that in the case of a sale he has a right to sell the goods, and in the case of an agreement to sell he will have such a right at the time when the property is to pass.

(2)    In a contract of sale, other than one to which subsection (3) below applies, there is also an implied warranty that—

(a)    the goods are free, and will remain free until the time when the property is to pass, from any charge or encumbrance not disclosed or known to the buyer before the contract is made, and

(b)    the buyer will enjoy quiet possession of the goods except so far as it may be disturbed by the owner or other person entitled to the benefit of any charge or encumbrance so disclosed or known.

(3)    This subsection applies to a contract of sale in the case of which there appears from the contract or is to be inferred from its circumstances an intention that the seller should transfer only such title as he or a third person may have.

(4)    In a contract to which subsection (3) above applies there is an implied warranty that all charges or encumbrances known to the seller and not known to the buyer have been disclosed to the buyer before the contract is made.

(5)    In a contract to which subsection (3) above applies there is also an implied warranty that none of the following will disturb the buyer's quiet possession of the goods, namely—

(a)    the seller;

(b)    in a case where the parties to the contract intend that the seller should transfer only such title as a third person may have, that person;

(c)    anyone claiming through or under the seller or that third person otherwise than under a charge or encumbrance disclosed or known to the buyer before the contract is made.

**13.    Sale by description.**

(1)    Where there is a contract for the sale of goods by description, there is an implied condition that the goods will correspond with the description.

(2)    If the sale is by sample as well as by description it is not sufficient that the bulk of the goods corresponds with the sample if the goods do not also correspond with the description.

(3)    A sale of goods is not prevented from being a sale by description by reason only that, being exposed for sale or hire, they are selected by the buyer.

## 14.    Implied terms about quality or fitness.

(1)    Except as provided by this section and section 15 below and subject to any other enactment, there is no implied condition or warranty about the quality or fitness for any particular purpose of goods supplied under a contract of sale.

(2)    Where the seller sells goods in the course of a business, there is an implied condition that the goods supplied under the contract are of merchantable quality, except that there is no such condition—

(a)    as regards defects specifically drawn to the buyer's attention before the contract is made; or

(b)    if the buyer examines the goods before the contract is made, as regards defects which that examination ought to reveal.

(3)    Where the seller sells goods in the course of a business and the buyer, expressly or by implication, makes known—

(a)    to the seller, or

(b)    where the purchase price or part of it is payable by instalments and the goods were previously sold by a credit-broker to the seller, to that credit-broker,

any particular purpose for which the goods are being bought, there is an implied condition that the goods supplied under the contract are reasonably fit for that purpose, whether or not that is a purpose for which such goods are commonly supplied, except where the circumstances show that the buyer does not rely, or that it is unreasonable for him to rely, on the skill or judgment of the seller or credit-broker.

(4)    An implied condition or warranty about quality or fitness for a particular purpose may be annexed to a contract of sale by usage.

(6)    Goods of any kind are of merchantable quality within the meaning of subsection (2) above if they are as fit for the purpose or purposes for which goods of that kind are commonly bought as it is reasonable to expect having regard to any description applied to them, the price (if relevant) and all the other relevant circumstances.

## 15.    Sale by sample.

(1)    A contract of sale is a contract for sale by sample where there is an express or implied term to that effect in the contract.

(2)    In the case of a contract for sale by sample there is an implied condition—

(a)    that the bulk will correspond with the sample in quality;

(b)    that the buyer will have a reasonable opportunity of comparing the bulk with the sample;

(c)    that the goods will be free from any defect, rendering them unmerchantable, which would not be apparent on reasonable examination of the sample.

(3)    In subsection (2)(c) above "unmerchantable" is to be construed in accordance with section 14(6) above.

## 20.    Risk prima facie passes with property.

(1)    Unless otherwise agreed, the goods remain at the sellers's risk until the property in them is transferred to the buyer, but when the property in them is transferred to the buyer the goods are at the buyer's risk whether delivery has been made or not.

(2)    But where delivery has been delayed through the fault of either buyer or seller the goods are at the risk of the party at fault as regards any loss which might not have occurred but for such fault.

(3)    Nothing in this section affects the duties or liabilities of either seller or buyer as a bailee or custodier of the goods of the other party.

## 28. Payment and delivery are concurrent conditions.

Unless otherwise agreed, delivery of the goods and payment of the price are concurrent conditions, that is to say, the seller must be ready and willing to give possession of the goods to the buyer in exchange for the price and the buyer must be ready and willing to pay the price in exchange for possession of the goods.

## 30. Delivery of wrong quantity.

(1) Where the seller delivers to the buyer a quantity of goods less than he contracted to sell, the buyer may reject them, but if the buyer accepts the goods so delivered he must pay for them at the contract rate.

(2) Where the seller delivers to the buyer a quantity of goods larger than he contracted to sell, the buyer may accept the goods included in the contract and reject the rest, or he may reject the whole.

(3) Where the seller delivers to the buyer a quantity of goods larger than he contracted to sell and the buyer accepts the whole of the goods so delivered he must pay for them at the contract rate.

(4) Where the seller delivers to the buyer the goods he contracted to sell mixed with goods of a different description not included in the contract, the buyer may accept the goods which are in accordance with the contract and reject the rest, or he may reject the whole.

(5) This section is subject to any usage of trade, special agreement, or course of dealing between the parties.

## 49. Action for price.

(1) Where, under a contract of sale, the property in the goods has passed to the buyer and he wrongfully neglects or refuses to pay for the goods according to the terms of the contract, the seller may maintain an action against him for the price of the goods.

## 50. Damages for non-acceptance.

(1) Where the buyer wrongfully neglects or refuses to accept and pay for the goods, the seller may maintain an action against him for damages for non-acceptance.

(2) The measure of damages is the estimated loss directly and naturally resulting, in the ordinary course of events, from the buyer's breach of contract.

(3) Where there is an available market for the goods in question the measure of damages is prima facie to be ascertained by the difference between the contract price and the market or current price at the time or times when the goods ought to have been accepted or (if no time was fixed for acceptance) at the time of the refusal to accept.

## 51. Damages for non-delivery.

(1) Where the seller wrongfully neglects or refuses to deliver the goods to the buyer, the buyer may maintain an action against the seller for damages for non-delivery.

(2) The measure of damages is the estimated loss directly and naturally resulting, in the ordinary course of events, from the seller's breach of contract.

(3) Where there is an available market for the goods in question the measure of damages is prima facie to be ascertained by the difference between the contract price and the market or current price of the goods at the time or times when they ought to have been delivered or (if no time was fixed) at the time of the refusal to deliver.

## 52. Specific performance.

(1) In any action for breach of contract to deliver specific or ascertained goods the court may, if it thinks fit, on the plaintiff's application, by its judgment or decree direct that the contract shall be performed specifically, without giving the defendant the option of retaining the goods on payment of damages.

(3) The judgment or decree may be unconditional, or on such terms and conditions as to damages, payment of the price and otherwise as seem just to the court.

### 53. Remedy for breach of warranty.

(1)    Where there is a breach of warranty by the seller, or where the buyer elects (or is compelled) to treat any breach of a condition on the part of the seller as a breach of warranty, the buyer is not by reason only of such breach of warranty entitled to reject the goods; but he may—

(a)    set up against the seller the breach of warranty in diminution or extinction of the price, or

(b)    maintain an action against the seller for damages for the breach of warranty.

(2)    The measure of damages for breach of warranty is the estimated loss directly and naturally resulting, in the ordinary course of events, from the breach of warranty.

(3)    In the case of breach of warranty of quality such loss is prima facie the difference between the value of the goods at the time of delivery to the buyer and the value they would have had if they had fulfilled the warranty.

(4)    The fact that the buyer has set up the breach of warranty in diminution or extinction of the price does not prevent him from maintaining an action for the same breach of warranty if he has suffered further damage.

### 54. Interest, etc.

Nothing in this Act affects the right of the buyer or the seller to recover interest or special damages in any case where by law interest or special damages may be recoverable, or to recover money paid where the consideration for the payment of it has failed.

### 55. Exclusion of implied terms.

(1)    Where a right, duty or liability would arise under a contract of sale of goods by implication of law, it may (subject to the Unfair Contract Terms Act 1977) be negatived or varied by express agreement, or by the course of dealing between the parties, or by such usage as binds both parties to the contract.

(2)    An express condition or warranty does not negative a condition or warranty implied by this Act unless inconsistent with it.

### 57. Auction sales.

(2)    A sale by auction is complete when the auctioneer announces its completion by the fall of the hammer, or in other customary manner; and until the announcement is made any bidder may retract his bid.

### 61. Interpretation.

(1)    In this Act, unless the context or subject matter otherwise requires,— . . .
"warranty" (as regards England and Wales and Northern Ireland) means an agreement with reference to goods which are the subject of a contract of sale, but collateral to the main purpose of such contract, the breach of which gives rise to a claim for damages, but not to a right to reject the goods and treat the contract as repudiated.

(3)    A thing is deemed to be done in good faith within the meaning of this Act when it is in fact done honestly, whether it is done negligently or not.

### 62. Savings: rules of law etc.

(2)    The rules of the common law, including the law merchant, except in so far as they are inconsistent with the provisions of this Act, and in particular the rules relating to the law of principal and agent and the effect of fraud, misrepresentation, duress or coercion, mistake, or other invalidating cause, apply to contracts for the sale of goods.

## THE VACCINE DAMAGE PAYMENTS ACT 1979
### (1979, c. 17)

### 1. Payments to persons severely disabled by vaccination.

(1)    If, on consideration of a claim, the Secretary of State is satisfied—

(a)    that a person is, or was immediately before his death, severely disabled as a result of vaccination against any of the diseases to which this Act applies; and

(b)    that the conditions of entitlement which are applicable in accordance with section 2 below are fulfilled,

he shall in accordance with this Act make a payment of £10,000 to or for the benefit of that person or to his personal representatives.

(2)    The diseases to which this Act applies are—

(a)    diphtheria,

(b)    tetanus,

(c)    whooping cough,

(d)    poliomyelitis,

(e)    measles,

(f)    rubella,

(g)    tuberculosis,

(h)    smallpox, and

(i)    any other disease which is specified by the Secretary of State for the purposes of this Act by order made by statutory instrument.

(3)    Subject to section 2(3) below, this Act has effect with respect to a person who is severely disabled as a result of a vaccination given to his mother before he was born as if the vaccination had been given directly to him and, in such circumstances as may be prescribed by regulations under this Act, this Act has effect with respect to a person who is severely disabled as a result of contracting a disease through contact with a third person who was vaccinated against it as if the vaccination had been given to him and the disablement resulted from it.

## 2.    Conditions of entitlement.

(1)    Subject to the provisions of this section, the conditions of entitlement referred to in section 1(1)(b) above are—

(a)    that the vaccination in question was carried out—

(i)    in the United Kingdom or the Isle of Man, and

(ii)    on or after 5 July 1948, and

(iii)    in the case of vaccination against smallpox, before 1st August 1971;

(b)    except in the case of vaccination against poliomyelitis or rubella, that the vaccination was carried out either at a time when the person to whom it was given was under the age of eighteen or at the time of an outbreak within the United Kingdom or the Isle of Man of the disease against which the vaccination was given; and

(c)    that the disabled person was over the age of two on the date when the claim was made or, if he died before that date, that he died after 9th May 1978 and was over the age of two when he died.

## 3.    Determination of claims.

(1)    Any reference in this Act, other than section 7, to a claim is a reference to a claim for a payment under section 1(1) above which is made—

(a)    by or on behalf of the disabled person concerned or, as the case may be, by his personal representatives; and

(b)    in the manner prescribed by regulations under this Act; and

(c)    within the period of six years beginning on the latest of the following dates, namely, the date of the vaccination to which the claim relates, the date on which the disabled person attained the age of two and 9th May 1978 . . .

## 6.    Payments to or for the benefit of disabled persons.

(1)    Where a payment under section 1(1) above falls to be made in respect of a disabled person who is over eighteen and capable of managing his own affairs, the payment shall be made to him.

(2)    Where such a payment falls to be made in respect of a disabled person who has died, the payment shall be made to his personal representatives.

(3)    Where such a payment falls to be made in respect of any other disabled person, the payment shall be made for his benefit by paying it to such trustees as the Secretary of State may appoint to be held by them upon such trusts or, in Scotland, for such purposes and upon such conditions as may be declared by the Secretary of State.

(4)    The making of a claim for, or the receipt of, a payment under section 1(1) above does not prejudice the right of any person to institute or carry on proceedings in respect of disablement suffered as a result of vaccination against any disease to which this Act applies; but in any civil proceedings brought in respect of disablement resulting from vaccination against such a disease, the court shall treat a payment made to or in repect of the disabled person concerned under section 1(1) above as paid on account of any damages which the court awards in respect of such disablement.

**12.    Financial provisions.**

(4)    There shall be paid out of moneys provided by Parliament—

(a)    any expenditure incurred by the Secretary of State in making payments under section 1(1) above . . .

## THE EMPLOYMENT ACT 1980
### (1980, c. 42)

**16.    Picketing.**

(2)    Nothing in section 13 of the 1974 Act shall prevent an act done in the course of picketing from being actionable in tort unless it is done in the course of attendance declared lawful by section 15 of that Act.

**17.    Secondary action.**

(1)    Nothing in section 13 of the 1974 Act shall prevent an act from being actionable in tort on a ground specified in subsection (1)(a) or (b) of that section in any case where—

(a)    the contract concerned is not a contract of employment, and

(b)    one of the facts relied upon for the purpose of establishing liability is that there has been secondary action which is not action satisfying the requirements of subsection (3), (4) or (5) below.

(2)    For the purposes of this section there is secondary action in relation to a trade dispute when, and only when, a person—

(a)    induces another to break a contract of employment or interferes or induces another to interfere with its performance, or

(b)    threatens that a contract of employment under which he or another is employed will be broken or its performance interfered with, or that he will induce another to break a contract of employment or to interfere with its performance,
if the employer under the contract of employment is not a party to the trade dispute.

(3)    Secondary action satisfies the requirements of this subsection if—

(a)    the purpose or principal purpose of the secondary action was directly to prevent or disrupt the supply during the dispute of goods or services between an employer who is a party to the dispute and the employer under the contract of employment to which the secondary action relates; and

(b)    the secondary action (together with any corresponding action relating to other contracts of employment with the same employer) was likely to achieve that purpose.

(4)    Secondary action satisfies the requirements of this subsection if—

(a)    the purpose or principal purpose of the secondary action was directly to prevent or disrupt the supply during the dispute of goods or services between any person and an associated employer or an employer who is a party to the dispute; and

(b)     the goods or services are in substitution for goods or services which but for the dispute would have fallen to be supplied to or by the employer who is a party to the dispute; and
(c)     the employer under the contract of employment to which the secondary action relates is either the said associated employer or the other party to the supply referred to in paragraph (a) above; and
(d)     the secondary action (together with any corresponding action relating to other contracts of employment with the same employer) was likely to achieve the purpose referred to in paragraph (a) above.
(5)     Secondary action satisfies the requirements of this subsection if it is done in the course of attendance declared lawful by section 15 of the 1974 Act—
(a)     by a worker employed (or, in the case of a worker not in employment, last employed) by a party to the dispute, or
(b)     by a trade union official whose attendance is lawful by virtue of subsection (1)(b) of that section.

**20.     Interpretation . . .**
(1)     In this Act—
"the 1974 Act" means the Trade Union and Labour Relations Act 1974 . . .

## THE HIGHWAYS ACT 1980
### (1980, c. 66)

**41.     Duty to maintain highways maintainable at public expense.**
(1)     The authority who are for the time being the highway authority for a highway maintainable at the public expense are under a duty, subject to subsections (2) and (4) below, to maintain the highway.

**58.     Special defence in action against a highway authority for damages for non-repair of highway.**
(1)     In an action against a highway authority in respect of damage resulting from their failure to maintain a highway maintainable at the public expense it is a defence (without prejudice to any other defence or the application of the law relating to contributory negligence) to prove that the authority had taken such care as in all the circumstances was reasonably required to secure that the part of the highway to which the action relates was not dangerous for traffic.

**102.     Provision of works for protecting highways against hazards of nature.**
(1)     The highway authority for a highway maintainable at the public expense may provide and maintain such barriers or other works as they consider necessary for the purpose of affording to the highway protection against snow, flood, landslide or other hazards of nature; and those works may be provided on the highway or on land which, or rights over which, has or have been acquired by the highway authority in the exercise of highway land acquisition powers for that purpose.
(3)     A highway authority shall pay compensation to any person who suffers damage by reason of the execution by them under this section of any works on a highway.

**165.     Dangerous land adjoining street.**
(1)     If, in or on any land adjoining a street, there is an unfenced or inadequately fenced source of danger to persons using the street, the local authority in whose area the street is situated may, by notice to the owner or occupier of that land, require him within such time as may be specified in the notice to execute such works of repair, protection, removal or enclosure as will obviate the danger.
(3)     Subject to any order made on appeal, if a person on whom a notice is served under this section fails to comply with the notice within the time specified in it, the authority by

whom the notice was served may execute such works as are necessary to comply with the notice and may recover the expenses reasonably incurred by them in so doing from that person.

## THE LIMITATION ACT 1980
## (1980, c. 58)
## PART I

**1.    Time limits under Part I subject to exclusion under Part II.**

(1)    This Part of this Act gives the ordinary time limits for bringing actions of the various classes mentioned in the following provisions of this Part.

(2)    The ordinary time limits given in this Part of this Act are subject to extension or exclusion in accordance with the provisions of Part II of this Act.

**2.    Time limit for actions founded on tort.**

An action founded on tort shall not be brought after the expiration of six years from the date on which the cause of action accrued.

**3.    Time limit in case of successive conversions and extinction of title of owner of converted goods.**

(1)    Where any cause of action in respect of the conversion of a chattel has accrued to any person and, before he recovers possession of the chattel, a further conversion takes place, no action shall be brought in respect of the further conversion after the expiration of six years from the accrual of the cause of action in respect of the original conversion.

(2)    Where any such cause of action has accrued to any person and the period prescribed for bringing that action has expired and he has not during that period recovered possession of the chattel, the title of that person to the chattel shall be extinguished.

**4.    Special time limit in case of theft.**

(1)    The right of any person from whom a chattel is stolen to bring an action in respect of the theft shall not be subject to the time limits under sections 2 and 3(1) of this Act, but if his title to the chattel is extinguished under section 3(2) of this Act he may not bring an action in respect of a theft preceding the loss of his title, unless the theft in question preceded the conversion from which time began to run for the purposes of section 3(2).

(2)    Subsection (1) above shall apply to any conversion related to the theft of a chattel as it applies to the theft of a chattel; and, except as provided below, every conversion following the theft of a chattel before the person from whom it is stolen recovers possession of it shall be regarded for the purposes of this section as related to the theft.

If anyone purchases the stolen chattel in good faith neither the purchase nor any conversion following it shall be regarded as related to the theft.

(3)    Any cause of action accruing in respect of the theft or any conversion related to the theft of a chattel to any person from whom the chattel is stolen shall be disregarded for the purpose of applying section 3(1) or (2) of this Act to his case.

(4)    Where in any action brought in respect of the conversion of a chattel it is proved that the chattel was stolen from the plaintiff or anyone through whom he claims it shall be presumed that any conversion following the theft is related to the theft unless the contrary is shown.

(5)    In this section "theft" includes—

(a)    any conduct outside England and Wales which would be theft if committed in England and Wales; and

(b)    obtaining any chattel (in England and Wales or elsewhere) in the circumstances described in section 15(1) of the Theft Act 1968 (obtaining by deception) or by blackmail within the meaning of section 21 of that Act;

and references in this section to a chattel being "stolen" shall be construed accordingly.

**[4A.    Time limit for actions for libel or slander.**
The time limit under section 2 of this Act shall not apply to an action for libel or slander, but no such action shall be brought after the expiration of three years from the date on which the cause of action accrued.]

**5.    Time limit for actions founded on simple contract.**
An action founded on simple contract shall not be brought after the expiration of six years from the date on which the cause of action accrued.

**6.    Special time limit for actions in respect of certain loans.**
(1)    Subject to subsection (3) below, section 5 of this Act shall not bar the right of action on a contract of loan to which this section applies.
(2)    This section applies to any contract of loan which—
(a)    does not provide for repayment of the debt on or before a fixed or determinable date; and
(b)    does not effectively (whether or not it purports to do so) make the obligation to repay the debt conditional on a demand for repayment made by or on behalf of the creditor or on any other matter;
except where in connection with taking the loan the debtor enters into any collateral obligation to pay the amount of the debt or any part of it (as, for example, by delivering a promissory note as security for the debt) on terms which would exclude the application of this section to the contract of loan if they applied directly to repayment of the debt.
(3)    Where a demand in writing for repayment of the debt under a contract of loan to which this section applies is made by or on behalf of the creditor (or, where there are joint creditors, by or on behalf of any one of them) section 5 of this Act shall thereupon apply as if the cause of action to recover the debt had accrued on the date on which the demand was made.
(4)    In this section "promissory note" has the same meaning as in the Bills of Exchange Act 1882.

**8.    Time limit for actions on a specialty.**
(1)    An action upon a specialty shall not be brought after the expiration of twelve years from the date on which the cause of action accrued.
(2)    Subsection (1) above shall not affect any action for which a shorter period of limitation is prescribed by any other provision of this Act.

**9.    Time limit for actions for sums recoverable by statute.**
(1)    An action to recover any sum recoverable by virtue of any enactment shall not be brought after the expiration of six years from the date on which the cause of action accrued.
(2)    Subsection (1) above shall not affect any action to which section 10 of this Act applies.

**10.    Special time limit for claiming contribution.**
(1)    Where under section 1 of the Civil Liability (Contribution) Act 1978 any person becomes entitled to a right to recover contribution in respect of any damage from any other person, no action to recover contribution by virtue of that right shall be brought after the expiration of two years from the date on which that right accrued.
(2)    For the purposes of this section the date on which a right to recover contribution in respect of any damage accrues to any person (referred to below in this section as "the relevant date") shall be ascertained as provided in subsections (3) and (4) below.
(3)    If the person in question is held liable in respect of that damage—
(a)    by a judgment given in any civil proceedings; or
(b)    by an award made on any arbitration;
the relevant date shall be the date on which the judgment is given, or the date of the award (as the case may be).

For the purposes of this subsection no account shall be taken of any judgment or award given or made on appeal in so far as it varies the amount of damages awarded against the person in question.

(4)    If, in any case not within subsection (3) above, the person in question makes or agrees to make any payment to one or more persons in compensation for that damage (whether he admits any liability in repect of the damage or not), the relevant date shall be the earliest date on which the amount to be paid by him is agreed between him (or his representative) and the person (or each of the persons, as the case may be) to whom the payment is to be made.

(5)    An action to recover contribution shall be one to which sections 28, 32 and 35 of this Act apply, but otherwise Parts II and III of this Act (except sections 34, 37 and 38) shall not apply for the purposes of this section.

## 11.    Special time limit for actions in respect of personal injuries.

(1)    This section applies to any action for damages for negligence, nuisance or breach of duty (whether the duty exists by virtue of a contract or of provision made by or under a statute or independently of any contract or any such provision) where the damages claimed by the plaintiff for the negligence, nuisance of action to recover the land had accrued to the person by whom the assurance was made or some person through whom he claimed or some person entitled to a preceding estate or interest, unless the action is brought within the period during which the person by whom the assurance was made could have brought such an action.

(3)    An action to which this section applies shall not be brought after the expiration of the period applicable in accordance with subsection (4) or (5) below.

(4)    Except where subsection (5) below applies, the period applicable is three years from—

   (a)    the date on which the cause of action accrued; or
   (b)    the date of knowledge (if later) of the person injured.

(5)    If the injured person dies before the expiration of the period mentioned in subsection (4) above, the period applicable as respects the cause of action surviving for the benefit of his estate by virtue of section 1 of the Law Reform (Miscellaneous Provisions) Act 1934 shall be three years from—

   (a)    the date of death; or
   (b)    the date of the personal representative's knowledge; whichever is the later.

## [11A    Actions in respect of defective products.

(1)    This section shall apply to an action for damages by virtue of any provision of Part I of the Consumer Protection Act 1987.

(2)    None of the time limits given in the preceding provisions of this Act shall apply to an action to which this section applies.

(3)    An action to which this section applies shall not be brought after the expiration of the period of ten years from the relevant time, within the meaning of section 4 of the said Act of 1987; and this subsection shall operate to extinguish a right of action and shall do so whether or not that right of action had accrued, or time under the following provisions of this Act had begun to run, at the end of the said period of ten years.

(4)    Subject to subsection (5) below, an action to which this section applies in which the damages claimed by the plaintiff consist of or include damages in respect of personal injuries to the plaintiff or any other person or loss of or damage to any property, shall not be brought after the expiration of the period of three years from whichever is the later of—

   (a)    the date on which the cause of action accrued; and
   (b)    the date of knowledge of the injured person or, in the case of loss of or damage to property, the date of knowledge of the plaintiff or (if earlier) of any person in whom his cause of action was previously vested.

(5)    If in a case where the damages claimed by the plaintiff consist of or include damages in respect of personal injuries to the plaintiff or any other person the injured person died before the expiration of the period mentioned in subsection (4) above, the subsection shall have effect as respects the cause of action surviving for the benefit of his estate by virtue of section I of the Law Reform (Miscellaneous Provisions) Act 1934 as if for the reference to that period there were substituted a reference to the period of three years from whichever is the later of—

(a)    the date of death; and

(b)    the date of the personal representative's knowledge.

(6)    For the purposes of this section "personal representative" includes any person who is or has been a personal representative of the deceased, including an executor who has not proved the will (whether or not he has renounced probate) but not anyone appointed only as a special personal representative in relation to settled land; and regard shall be had to any knowledge acquired by any such person while a personal representative or previously.

(7)    If there is more than one personal representative and their dates of knowledge are different, subsection (5)(b) above shall be read as referring to the earliest of those dates.

(8)    Expressions used in this section or section 14 of this Act and in Part I of the Consumer Protection Act 1987 have the same meanings in this section or that section as in that Part; and section 1(1) of that Act (Part I to be construed as enacted for the purpose of complying with the product liability Directive) shall apply for the purpose of construing this section and the following provisions of this Act so far as they relate to an action by virtue of any provision of that Part as it applies for the purpose of construing that Part.]

**12.    Special time limit for actions under Fatal Accidents legislation.**

(1)    An action under the Fatal Accidents Act 1976 shall not be brought if the death occurred when the person injured could no longer maintain an action and recover damages in respect of the injury (whether because of a time limit in this Act or in any other Act, or for any other reason).

Where any such action by the injured person would have been barred by the time limit in section 11 [or 11A] of this Act, no account shall be taken of the possibility of that time limit being overridden under section 33 of this Act.

(2)    None of the time limits given in the preceding provisions of this Act shall apply to an action under the Fatal Accidents Act 1976, but no such action shall be brought after the expiration of three years from—

(a)    the date of death; or

(b)    the date of knowledge of the person for whose benefit the action is brought;

whichever is the later.

(3)    An action under the Fatal Accidents Act 1976 shall be one to which sections 28, 33 and 35 of this Act apply, and the application to any such action of the time limit under subsection (2) above shall be subject to section 39; but otherwise Parts II and III of this Act shall not apply to any such action.

**13.    Operation of time limit under section 12 in relation to different dependants.**

(1)    Where there is more than one person for whose benefit an action under the Fatal Accidents Act 1976 is brought, section 12(2)(b) of this Act shall be applied separately to each of them.

(2)    Subject to subsection (3) below, if by virtue of subsection (1) above the action would be outside the time limit given by section 12(2) as regards one or more, but not all, of the persons for whose benefit it is brought, the court shall direct that any person as regards whom the action would be outside that limit shall be excluded from those for whom the action is brought.

(3)    The court shall not give such a direction if it is shown that if the action were brought exclusively for the benefit of the person in question it would not be defeated by a

defence of limitation (whether in consequence of section 28 of this Act or an agreement between the parties not to raise the defence, or otherwise).

## 14.    Definition of date of knowledge for purposes of sections 11 and 12.

(1)    [Subject to subsection (1A) below,] In sections 11 and 12 of this Act references to a person's date of knowledge are references to the date on which he first had knowledge of the following facts—

(a)    that the injury in question was significant; and

(b)    that the injury was attributable in whole or in part to the act or omission which is alleged to constitute negligence, nuisance or breach of duty; and

(c)    the identity of the defendant; and

(d)    if it is alleged that the act or omission was that of a person other than the defendant, the identity of that person and the additional facts supporting the bringing of an action against the defendant;

and knowledge that any acts or omissions did or did not, as a matter of law, involve negligence, nuisance or breach of duty is irrelevant.

[(1A) In section 11A of this Act and in section 12 of this Act so far as that section applies to an action by virtue of section 6(1)(a) of the Consumer Protection Act 1987 (death caused by defective product) references to a person's date of knowledge are references to the date on which he first had knowledge of the following facts—

(a)    such facts about the damage caused by the defect as would lead a reasonable person who had suffered such damage to consider it sufficiently serious to justify his instituting proceedings for damages against a defendant who did not dispute liability and was able to satisfy a judgment; and

(b)    that the damage was wholly or partly attributable to the facts and circumstances alleged to constitute the defect; and

(c)    the identity of the defendant;

but, in determining the date on which a person first had such knowledge there shall be disregarded both the extent (if any) of that person's knowledge on any date of whether particular facts or circumstances would or would not, as a matter of law, constitute a defect and, in a case relating to loss of or damage to property, any knowledge which that person had on a date on which he had no right of action by virtue of Part of I of that Act in respect of the loss or damage.]

(2)    For the purposes of this section an injury is significant if the person whose date of knowledge is in question would reasonably have considered it sufficiently serious to justify his instituting proceedings for damages against a defendant who did not dispute liability and was able to satisfy a judgment.

(3)    For the purposes of this section a person's knowledge includes knowledge which he might reasonably have been expected to acquire—

(a)    from facts observable or ascertainable by him; or

(b)    from facts ascertainable by him with the help of medical or other appropriate expert advice which it is reasonable for him to seek;

but a person shall not be fixed under this subsection with knowledge of a fact ascertainable only with the help of expert advice so long as he has taken all reasonable steps to obtain (and, where appropriate, to act on) that advice.

## [14A.    Special time limit for negligence actions where facts relevant to cause of action are not known at date of accrual.

(1)    This section applies to any action for damages for negligence, other than one to which section 11 of this Act applies, where the starting date for reckoning the period of limitation under subsection (4)(b) below falls after the date on which the cause of action accrued.

(2)    Section 2 of this Act shall not apply to an action to which this section applies.

(3)    An action to which this section applies shall not be brought after the expiration of the period applicable in accordance with subsection (4) below.

(4) That period is either—
    (a) six years from the date on which the cause of action accrued; or
    (b) three years from the starting date as defined by subsection (5) below, if that period expires later than the period mentioned in paragraph (a) above.

(5) For the purposes of this section, the starting date for reckoning the period of limitation under subsection (4)(b) above is the earliest date on which the plaintiff or any person in whom the cause of action was vested before him first had both the knowledge required for bringing an action for damages in respect of the relevant damage and a right to bring such an action.

(6) In subsection (5) above "the knowledge required for bringing an action for damages in respect of the relevant damage" means knowledge both—
    (a) of the material facts about the damage in respect of which damages are claimed; and
    (b) of the other facts relevant to the current action mentioned in subsection (8) below.

(7) For the purposes of subsection (6)(a) above, the material facts about the damage are such facts about the damage as would lead a reasonable person who had suffered such damage to consider it sufficiently serious to justify his instituting proceedings for damages against a defendant who did not dispute liability and was able to satisfy a judgment.

(8) The other facts referred to in subsection (6)(b) above are—
    (a) that the damage was attributable in whole or in part to the act or omission which is alleged to constitute negligence; and
    (b) the identity of the defendant; and
    (c) if it is alleged that the act or omission was that of a person other than the defendant, the identity of that person and the additional facts supporting the bringing of an action against the defendant.

(9) Knowledge that any acts or omissions did or did not, as a matter of law, involve negligence is irrelevant for the purposes of subsection (5) above.

(10) For the purposes of this section a person's knowledge includes knowledge which he might reasonably have been expected to acquire—
    (a) from facts observable or ascertainable by him; or
    (b) from facts ascertainable by him with the help of appropriate expert advice which it is reasonable for him to seek;
but a person shall not be taken by virtue of this subsection to have knowledge of a fact ascertainable only with the help of expert advice so long as he has taken all reasonable steps to obtain (and, where appropriate, to act on) that advice.]

**[14B. Overriding time limit for negligence actions not involving personal injuries.**

(1) An action for damages for negligence, other than one to which section 11 of this Act applies, shall not be brought after the expiration of fifteen years from the date (or, if more than one, from the last of the dates) on which there occurred any act or omission—
    (a) which is alleged to constitute negligence; and
    (b) to which the damage in respect of which damages are claimed is alleged to be attributable (in whole or in part).

(2) This section bars the right of action in a case to which subsection (1) above applies notwithstanding that—
    (a) the cause of action has not yet accrued; or
    (b) where section 14A of this Act applies to the action, the date which is for the purposes of that section the starting date for reckoning the period mentioned in subsection (4)(b) of that section has not yet occurred;
before the end of the period of limitation prescribed by this section.]

**15.    Time limit for actions to recover land.**

(1)    No action shall be brought by any person to recover any land after the expiration of twelve years from the date on which the right of action accrued to him or, if it first accrued to some person through whom he claims, to that person.

## PART II

**28.    Extension of limitation period in case of disability.**

(1)    Subject to the following provisions of this section, if on the date when any right of action accrued for which a period of limitation is prescribed by this Act, the person to whom it accrued was under a disability, the action may be brought at any time before the expiration of six years from the date when he ceased to be under a disability or died (whichever first occurred) notwithstanding that the period of limitation has expired.

(2)    This section shall not affect any case where the right of action first accrued to some person (not under a disability) through whom the person under a disability claims.

(3)    When a right of action which has accrued to a person under a disability accrues, on the death of that person while still under a disability, to another person under a disability, no further extension of time shall be allowed by reason of the disability of the second person.

[(4A) If the action is one to which section 4A of this Act applies, subsection (1) above shall have effect as if for the words from "at any time" to "occurred)" there were substituted the words "by him at any time before the expiration of three years from the date when he ceased to be under a disability".]

(5)    If the action is one to which section 10 of this Act applies, subsection (1) above shall have effect as if for the words "six years" there were substituted the words "two years".

(6)    If the action is one to which section 11 or 12(2) of this Act applies, subsection (1) above shall have effect as if for the words "six years" there were substituted the words "three years".

[(7)    If the action is one to which section 11A of this Act applies or one by virtue of section 6(1)(a) of the Consumer Protection Act 1987 (death caused by defective product), subsection (1) above—

(a)    shall not apply to the time limit prescribed by subsection (3) of the said section 11A or to that time limit as applied by virtue of section 12(1) of this Act; and

(b)    in relation to any other time limit prescribed by this Act shall have effect as if for the words "six years" there were substituted the words "three years".]

**[28A.    Extension for cases where the limitation period is the period under section 14A(4)(b).**

(1)    Subject to subsection (2) below, if in the case of any action for which a period of limitation is prescribed by section 14A of this Act—

(a)    the period applicable in accordance with subsection (4) of that section is the period mentioned in paragraph (b) of that subsection;

(b)    on the date which is for the purposes of that section the starting date for reckoning that period the person by reference to whose knowledge that date fell to be determined under subsection (5) of that section was under a disability; and

(c)    section 28 of this Act does not apply to the action;

the action may be brought at any time before the expiration of three years from the date when he ceased to be under a disability or died (whichever first occurred) notwithstanding that the period mentioned above has expired.

(2)    An action may not be brought by virtue of subsection (1) above after the end of the period of limitation prescribed by section 14B of this Act.]

**29. Fresh accrual of action on acknowledgment or part payment.**

(5)   Subject to subsection (6) below, where any right of action has accrued to recover—

(a)   any debt or other liquidated pecuniary claim; or

(b)   any claim to the personal estate of a deceased person or to any share or interest in any such estate;

and the person liable or accountable for the claim acknowledges the claim or makes any payment in respect of it the right shall be treated as having accrued on and not before the date of the acknowledgment or payment.

(6)   A payment of a part of the rent or interest due at any time shall not extend the period for claiming the remainder then due, but any payment of interest shall be treated as a payment in respect of the principal debt.

(7)   Subject to subsection (6) above, a current period of limitation may be repeatedly extended under this section by further acknowledgments or payments, but a right of action, once barred by this Act shall not be revived by any subsequent acknowledgment or payment.

**30. Formal provisions as to acknowledgments and part payments.**

(1)   To be effective for the purposes of section 29 of this Act, an acknowledgment must be in writing and signed by the person making it.

(2)   For the purposes of section 29, any acknowledgment or payment—

(a)   may be made by the agent of the person by whom it is required to be made under that section; and

(b)   shall be made to the person, or to an agent of the person, whose title or claim is being acknowledged or, as the case may be, in respect of whose claim the payment is being made.

**31. Effect of acknowledgment or part payment on persons other than the maker or recipient.**

(6)   An acknowledgment of any debt or other liquidated pecuniary claim shall bind the acknowledgor and his successors but not any other person.

(7)   A payment made in respect of any debt or other liquidated pecuniary claim shall bind all persons liable in respect of the debt or claim.

(8)   An acknowledgment by one of several personal representatives of any claim to the personal estate of a deceased person or to any share or interest in any such estate, or a payment by one of several personal representatives in respect of any such claim, shall bind the estate of the deceased person.

(9)   In this section "successor", in relation to any mortgagee or person liable in respect of any debt or claim, means his personal representatives and any other person on whom the rights under the mortgage or, as the case may be, the liability in respect of the debt or claim devolve (whether on death or bankruptcy or the disposition of property or the determination of a limited estate or interest in settled property or otherwise).

**32. Postponement of limitation period in case of fraud, concealment or mistake.**

(1)   Subject to [subsections (3) and (4A)] below, where in the case of any action for which a period of limitation is prescribed by this Act, either—

(a)   the action is based upon the fraud of the defendant; or

(b)   any fact relevant to the plaintiff's right of action has been deliberately concealed from him by the defendant; or

(c)   the action is for relief from the consequences of a mistake;

the period of limitation shall not begin to run until the plaintiff has discovered the fraud, concealment or mistake (as the case may be) or could with reasonable diligence have discovered it.

References in this subsection to the defendant include references to the defendant's agent and to any person through whom the defendant claims and his agent.

(2)    For the purposes of subsection (1) above, deliberate commission of a breach of duty in circumstances in which it is unlikely to be discovered for some time amounts to deliberate concealment of the facts involved in that breach of duty.

(3)    Nothing in this section shall enable any action—

    (a)    to recover, or recover the value of, any property; or

    (b)    to enforce any charge against, or set aside any transaction affecting, any property;

to be brought against the purchaser of the property or any person claiming through him in any case where the property has been purchased for valuable consideration by an innocent third party since the fraud or concealment or (as the case may be) the transaction in which the mistake was made took place.

(4)    A purchaser is an innocent third party for the purposes of this section—

    (a)    in the case of fraud or concealment of any fact relevant to the plaintiff's right of action, if he was not a party to the fraud or (as the case may be) to the concealment of that fact and did not at the time of the purchase know or have reason to believe that the fraud or concealment had taken place; and

    (b)    in the case of mistake, if he did not at the time of the purchase know or have reason to believe that the mistake had been made.

[(4A) Subsection (1) above shall not apply in relation to the time limit prescribed by section 11A(3) of this Act or in relation to that time limit as applied by virtue of section 12(1) of this Act.]

[(5)    Sections 14A and 14B of this Act shall not apply to any action to which subsection (1)(b) above applies (and accordingly the period of limitation referred to in that subsection, in any case to which either of those sections would otherwise apply, is the period applicable under section 23 of this Act).]

**[32A.    Discretionary extension of time limit for actions for libel or slander.**
Where a person to whom a cause of action for libel or slander has accrued has not brought such an action within the period of three years mentioned in section 4A of this Act (or, where applicable, the period allowed by section 28(1) as modified by section 28(4A)) because all or any of the facts relevant to that cause of action did not become known to him until after the expiration of that period, such an action—

    (a)    may be brought by him at any time before the expiration of one year from the earliest date on which he knew all the facts relevant to that cause of action; but

    (b)    shall not be so brought without the leave of the High Court.]

**33.    Discretionary exclusion of time limit for actions in respect of personal injuries or death.**

(1)    If it appears to the court that it would be equitable to allow an action to proceed having regard to the degree to which—

    (a)    the provisions of section 11 [or 11A] or 12 of this Act prejudice the plaintiff or any person whom he represents; and

    (b)    any decision of the court under this subsection would prejudice the defendant or any person whom he represents;

the court may direct that those provisions shall not apply to the action, or shall not apply to any specified cause of action to which the action relates.

[(1A) The court shall not under this section disapply—

    (a)    subsection (3) of section 11A; or

    (b)    where the damages claimed by the plaintiff are confined to damages for loss of or damage to any property, any other provision in its application to an action by virtue of Part I of the Consumer Protection Act 1987.]

(2)    The court shall not under this section disapply section 12(1) except where the reason why the person injured could no longer maintain an action was because of the time limit in section 11 [or subsection (4) of section 11A].

If, for example, the person injured could at his death no longer maintain an action under the Fatal Accidents Act 1976 because of the time limit in Article 29 in Schedule 1 to the Carriage by Air Act 1961, the court has no power to direct that section 12(1) shall not apply.

(3)    In acting under this section the court shall have regard to all the circumstances of the case and in particular to—

(a)    the length of, and the reasons for, the delay on the part of the plaintiff;

(b)    the extent to which, having regard to the delay, the evidence adduced or likely to be adduced by the plaintiff or the defendant is or is likely to be less cogent than if the action had been brought within the time allowed by section 11 [, by section 11A] or (as the case may be) by section 12;

(c)    the conduct of the defendant after the cause of action arose, including the extent (if any) to which he responded to requests reasonably made by the plaintiff for information or inspection for the purpose of ascertaining facts which were or might be relevant to the plaintiff's cause of action against the defendant;

(d)    the duration of any disability of the plaintiff arising after the date of the accrual of the cause of action;

(e)    the extent to which the plaintiff acted promptly and reasonably once he knew whether or not the act or omission of the defendant, to which the injury was attributable, might be capable at that time of giving rise to an action for damages;

(f)    the steps, if any, taken by the plaintiff to obtain medical, legal or other expert advice and the nature of any such advice he may have received.

(4)    In a case where the person injured died when, because of section 11 [or subsection (4) of section 11A], he could no longer maintain an action and recover damages in respect of the injury, the court shall have regard in particular to the length of, and the reasons for, the delay on the part of the deceased.

(5)    In a case under subsection (4) above, or any other case where the time limit, or one of the time limits, depends on the date of knowledge of a person other than the plaintiff, subsection (3) above shall have effect with appropriate modifications, and shall have effect in particular as if references to the plaintiff included references to any person whose date of knowledge is or was relevant in determining a time limit.

(6)    A direction by the court disapplying the provisions of section 12(1) shall operate to disapply the provisions to the same effect in section 1(1) of the Fatal Accidents Act 1976.

(7)    In this section "the court" means the court in which the action has been brought.

(8)    References in this section to section 11 [or 11A] include references to that section as extended by any of the preceding provisions of this Part of this Act or by any provision of Part III of this Act.

**35.    New claims in pending actions; rules of court.**

(1)    For the purposes of this Act, any new claim made in the course of any action shall be deemed to be a separate action and to have been commenced—

(a)    in the case of a new claim made in or by way of third party proceedings, on the date on which those proceedings were commenced; and

(b)    in the case of any other new claim, on the same date as the original action.

(2)    In this section a new claim means any claim by way of set-off or counterclaim, and any claim involving either—

(a)    the addition or substitution of a new cause of action; or

(b)    the addition or substitution of a new party;

and "third party proceedings" means any proceedings brought in the course of any action by any party to the action against a person not previously a party to the action, other than proceedings brought by joining any such person as defendant to any claim already made in the original action by the party bringing the proceedings.

(3)    Except as provided by section 33 of this Act or by rules of court, neither the High Court nor any county court shall allow a new claim within subsection (1)(b) above, other than an original set-off or counterclaim, to be made in the course of any action after the

expiry of any time limit under this Act which would affect a new action to enforce that claim.

For the purposes of this subsection, a claim is an original set-off or an original counterclaim if it is a claim made by way of set-off or (as the case may be) by way of counterclaim by a party who has not previously made any claim in the action.

(4) Rules of court may provide for allowing a new claim to which subsection (3) above applies to be made as there mentioned, but only if the conditions specified in subsection (5) below are satisfied, and subject to any further restrictions the rules may impose.

(5) The conditions referred to in subsection (4) above are the following—

(a) in the case of a claim involving a new cause of action, if the new cause of action arises out of the same facts or substantially the same facts as are already in issue on any claim previously made in the original action; and

(b) in the case of a claim involving a new party, if the addition or substitution of the new party is necessary for the determination of the original action.

(6) The addition or substitution of a new party shall not be regarded for the purposes of subsection (5)(b) above as necessary for the determination of the original action unless either—

(a) the new party is substituted for a party whose name was given in any claim made in the original action in mistake for the new party's name; or

(b) any claim already made in the original action cannot be maintained by or against an existing party unless the new party is joined or substituted as plaintiff or defendant in that action.

(7) Subject to subsection (4) above, rules of court may provide for allowing a party to any action to claim relief in a new capacity in respect of a new cause of action notwithstanding that he had no title to make that claim at the date of the commencement of the action.

This subsection shall not be taken as prejudicing the power of rules of court to provide for allowing a party to claim relief in a new capacity without adding or substituting a new cause of action.

(8) Subsections (3) to (7) above shall apply in relation to a new claim made in the course of third party proceedings as if those proceedings were the original action, and subject to such other modifications as may be prescribed by rules of court in any case or class of case.

## PART III

### 36. Equitable jurisdiction and remedies.

(1) The following time limits under this Act, that is to say—

(a) the time limit under section 2 for actions founded on tort;

[(aa) the time limit under section 4A for actions for libel or slander;]

(b) the time limit under section 5 for actions founded on simple contract;

(c) the time limit under section 7 for actions to enforce awards where the submission is not by an instrument under seal;

(d) the time limit under section 8 for actions on a specialty;

(e) the time limit under section 9 for actions to recover a sum recoverable by virtue of any enactment; and

(f) the time limit under section 24 for actions to enforce a judgment;

shall not apply to any claim for specific performance of a contract or for an injunction or for other equitable relief, except in so far as any such time limit may be applied by the court by analogy in like manner as the corresponding time limit under any enactment repealed by the Limitation Act 1939 was applied before 1st July 1940.

(2) Nothing in this Act shall affect any equitable jurisdiction to refuse relief on the ground of acquiescence or otherwise.

**37. Application to the Crown and the Duke of Cornwall.**

(1) Except as otherwise expressly provided in this Act, and without prejudice to section 39, this Act shall apply to proceedings by or against the Crown in like manner as it applies to proceedings between subjects.

**38. Interpretation.**

(1) In this Act, unless the context otherwise requires— . . .

"personal injuries" includes any disease and any impairment of a person's physical or mental condition, and "injury" and cognate expressions shall be construed accordingly;

(2) For the purposes of this Act a person shall be treated as under a disability while he is an infant, or of unsound mind.

(3) For the purposes of subsection (2) above a person is of unsound mind if he is a person who, by reason of mental disorder within the meaning of the [Mental Health Act 1983], is incapable of managing and administering his property and affairs.

(4) Without prejudice to the generality of subsection (3) above, a person shall be conclusively presumed for the purposes of subsection (2) above to be of unsound mind—

(a) while he is liable to be detained or subject to guardianship under [the Mental Health Act 1983 (otherwise than by virtue of section 35 or 89)]; . . .

**39. Saving for other limitation enactments.**

This Act shall not apply to any action or arbitration for which a period of limitation is prescribed by or under any other enactment (whether passed before or after the passing of this Act) or to any action or arbitration to which the Crown is a party and for which, if it were between subjects, a period of limitation would be prescribed by or under any such other enactment.

## THE BRITISH TELECOMMUNICATIONS ACT 1981
### (1981, c. 38)

**23. Exclusion of certain liabilities in tort in relation to telecommunications.**

(1) No proceedings in tort shall lie against the Corporation in respect of any loss or damage suffered by any person by reason of—

(a) failure to provide, or delay in providing, a telecommunication service, apparatus associated therewith or a service ancillary thereto;

(b) failure, interruption, suspension or restriction of a telecommunication service or a service ancillary thereto or delay of, or fault in, communication by means of a telecommunication service; or

(c) error in, or omission from, a directory for use in connection with a telecommunication service.

## THE CONTEMPT OF COURT ACT 1981
### (1981, c. 49)

**4. Contemporary reports of proceedings.**

(3) For the purposes of subsection (1) of this section and of section 3 of the Law of Libel Amendment Act 1888 (privilege) a report of proceedings shall be treated as published contemporaneously—

(a) in the case of a report of which publication is postponed pursuant to an order under subsection (2) of this section, if published as soon as practicable after that order expires;

(b) in the case of a report of committal proceedings of which publication is permitted by virtue only of subsection (3) of section 8 of the Magistrates' Court Act 1980, if published as soon as practicable after publication is so permitted.

## THE SUPREME COURT ACT 1981
### (1981, c. 54)

**32. Orders for interim payment.**

(1)    As regards proceedings pending in the High Court, provision may be made by rules of court for enabling the court, in such circumstances as may be prescribed, to make an order requiring a party to the proceedings to make an interim payment of such amount as may be specified in the order, with provision for the payment to be made to such other party to the proceedings as may be so specified or, if the order so provides, by paying it into court.

(2)    Any rules of court which make provision in accordance with subsection (1) may include provision for enabling a party to any proceedings who, in pursuance of such an order, has made an interim payment to recover the whole or part of the amount of the payment in such circumstances, and from such other party to the proceedings, as may be determined in accordance with the rules.

(3)    Any rules made by virtue of this section may include such incidental, supplementary and consequential provisions as the rule-making authority may consider necessary or expedient.

(4)    Nothing in this section shall be construed as affecting the exercise of any power relating to costs, including any power to make rules of court relating to costs.

(5)    In this section "interim payment", in relation to a party to any proceedings, means a payment on account of any damages, debt or other sum (excluding any costs) which that party may be held liable to pay to or for the benefit of another party to the proceedings if a final judgment or order of the court in the proceedings is given or made in favour of that other party.

**[32A.    Orders for provisional damages for personal injuries.**

(1)    This section applies to an action for damages for personal injuries in which there is proved or admitted to be a chance that at some definite or indefinite time in the future the injured person will, as a result of the act or omission which gave rise to the cause of action, develop some serious disease or suffer some serious deterioration in his physical or mental condition.

(2)    Subject to subsection (4) below, as regards any action for damages to which this section applies in which a judgment is given in the High Court, provision may be made by rules of court for enabling the court, in such circumstances as may be prescribed, to award the injured person—

(a)    damages assessed on the assumption that the injured person will not develop the disease or suffer the deterioration in his condition; and

(b)    further damages at a future date if he develops the disease or suffers the deterioration.

(3)    Any rules made by virtue of this section may include such incidental, supplementary and consequential provisions as the rule-making authority may consider necessary or expedient.

(4)    Nothing in this section shall be construed—

(a)    as affecting the exercise of any power relating to costs, including any power to make rules of court relating to costs; or

(b)    as prejudicing any duty of the court under any enactment or rule of law to reduce or limit the total damages which would have been recoverable apart from any such duty.]

**35. Provisions supplementary to ss. 33 and 34.**

(5)    In sections [32A,] 33 and 34 and this section— . . .

"personal injuries" includes any disease and any impairment of a person's physical or mental condition.

**[35A.   Powers of High Court to award interest on debts and damages.**

(1)   Subject to rules of court, in proceedings (whenever instituted) before the High Court for the recovery of a debt or damages there may be included in any sum for which judgment is given simple interest, at such rate as the court thinks fit or as rules of court may provide, on all or any part of the debt or damages in respect of which judgment is given, or payment is made before judgment, for all or any part of the period between the date when the cause of action arose and—

(a)   in the case of any sum paid before judgment, the date of the payment; and

(b)   in the case of the sum for which judgment is given, the date of the judgment.

(2)   In relation to a judgment given for damages for personal injuries or death which exceed £200 subsection (1) shall have effect—

(a)   with the substitution of "shall be included" for "may be included"; and

(b)   with the addition of "unless the court is satisfied that there are special reasons to the contrary" after "given", where first occurring.

(3)   Subject to rules of court, where—

(a)   there are proceedings (whenever instituted) before the High Court for the recovery of a debt; and

(b)   the defendant pays the whole debt to the plaintiff (otherwise than in pursuance of a judgment in the proceedings),

the defendant shall be liable to pay the plaintiff simple interest at such rate as the court thinks fit or as rules of court may provide on all or any part of the debt for all or any part of the period between the date when the cause of action arose and the date of the payment.

(4)   Interest in respect of a debt shall not be awarded under this section for a period during which, for whatever reason, interest on the debt already runs.

(5)   Without prejudice to the generality of section 84, rules of court may provide for a rate of interest by reference to the rate specified in section 17 of the Judgments Act 1838 as that section has effect from time to time or by reference to a rate for which any other enactment provides.

(6)   Interest under this section may be calculated at different rates in respect of different periods.

(7)   In this section "plaintiff" means the person seeking the debt or damages and "defendant" means the person from whom the plaintiff seeks the debt or damages and "personal injuries" includes any disease and any impairment of a person's physical or mental condition.]

**37.   Powers of High Court with respect to injunctions and receivers.**

(1)   The High Court may by order (whether interlocutory or final) grant an injunction or appoint a receiver in all cases in which it appears to the court to be just and convenient to do so.

**49.   Concurrent administration of law and equity.**

(1)   Subject to the provisions of this or any other Act, every court exercising jurisdiction in England and Wales in any civil cause or matter shall continue to administer law and equity on the basis that, wherever there is any conflict or variance between the rules of equity and the rules of the common law with reference to the same matter, the rules of equity shall prevail.

**50.   Power to award damages as well as, or in substitution for, injunction or specific performance.**

Where the Court of Appeal or the High Court has jurisdiction to entertain an application for an injunction or specific performance, it may award damages in addition to, or in substitution for, an injunction or specific performance.

**69.    Trial by jury.**
  (1)    Where, on the application of any party to an action to be tried in the Queen's Bench Division, the court is satisfied that there is in issue—
    (a)    a charge of fraud against that party; or
    (b)    a claim in respect of libel, slander, malicious prosecution or false imprisonment; or
    (c)    any question or issue of a kind prescribed for the purposes of this paragraph,
the action shall be tried with a jury, unless the court is of opinion that the trial requires any prolonged examination of documents or accounts or any scientific or local investigation which cannot conveniently be made with a jury.

## THE ADMINISTRATION OF JUSTICE ACT 1982
### (1982, c. 53)

**1.    Abolition of right to damages for loss of expectation of life.**
  (1)    In an action under the law of England and Wales or the law of Northern Ireland for damages for personal injuries—
    (a)    no damages shall be recoverable in respect of any loss of expectation of life caused to the injured person by the injuries; but
    (b)    if the injured person's expectation of life has been reduced by the injuries, the court, in assessing damages in respect of pain and suffering caused by the injuries, shall take account of any suffering caused or likely to be caused to him by awareness that his expectation of life has been so reduced.
  (2)    The reference in subsection (1)(a) above to damages in respect of loss of expectation of life does not include damages in respect of loss of income.

**2.    Abolition of actions for loss of services, etc.**
No person shall be liable in tort under the law of England and Wales or the law of Northern Ireland—
    (a)    to a husband on the ground only of having deprived him of the services or society of his wife;
    (b)    to a parent (or person standing in the place of a parent) on the ground only of his having deprived him of the services of a child; or
    (c)    on the ground only—
        (i)    of having deprived another of the services of his menial servant;
        (ii)    of having deprived another of the services of his female servant by raping or seducing her; or
        (iii)    of enticement of a servant or harbouring a servant.

**5.    Maintenance at public expense to be taken into account in assessment of damages.**
In an action under the law of England and Wales or the law of Northern Ireland for damages for personal injuries (including any such action arising out of a contract) any saving to the injured person which is attributable to his maintenance wholly or partly at public expense in a hospital, nursing home or other institution shall be set off against any income lost by him as a result of his injuries.

## THE CIVIL AVIATION ACT 1982
### (1982, c. 16)

**76.    Liability of aircraft in respect of trespass, nuisance and surface damage.**
  (1)    No action shall lie in respect of trespass or in respect of nuisance, by reason only of the flight of an aircraft over any property at a height above the ground which, having regard to wind, weather and all the circumstances of the case is reasonable, or the ordinar

incidents of such flight, so long as the provisions of any Air Navigation Order and of any orders under section 62 above have been duly complied with and there has been no breach of section 81 below.

(2)    Subject to subsection (3) below, where material loss or damage is caused to any person or property on land or water by, or by a person in, or an article, animal or person falling from, an aircraft while in flight, taking off or landing, then unless the loss or damage was caused or contributed to by the negligence of the person by whom it was suffered, damages in respect of the loss or damage shall be recoverable without proof of negligence or intention or other cause of action, as if the loss or damage had been caused by the wilful act, neglect, or default of the owner of the aircraft.

(3)    Where material loss or damage is caused as aforesaid in circumstances in which—

(a)    damages are recoverable in respect of the said loss or damage by virtue only of subsection (2) above, and

(b)    a legal liability is created in some person other than the owner to pay damages in respect of the said loss or damage,

the owner shall be entitled to be indemnified by that other person against any claim in respect of the said loss or damage.

### 77.    Nuisance caused by aircraft on aerodromes.

(1)    An Air Navigation Order may provide for regulating the conditions under which noise and vibration may be caused by aircraft on aerodromes and may provide that subsection (2) below shall apply to any aerodrome as respects which provision as to noise and vibration caused by aircraft is so made.

(2)    No action shall lie in respect of nuisance by reason only of the noise and vibration caused by aircraft on an aerodrome to which this subsection applies by virtue of an Air Navigation Order, as long as the provisions of any such Order are duly complied with.

### THE EMPLOYMENT ACT 1982
### (1982, c. 46)

### 12.    Prohibition on union membership requirements.

(1)    Any term or condition of a contract for the supply of goods or services is void in so far as it purports—

(a)    to require that the whole, or some part, of the work done for the purposes of the contract is to be done only by persons who are not members of trade unions or not members of a particular trade union; or

(b)    to require that the whole, or some part, of such work is to be done only by persons who are members of trade unions or members of a particular trade union.

(2)    A person contravenes this subsection if, on the ground of union membership, he—

(a)    fails, in a case where he maintains (in whatever form) a list of approved suppliers of goods or services or a list of persons from whom tenders for the supply of goods or services may be invited to include the name of a particular person in that list;

(b)    terminates a contract for the supply of goods or services; or

(c)    does, in relation to a proposed contract for the supply of goods or services, any of the acts mentioned in subsection (3) below.

(3)    The acts are—

(a)    excluding a particular person from the group of persons from whom tenders for the supply of the goods or services are invited;

(b)    failing to permit a particular person to submit such a tender;

(c)    otherwise determining not to enter into a contract with a particular person for the supply of the goods or services.

(7)    Subsection (2) above does not create an offence but the obligation to comply with it is a duty owed to each of the following—

(a)    in a case falling within subsection (2)(a) above, the person referred to in subsection (4) as the supplier;

(b)    in a case falling within subsection (2)(b) above, any other party to the contract;

(c)    in a case falling within subsection (2)(c) above, the person referred to in subsection (3) above; and

(d)    in any case, any other person who may be adversely affected by its contravention;

and any breach of that duty shall be actionable accordingly (subject to the defences and other incidents applying to actions for breach of statutory duty).

**14.    Pressure to impose union membership or recognition requirements.**

(1)    Nothing in section 13 of the 1974 Act shall prevent an act being actionable in tort in any case where a person induces, or attempts to induce, another—

(a)    to incorporate in a contract to which that other person is a party, or proposed contract to which that other person intends to be a party, any term or condition which is, or would be, void by virtue of section 12(1) or 13(1) of this Act; or

(b)    to contravene section 12(2) or 13(2);

and the act constitutes, or is one of a number of acts which together constitute, the inducement or attempted inducement.

(2)    Nothing in section 13 of the 1974 Act shall prevent an act which interferes with the supply (whether or not under a contract) of goods or services, or can reasonably be expected to have such an effect, being actionable in tort in any case where subsection (3) below is satisfied and one of the facts relied upon for the purpose of establishing liability is that any person has—

(a)    induced another to break a contract of employment or interfered or induced another to interfere with its performance; or

(b)    threatened that a contract of employment under which he or another is employed will be broken or its performance interfered with, or that he will induce another to break a contract of employment or to interfere with its performance.

(3)    This subsection is satisfied if—

(a)    the reason, or one of the reasons, for doing the act is that work done or to be done in connection with the supply of the goods or services in question has been, or is likely to be, done by persons (other than persons employed by the relevant employer) who are not members of trade unions or of a particular trade union;

(b)    the reason, or one of the reasons, for doing the act is that such work has been, or is likely to be, done by persons (other than persons employed by the relevant employer) who are members of trade unions or of a particular trade union; or

(c)    the supplier of the goods or services in question is not the relevant employer and the reason, or one of the reasons, for doing the act is that the supplier does not, or is not likely to, recognise, negotiate or consult as mentioned in section 13.

(4)    In subsection (3) above "the relevant employer" means the employer under the contract of employment mentioned in subsection (2) above.

**16.    Limit on damages awarded against trade unions in actions in tort.**

(1)    Subject to subsection (2) below, in any proceedings in tort brought against a trade union the amount which may be awarded against the union by way of damages in those proceedings shall not exceed the appropriate limit.

(2)    Subsection (1) above does not apply to any proceedings—

(a)    for any of the following resulting in personal injury to any person, that is to say negligence, nuisance or breach of duty; or

(b)    without prejudice to paragraph (a) above, for breach of duty in connection with the ownership, occupation, possession, control or use of property (whether real or personal or, in Scotland, heritable or moveable) [or to any proceedings by virtue of Part I of the Consumer Protection Act 1987 (product liability)].

(3)    The appropriate limit is—
    (a)    £10,000, if the union has less than 5,000 members;
    (b)    £50,000, if it has 5,000 or more members but less than 25,000 members;
    (c)    £125,000, if it has 25,000 or more members but less than 100,000 members;
and
    (d)    £250,000, if it has 100,000 or more members.
(4)    The Secretary of State may by order vary any of the sums for the time being specified in subsection (3) above.
(6)    In this section—
"duty" means a duty imposed by any rule of law or by or under any enactment; and
"personal injury" includes any disease and any impairment of a person's physical or mental condition.

**21.    Interpretation, minor and consequential amendments and repeals.**
(1)    In this Act—
"the 1974 Act" means the Trade Union and Labour Relations Act 1974; . . .

## THE FORFEITURE ACT 1982
### (1982, c. 34)

**1.    The "forfeiture rule".**
(1)    In this Act, the "forfeiture rule" means the rule of public policy which in certain circumstances precludes a person who has unlawfully killed another from acquiring a benefit in consequence of the killing. . . .

**2.    Power to modify the rule.**
(1)    Where a court determines that the forfeiture rule has precluded a person (in this section referred to as "the offender") who has unlawfully killed another from acquiring any interest in property mentioned in subsection (4) below, the court may make an order under this section modifying the effect of that rule.
(2)    The court shall not make an order under this section modifying the effect of the forfeiture rule in any case unless it is satisfied that, having regard to the conduct of the offender and of the deceased and to such other circumstances as appear to the court to be material, the justice of the case requires the effect of the rule to be so modified in that case.
(3)    In any case where a person stands convicted of an offence of which unlawful killing is an element, the court shall not make an order under this section modifying the effect of the forfeiture rule in that case unless proceedings for the purpose are brought before the expiry of the period of three months beginning with his conviction.
(4)    The interests in property referred to in subsection (1) above are—
    (a)    any beneficial interest in property which (apart from the forfeiture rule) the offender would have acquired—
        (i)    under the deceased's will (including, as respects Scotland, any writing having testamentary effect) or the law relating to intestacy or by way of ius relicti, ius relictae or legitim;
        (ii)    on the nomination of the deceased in accordance with the provisions of any enactment;
        (iii)    as a donatio mortis causa made by the deceased; or
        (iv)    under a special destination (whether relating to heritable or moveable property); or
    (b)    any beneficial interest in property which (apart from the forfeiture rule) the offender would have acquired in consequence of the death of the deceased, being property which, before the death, was held on trust for any person.

(5)    An order under this section may modify the effect of the forfeiture rule in respect of any interest in property to which the determination referred to in subsection (1) above relates and may do so in either or both of the following ways, that is—
(a)    where there is more than one such interest, by excluding the application of the rule in respect of any (but not all) of those interests; and
(b)    in the case of any such interest in property, by excluding the application of the rule in respect of part of the property.
(6)    On the making of an order under this section, the forfeiture rule shall have effect for all purposes (including purposes relating to anything done before the order is made) subject to the modifications made by the order. . . .

## 5.    Exclusion of murderers.
Nothing in this Act or in any order made under section 2 or referred to in section 3(1) of this Act shall affect the application of the forfeiture rule in the case of a person who stands convicted of murder.

## THE INSURANCE COMPANIES ACT 1982
### (1982, c. 50)

## 2.    Restriction on carrying on insurance business.
(1)    Subject to the following provisions of this section, no person shall carry on any insurance business in the United Kingdom unless authorised to do so under section 3 or 4 below.

## THE SUPPLY OF GOODS AND SERVICES ACT 1982
### (1982, c. 29)

### PART I
### SUPPLY OF GOODS
*Contracts for the transfer of property in goods*

## 1.    The contracts concerned.
(1)    In this Act a "contract for the transfer of goods" means a contract under which one person transfers or agrees to transfer to another the property in goods, other than an excepted contract.
(2)    For the purposes of this section an excepted contract means any of the following:—
(a)    a contract of sale of goods;
(b)    a hire-purchase agreement;
(c)    a contract under which the property in goods is (or is to be) transferred in exchange for trading stamps on their redemption;
(d)    a transfer or agreement to transfer which is made by deed and for which there is no consideration other than the presumed consideration imported by the deed;
(e)    a contract intended to operate by way of mortgage, pledge, charge or other security.
(3)    For the purposes of this Act a contract is a contract for the transfer of goods whether or not services are also provided or to be provided under the contract, and (subject to subsection (2) above) whatever is the nature of the consideration for the transfer or agreement to transfer.

## 2.    Implied terms about title, etc.
(1)    In a contract for the transfer of goods, other than one to which subsection (3) below applies, there is an implied condition on the part of the transferor that in the case of a transfer of the property in the goods he has a right to transfer the property and in the case of

an agreement to transfer the property in the goods he will have such a right at the time when the property is to be transferred.

(2)    In a contract for the transfer of goods, other than one to which subsection (3) below applies, there is also an implied warranty that—

(a)    the goods are free, and will remain free until the time when the property is to be transferred, from any charge or encumbrance not disclosed or known to the transferee before the contract is made, and

(b)    the transferee will enjoy quiet possession of the goods except so far as it may be disturbed by the owner or other person entitled to the benefit of any charge or encumbrance so disclosed or known.

(3)    This subsection applies to a contract for the transfer of goods in the case of which there appears from the contract or is to be inferred from its circumstances an intention that the transferor should transfer only such title as he or a third person may have.

(4)    In a contract to which subsection (3) above applies there is an implied warranty that all charges or encumbrances known to the transferor and not known to the transferee have been disclosed to the transferee before the contract is made.

(5)    In a contract to which subsection (3) above applies there is also an implied warranty that none of the following will disturb the transferee's quiet possession of the goods, namely—

(a)    the transferor;

(b)    in a case where the parties to the contract intend that the transferor should transfer only such title as a third person may have, that person;

(c)    anyone claiming through or under the transferor or that third person otherwise than under a charge or encumbrance disclosed or known to the transferee before the contract is made.

**3.    Implied terms where transfer is by description.**

(1)    This section applies where, under a contract for the transfer of goods, the transferor transfers or agrees to transfer the property in the goods by description.

(2)    In such case there is an implied condition that the goods will correspond with the description.

(3)    If the transferor transfers or agrees to transfer the property in the goods by sample as well as by description it is not sufficient that the bulk of the goods corresponds with the sample if the goods do not also correspond with the description.

(4)    A contract is not prevented from falling within subsection (1) above by reason only that, being exposed for supply, the goods are selected by the transferee.

**4.    Implied terms about quality or fitness.**

(1)    Except as provided by this section and section 5 below and subject to the provisions of any other enactment, there is no implied condition or warranty about the quality or fitness for any particular purpose of goods supplied under a contract for the transfer of goods.

(2)    Where, under such a contract, the transferor transfers the property in goods in the course of a business, there is (subject to subsection (3) below) an implied condition that the goods supplied under the contract are of merchantable quality.

(3)    There is no such condition as is mentioned in subsection (2) above—

(a)    as regards defects specifically drawn to the transferee's attention before the contract is made; or

(b)    if the transferee examines the goods before the contract is made, as regards defects which that examination ought to reveal.

(4)    Subsection (5) below applies where, under a contract for the transfer of goods, the transferor transfers the property in goods in the course of a business and the transferee, expressly or by implication, makes known—

(a)    to the transferor, or

(b)    where the consideration or part of the consideration for the transfer is a sum payable by instalments and the goods were previously sold by a credit-broker to the transferor, to that credit-broker,
any particular purpose for which the goods are being acquired.

(5)    In that case there is (subject to subsection (6) below) an implied condition that the goods supplied under the contract are reasonably fit for that purpose, whether or not that is a purpose for which such goods are commonly supplied.

(6)    Subsection (5) above does not apply where the circumstances show that the transferee does not rely, or that it is unreasonable for him to rely, on the skill or judgment of the transferor or credit-broker.

(7)    An implied condition or warranty about quality or fitness for a particular purpose may be annexed by usage to a contract for the transfer of goods.

(8)    The preceding provisions of this section apply to a transfer by a person who in the course of a business is acting as agent for another as they apply to a transfer by a principal in the course of a business, except where that other is not transferring in the course of a business and either the transferee knows that fact or reasonable steps are taken to bring it to the transferee's notice before the contract concerned is made.

(9)    Goods of any kind are of merchantable quality within the meaning of subsection (2) above if they are as fit for the purpose or purposes for which goods of that kind are commonly supplied as it is reasonable to expect having regard to any description applied to them, the price (if relevant) and all the other relevant circumstances.

## 5.    Implied terms where transfer is by sample.

(1)    This section applies where, under a contract for the transfer of goods, the transferor transfers or agrees to transfer the property in the goods by reference to a sample.

(2)    In such a case there is an implied condition—
        (a)    that the bulk will correspond with the sample in quality; and
        (b)    that the transferee will have a reasonable opportunity of comparing the bulk with the sample; and
        (c)    that the goods will be free from any defect, rendering them unmerchantable, which would not be apparent on reasonable examination of the sample.

(3)    In subsection (2)(c) above "unmerchantable" is to be construed in accordance with section 4(9) above.

(4)    For the purposes of this section a transferor transfers or agrees to transfer the property in goods by reference to a sample where there is an express or implied term to that effect in the contract concerned.

*Contracts for the hire of goods*

## 6.    The contracts concerned.

(1)    In this Act a "contract for the hire of goods" means a contract under which one person bails or agrees to bail goods to another by way of hire, other than an excepted contract.

(2)    For the purposes of this section an excepted contract means any of the following:—
        (a)    a hire-purchase agreement;
        (b)    a contract under which goods are (or are to be) bailed in exchange for trading stamps on their redemption.

(3)    For the purposes of this Act a contract is a contract for the hire of goods whether or not services are also provided or to be provided under the contract, and (subject to subsection (2) above) whatever is the nature of the consideration for the bailment or agreement to bail by way of hire.

**7.   Implied terms about right to transfer possession, etc.**

(1)   In a contract for the hire of goods there is an implied condition on the part of the bailor that in the case of a bailment he has a right to transfer possession of the goods by way of hire for the period of the bailment and in the case of an agreement to bail he will have such a right at the time of the bailment.

(2)   In a contract for the hire of goods there is also an implied warranty that the bailee will enjoy quiet possession of the goods for the period of the bailment except so far as the possession may be disturbed by the owner or other person entitled to the benefit of any charge or encumbrance disclosed or known to the bailee before the contract is made.

(3)   The preceding provisions of this section do not affect the right of the bailor to repossess the goods under an express or implied term of the contract.

**8.   Implied terms where hire is by description.**

(1)   This section applies where, under a contract for the hire of goods, the bailor bails or agrees to bail the goods by description.

(2)   In such a case there is an implied condition that the goods will correspond with the description.

(3)   If under the contract the bailor bails or agrees to bail the goods by reference to a sample as well as a description it is not sufficient that the bulk of the goods corresponds with the sample if the goods do not also correspond with the description.

(4)   A contract is not prevented from falling within subsection (1) above by reason only that, being exposed for supply, the goods are selected by the bailee.

**9.   Implied terms about quality or fitness.**

(1)   Except as provided by this section and section 10 below and subject to the provisions of any other enactment, there is no implied condition or warranty about the quality or fitness for any particular purpose of goods bailed under a contract for the hire of goods.

(2)   Where, under such a contract, the bailor bails goods in the course of a business, there is (subject to subsection (3) below) an implied condition that the goods supplied under the contract are of merchantable quality.

(3)   There is no such condition as is mentioned in subsection (2) above—

(a)   as regards defects specifically drawn to the bailee's attention before the contract is made; or

(b)   if the bailee examines the goods before the contract is made, as regards defects which that examination ought to reveal.

(4)   Subsection (5) below applies where, under a contract for the hire of goods, the bailor bails goods in the course of a business and the bailee, expressly or by implication, makes known—

(a)   to the bailor in the course of negotiations conducted by him in relation to the making of the contract, or

(b)   to a credit-broker in the course of negotiations conducted by that broker in relation to goods sold by him to the bailor before forming the subject matter of the contract, any particular purpose for which the goods are being bailed.

(5)   In that case there is (subject to subsection (6) below) an implied condition that the goods supplied under the contract are reasonably fit for that purpose, whether or not that is a purpose for which such goods are commonly supplied.

(6)   Subsection (5) above does not apply where the circumstances show that the bailee does not rely, or that it is unreasonable for him to rely, on the skill or judgment of the bailor or credit-broker.

(7)   An implied condition or warranty about quality or fitness for a particular purpose may be annexed by usage to a contract for the hire of goods.

(8)   The preceding provisions of this section apply to a bailment by a person who in the course of a business is acting as agent for another as they apply to a bailment by a

principal in the course of a business, except where that other is not bailing in the course of a business and either the bailee knows that fact or reasonable steps are taken to bring it to the bailee's notice before the contract concerned is made.

(9)   Goods of any kind are of merchantable quality within the meaning of subsection (2) above if they are as fit for the purpose or purposes for which goods of that kind are commonly supplied as it is reasonable to expect having regard to any description applied to them, the consideration for the bailment (if relevant) and all the other relevant circumstances.

**10.   Implied terms where hire is by sample.**

(1)   This section applies where, under a contract for the hire of goods, the bailor bails or agrees to bail the goods by reference to a sample.

(2)   In such a case there is an implied condition—

(a)   that the bulk will correspond with the sample in quality; and

(b)   that the bailee will have a reasonable opportunity of comparing the bulk with the sample; and

(c)   that the goods will be free from any defect, rendering them unmerchantable, which would not be apparent on reasonable examination of the sample.

(3)   In subsection (2)(c) above "unmerchantable" is to be construed in accordance with section 9(9) above.

(4)   For the purposes of this section a bailor bails or agrees to bail goods by reference to a sample where there is an express or implied term to that effect in the contract concerned.

*Exclusion of implied terms, etc.*

**11.   Exclusion of implied terms, etc.**

(1)   Where a right, duty or liability would arise under a contract for the transfer of goods or a contract for the hire of goods by implication of law, it may (subject to subsection (2) below and the 1977 Act) be negatived or varied by express agreement, or by the course of dealing between the parties, or by such usage as binds both parties to the contract.

(2)   An express condition or warranty does not negative a condition or warranty implied by the preceding provisions of this Act unless inconsistent with it.

(3)   Nothing in the preceding provisions of this Act prejudices the operation of any other enactment or any rule of law whereby any condition or warranty (other than one relating to quality or fitness) is to be implied in a contract for the transfer of goods or a contract for the hire of goods.

PART II
SUPPLY OF SERVICES

**12.   The contracts concerned.**

(1)   In this Act a "contract for the supply of a service" means, subject to subsection (2) below, a contract under which a person ("the supplier") agrees to carry out a service.

(2)   For the purposes of this Act, a contract of service or apprenticeship is not a contract for the supply of a service.

(3)   Subject to subsection (2) above, a contract is a contract for the supply of a service for the purposes of this Act whether or not goods are also—

(a)   transferred or to be transferred, or

(b)   bailed or to be bailed by way of hire,

under the contract, and whatever is the nature of the consideration for which the service is to be carried out.

(4)   The Secretary of State may by order provide that one or more of sections 13 to 15 below shall not apply to services of a description specified in the order, and such an order may make different provision for different circumstances.

(5)    The power to make an order under subsection (4) above shall be exercisable by statutory instrument subject to annulment in pursuance of a resolution of either House of Parliament.

**13.    Implied term about care and skill.**

In a contract for the supply of a service where the supplier is acting in the course of a business, there is an implied term that the supplier will carry out the service with reasonable care and skill.

**14.    Implied term about time of performance.**

(1)    Where, under a contract for the supply of a service by a supplier acting in the course of a business, the time for the service to be carried out is not fixed by the contract, left to be fixed in a manner agreed by the contract or determined by the course of dealing between the parties, there is an implied term that the supplier will carry out the service within a reasonable time.

(2)    What is a reasonable time is a question of fact.

**15.    Implied term about consideration.**

(1)    Where, under a contract for the supply of a service, the consideration for the service is not determined by the contract, left to be determined in a manner agreed by the contract or determined by the course of dealing between the parties, there is an implied term that the party contracting with the supplier will pay a reasonable charge.

(2)    What is a reasonable charge is a question of fact.

**16.    Exclusion of implied terms, etc.**

(1)    Where a right, duty or liability would arise under a contract for the supply of a service by virtue of this Part of this Act, it may (subject to subsection (2) below and the 1977 Act) be negatived or varied by express agreement, or by the course of dealing between the parties, or by such usage as binds both parties to the contract.

(2)    An express term does not negative a term implied by this Part of this Act unless inconsistent with it.

(3)    Nothing in this Part of this Act prejudices—

(a)    any rule of law which imposes on the supplier a duty stricter than that imposed by section 13 or 14 above; or

(b)    subject to paragraph (a) above, any rule of law whereby any term not inconsistent with this Part of this Act is to be implied in a contract for the supply of a service.

(4)    This Part of this Act has effect subject to any other enactment which defines or restricts the rights, duties or liabilities arising in connection with a service of any description.

PART III
SUPPLEMENTARY

**18.    Interpretation: general.**

(1)    In the preceding provisions of this Act and this section—

"bailee", in relation to a contract for the hire of goods means (depending on the context) a person to whom the goods are bailed under the contract, or a person to whom they are to be so bailed, or a person to whom the rights under the contract of either of those persons have passed;

"bailor", in relation to a contract for the hire of goods, means (depending on the context) a person who bails the goods under the contract, or a person who agrees to do so, or a person to whom the duties under the contract of either of those persons have passed;

"business" includes a profession and the activities of any government department or local or public authority;

"credit-broker" means a person acting in the course of a business of credit brokerage carried on by him;

"credit brokerage" means the effecting of introductions—

(a)    of individuals desiring to obtain credit to persons carrying on any business so far as it relates to the provision of credit; or

(b)    of individuals desiring to obtain goods on hire to persons carrying on a business which comprises or relates to the bailment of goods under a contract for the hire of goods; or

(c)    of individuals desiring to obtain credit, or to obtain goods on hire, to other credit-brokers;

"enactment" means any legislation (including subordinate legislation) of the United Kingdom or Northern Ireland;

"goods" include all personal chattels (including emblements, industrial growing crops, and things attached to or forming part of the land which are agreed to be severed before the transfer or bailment concerned or under the contract concerned), other than things in action and money;

"hire-purchase agreement" has the same meaning as in the 1974 Act;

"property", in relation to goods, means the general property in them and not merely a special property;

"quality", in relation to goods, includes their state or condition;

"redemption", in relation to trading stamps, has the same meaning as in the Trading Stamps Act 1964 or, as respects Northern Ireland, the Trading Stamps Act (Northern Ireland) 1965;

"trading stamps" has the same meaning as in the said Act of 1964 or, as respects Northern Ireland, the said Act of 1965;

"transferee", in relation to a contract for the transfer of goods, means (depending on the context) a person to whom the property in the goods is transferred under the contract, or a person to whom the property is to be so transferred, or a person to whom the rights under the contract of either of those persons have passed;

"transferor", in relation to a contract for the transfer of goods, means (depending on the context) a person who transfers the property in the goods under the contract, or a person who agrees to do so, or a person to whom the duties under the contract of either of those persons have passed.

(2)    In subsection (1) above, in the definitions of bailee, bailor, transferee and transferor, a reference to rights or duties passing is to their passing by assignment, operation of law or otherwise.

### 19.    Interpretation: references to Acts.
In this Act—

"the 1973 Act" means the Supply of Goods (Implied Terms) Act 1973;

"the 1974 Act" means the Consumer Credit Act 1974;

"the 1977 Act" means the Unfair Contract Terms Act 1977; and

"the 1979 Act" means the Sale of Goods Act 1979.

## THE INTERNATIONAL TRANSPORT CONVENTIONS ACT 1983
### (1983, c. 14)

### 1.    Convention to have the force of law.
(1)    The Convention concerning International Carriage by Rail signed on behalf of the United Kingdom on 9th May 1980 shall have the force of law in the United Kingdom.

### 3.    Fatal accidents.
(1)    Where by virtue of the Convention any person has a right of action in respect of the death of a passenger by reason of his being a person whom the passenger was under a legal duty to maintain—

(a)    subject to subsection (2) below, no action in respect of the passenger's death shall be brought for the benefit of that person under the Fatal Accidents Act 1976; but

(b)    nothing in section 2(3) of that Act (not more than one action in respect of the same subject-matter of complaint) shall prevent an action being brought under that Act for the benefit of any other person.

(2)    Nothing in subsection (1)(a) above affects the right of any person to claim damages for bereavement under section 1A of the said Act of 1976.

(3)    Section 4 of the said Act of 1976 (exclusion of certain benefits in assessment of damages) shall apply in relation to an action brought by any person under the Convention as it applies in relation to an action under that Act.

(4)    Where separate proceedings are brought under the Convention and under the said Act of 1976 in respect of the death of a passenger, a court, in awarding damages under that Act, shall take into account any damages awarded in the proceedings brought under the Convention and shall have jurisdiction to make any part of its award conditional on the result of those proceedings.

## THE MENTAL HEALTH ACT 1983
### (1983,c. 20)

**95.    General functions of the judge with respect to property and affairs of patient.**

(1)    The judge may, with respect to the property and affairs of a patient, do or secure the doing of all such things as appear necessary or expedient—

(a)    for the maintenance or other benefit of the patient,

(b)    for the maintenance or other benefit of members of the patient's family,

(c)    for making provision for other persons or purposes for whom or which the patient might be expected to provide if he were not mentally disordered, or

(d)    otherwise for administering the patient's affairs.

(2)    In the exercise of the powers conferred by this section regard shall be had first of all to the requirements of the patient, and the rules of law which restricted the enforcement by a creditor of rights against property under the control of the judge in lunacy shall apply to property under the control of the judge; but, subject to the foregoing provisions of this subsection, the judge shall, in administering a patient's affairs, have regard to the interests of creditors and also to the desirability of making provision for obligations of the patient notwithstanding that they may not be legally enforceable.

**139.    Protection for acts done in pursuance of this Act.**

(1)    No person shall be liable, whether on the ground of want of jurisdiction or on any other ground, to any civil or criminal proceedings to which he would have been liable apart from this section in respect of any act purporting to be done in pursuance of this Act or any regulations or rules made under this Act, or in, or in pursuance of anything done in, the discharge of functions conferred by any other enactment on the authority having jurisdiction under Part VII of this Act, unless the act was done in bad faith or without reasonable care.

(2)    No civil proceedings shall be brought against any person in any court in respect of any such act without the leave of the High Court; and no criminal proceedings shall be brought against any person in any court in respect of any such act except by or with the consent of the Director of Public Prosecutions.

## THE BUILDING ACT 1984
### (1984, c. 55)

**1.    Power to make building regulations.**

(1)    The Secretary of State may, for any of the purposes of—

(a)    securing the health, safety, welfare and convenience of persons in or about buildings and of others who may be affected by buildings or matters connected with buildings,

(b)    furthering the conservation of fuel and power, and

(c)    preventing waste, undue consumption, misuse or contamination of water, make regulations with respect to the design and construction of buildings and the provision of services, fittings and equipment in or in connection with buildings.

## 38.    Civil liability.

(1)    Subject to this section—

(a)    breach of a duty imposed by building regulations, so far as it causes damage, is actionable, except in so far as the regulations provide otherwise, and

(b)    as regards such a duty, building regulations may provide for a prescribed defence to be available in an action for breach of that duty brought by virtue of this subsection.

(2)    Subsection (1) above, and any defence provided for in regulations made by virtue of it, do not apply in the case of a breach of such a duty in connection with a building erected before the date on which that subsection comes into force unless the regulations imposing the duty apply to or in connection with the building by virtue of section 2(2) above or paragraph 8 of Schedule 1 to this Act.

(3)    This section does not affect the extent (if any) to which breach of—

(a)    a duty imposed by or arising in connection with this Part of this Act or any other enactment relating to building regulations, or

(b)    a duty imposed by building regulations in a case to which subsection (1) above does not apply,

is actionable, or prejudice a right of action that exists apart from the enactments relating to building regulations.

(4)    In this section, "damage" includes the death of, or injury to, any person (including any disease and any impairment of a person's physical or mental condition).

## THE CABLE AND BROADCASTING ACT 1984
### (1984, c. 46)

## 28.    Amendment of law of defamation.

(1)    For the purposes of the law of libel and slander (including the law of criminal libel so far as it relates to the publication of defamatory matter) the publication of words in the course of a programme included in a cable programme service shall be treated as publication in permanent form.

(2)    Subsection (1) above shall apply for the purposes of section 3 of each of the Defamation Acts (slander of title etc.) as it applies for the purposes of the law of libel and slander.

(3)    Section 7 of each of those Acts (qualified privilege of newspapers) shall apply in relation to reports or matters included in a cable programme service which is or does not require to be licensed, and in relation to any inclusion in such a service of any such report or matter, as it applies in relation to reports and matters published in a newspaper and to publication in a newspaper; and subsection (2) of that section shall have effect, in relation to any such inclusion, as if for the words "in the newspaper in which" there were substituted the words "in the matter in which".

(4)    In this section "the Defamation Act" means the Defamation Act 1952 and the Defamation Act (Northern Ireland) 1955.

## THE DATA PROTECTION ACT 1984
### (1984, c. 35)

**22.  Compensation for inaccuracy.**

(1)    An individual who is the subject of personal data held by a data user and who suffers damage by reason of the inaccuracy of the data shall be entitled to compensation from the data user for that damage and for any distress which the individual has suffered by reason of the inaccuracy. . . .

(3)    In proceedings brought against any person by virtue of this section it shall be a defence to prove that he had taken such care as in all the circumstances was reasonably required to ensure the accuracy of the data at the material time.

(4)    Data are inaccurate for the purposes of this section if incorrect or misleading as to any matter of fact.

## THE OCCUPIERS' LIABILITY ACT 1984
### (1984, c. 3)

**1.    Duty of occupier to persons other than his visitors.**

(1)    The rules enacted by this section shall have effect, in place of the rules of the common law, to determine—

   (a)    whether any duty is owed by a person as occupier of premises to persons other than his visitors in respect of any risk of their suffering injury on the premises by reason of any danger due to the state of the premises or to things done or omitted to be done on them; and

   (b)    if so, what that duty is.

(2)    For the purposes of this section, the persons who are to be treated respectively as an occupier of any premises (which, for those purposes, include any fixed or movable structure) and as his visitors are—

   (a)    any person who owes in relation to the premises the duty referred to in section 2 of the Occupiers' Liability Act 1957 (the common duty of care), and

   (b)    those who are his visitors for the purposes of that duty.

(3)    An occupier of premises owes a duty to another (not being his visitor) in respect of any such risk as is referred to in subsection (1) above if—

   (a)    he is aware of the danger or has reasonable grounds to believe that it exists;

   (b)    he knows or has reasonable grounds to believe that the other is in the vicinity of the danger concerned or that he may come into the vicinity of the danger (in either case, whether the other has lawful authority for being in that vicinity or not); and

   (c)    the risk is one against which, in all the circumstances of the case, he may reasonably be expected to offer the other some protection.

(4)    Where, by virtue of this section, an occupier of premises owes a duty to another in respect of such a risk, the duty is to take such care as is reasonable in all the circumstances of the case to see that he does not suffer injury on the premises by reason of the danger concerned.

(5)    Any duty owed by virtue of this section in respect of a risk may, in an appropriate case, be discharged by taking such steps as are reasonable in all the circumstances of the case to give warning of the danger concerned or to discourage persons from incurring the risk.

(6)    No duty is owed by virtue of this section to any person in respect of risks willingly accepted as his by that person (the question whether a risk was so accepted to be decided on the same principles as in other cases in which one person owes a duty of care to another).

(7)    No duty is owed by virtue of this section to persons using the highway, and this section does not affect any duty owed to such persons.

(8)    Where a person owes a duty by virtue of this section, he does not, by reason of any breach of the duty, incur any liability in respect of any loss of or damage to property.
(9)    In this section—
"highway" means any part of a highway other than a ferry or waterway;
"injury" means anything resulting in death or personal injury, including any disease and any impairment of physical or mental condition; and
"movable structure" includes any vessel, vehicle or aircraft.

### 3.    Application to Crown.
Section 1 of this Act shall bind the Crown, but as regards the Crown's liability in tort shall not bind the Crown further than the Crown is made liable in tort by the Crown Proceedings Act 1947.

## THE POLICE AND CRIMINAL EVIDENCE ACT 1984
### (1984, c. 60)

### 17.    Entry for purpose of arrest etc.
(1)    Subject to the following provisions of this section, and without prejudice to any other enactment, a constable may enter and search any premises for the purpose—
    (a)    of executing—
        (i)    a warrant of arrest issued in connection with or arising out of criminal proceedings; or
        (ii)    a warrant of commitment issued under section 76 of the Magistrates' Courts Act 1980;
    (b)    of arresting a person for an arrestable offence; . . .
    (e)    of saving life or limb or preventing serious damage to property.
(4)    The power of search conferred by this section is only a power to search to the extent that is reasonably required for the purpose for which the power of entry is exercised.
(5)    Subject to subsection (6) below, all the rules of common law under which a constable has power to enter premises without a warrant are hereby abolished.
(6)    Nothing in subsection (5) above affects any power of entry to deal with or prevent a breach of the peace.

### 19.    General power of seizure etc.
(1)    The powers conferred by subsections (2), (3) and (4) below are exercisable by a constable who is lawfully on any premises.
(2)    The constable may seize anything which is on the premises if he has reasonable grounds for believing—
    (a)    that it has been obtained in consequence of the commission of an offence; and
    (b)    that it is necessary to seize it in order to prevent it being concealed, lost, damaged, altered or destroyed.

### 22.    Retention.
(1)    Subject to subsection (4) below, anything which has been seized by a constable or taken away by a constable following a requirement made by virtue of section 19 or 20 above may be retained so long as is necessary in all the circumstances.
(3)    Nothing seized on the ground that it may be used—
    (a)    to cause physical injury to any person;
    (b)    to damage property;
    (c)    to interfere with evidence; or
    (d)    to assist in escape from police detention or lawful custody,
may be retained when the person from whom it was seized is no longer in police detention or the custody of a court or is in the custody of a court but has been released on bail.

### 24.   Arrest without warrant for arrestable offences.

(4)   Any person may arrest without a warrant—
    (a)   anyone who is in the act of committing an arrestable offence;
    (b)   anyone whom he has reasonable grounds for suspecting to be committing such an offence.

(5)   Where an arrestable offence has been committed, any person may arrest without a warrant—
    (a)   anyone who is guilty of the offence;
    (b)   anyone whom he has reasonable grounds for suspecting to be guilty of it.

(6)   Where a constable has reasonable grounds for suspecting that an arrestable offence has been committed, he may arrest without a warrant anyone whom he has reasonable grounds for suspecting to be guilty of the offence.

(7)   A constable may arrest without a warrant—
    (a)   anyone who is about to commit an arrestable offence;
    (b)   anyone whom he has reasonable grounds for suspecting to be about to commit an arrestable offence.

### 25.   General arrest conditions.

(1)   Where a constable has reasonable grounds for suspecting that any offence which is not an arrestable offence has been committed or attempted, or is being committed or attempted, he may arrest the relevant person if it appears to him that service of a summons is impracticable or inappropriate because any of the general arrest conditions is satisfied.

### 32.   Search upon arrest.

(1)   A constable may search an arrested person, in any case where the person to be searched has been arrested at a place other than a police station, if the constable has reasonable grounds for believing that the arrested person may present a danger to himself or others.

### 34.   Limitations on police detention.

(1)   A person arrested for an offence shall not be kept in police detention except in accordance with the provisions of this Part of this Act.

(2)   Subject to subsection (3) below, if at any time a custody officer—
    (a)   becomes aware, in relation to any person in police detention, that the grounds for the detention of that person have ceased to apply; and
    (b)   is not aware of any other grounds on which the continued detention of that person could be justified under the provisions of this Part of this Act,
it shall be the duty of the custody officer, subject to subsection (4) below, to order his immediate release from custody.

### 55.   Intimate searches.

(2)   An officer may not authorise an intimate search of a person for anything unless he has reasonable grounds for believing that it cannot be found without his being intimately searched.

### 62.   Intimate samples.

(1)   An intimate sample may be taken from a person in police detention only—
    (a)   if a police officer of at least the rank of superintendent authorises it to be taken; and
    (b)   if the appropriate consent is given.

### 65.   Part V — supplementary.

In this Part of this Act— . . .
    "intimate sample" means a sample of blood, semen or any other tissue fluid, urine, saliva or pubic hair, or a swab taken from a person's body [orifices]; . . .

## THE TRADE UNION ACT 1984
### (1984, c. 49)

**10.    Industrial action authorised or endorsed by trade union without reference to a ballot.**

(1)    Nothing in section 13 of the 1974 Act shall prevent an act done by a trade union without the support of a ballot from being actionable in tort (whether or not against the trade union) on the ground that it induced a person to break his contract of employment or to interfere with its performance.

(2)    Nothing in section 13 of the 1974 Act shall prevent an act done by a trade union from being actionable in tort (whether or not against the trade union) on the ground that it induced a person to break a commercial contract or to interfere with its performance where—

(a)    one of the facts relied upon for the purpose of establishing liability is that the union induced another person to break his contract of employment or to interfere with its performance; and

(b)    by virtue of subsection (1) above, nothing in section 13 of the 1974 Act would prevent the act of inducement referred to in paragraph (a) above from being actionable in tort.

(5)    In this Part—

"the 1974 Act" means the Trade Union and Labour Relations Act 1974; . . .

"commercial contract" means any contract which is not a contract of employment;

"contract of employment" has the same meaning as it has in the 1974 Act by virtue of section 30; . . .

"trade union" has the same meaning as it has in the 1974 Act by virtue of section 28; and any reference to a breach or interference occurring in the course of a strike or other industrial action includes a reference to a breach or interference which taken together with any corresponding action relating to other contracts of employment, constitutes that action.

## THE ADMINISTRATION OF JUSTICE ACT 1985
### (1985, c. 61)

### PART II

**12.    Establishment of the Council.**

(1)    For the purposes of this Part there shall be a body to be known as the Council for Licensed Conveyancers.

**21.    Professional indemnity and compensation.**

(1)    The Council shall make rules for indemnifying licensed conveyancers and former licensed conveyancers against losses arising from claims in respect of any description of civil liability incurred by them, or by employees or associates or former employees or associates of theirs, in connection with their practices as licensed conveyancers.

(2)    The Council shall also make rules for the making of grants or other payments for the purpose of relieving or mitigating losses suffered by persons in consequence of—

(a)    negligence or fraud or other dishonesty on the part of licensed conveyancers, or of employees or associates of theirs, in connection with their practices (or purported practices) as licensed conveyancers; or

(b)    failure on the part of licensed conveyancers to account for money received by them in connection with their practices (or purported practices) as licensed conveyancers.

# THE COMPANIES ACT 1985
## (1985, c. 6)

### 14. Effect of memorandum and articles.

(1)  Subject to the provisions of this Act, the memorandum and articles, when registered, bind the company and its members to the same extent as if they respectively had been signed and sealed by each member, and contained covenants on the part of each member to observe all the provisions of the memorandum and of the articles.

### 35. Company's capacity: power of directors to bind it.

(1)  In favour of a person dealing with a company in good faith, any transaction decided on by the directors is deemed to be one which it is within the capacity of the company to enter into, and the power of the directors to bind the company is deemed to be free of any limitation under the memorandum or articles.

(2)  A party to a transaction so decided on is not bound to enquire as to the capacity of the company to enter into it or as to any such limitation on the powers of the directors, and is presumed to have acted in good faith unless the contrary is proved.

### 36. Form of company contracts.

(4)  Where a contract purports to be made by a company, or by a person as agent for a company, at a time when the company has not been formed, then subject to any agreement to the contrary the contract has effect as one entered into by the person purporting to act for the company or as agent for it, and he is personally liable on the contract accordingly.

# THE HOUSING ACT 1985
## (1985, c. 68)

### 118. The right to buy.

(1)  A secure tenant has the right to buy, that is to say, the right, in the circumstances and subject to the conditions and exceptions stated in the following provisions of this Part—

(a)  if the dwelling-house is a house and the landlord owns the freehold, to acquire the freehold of the dwelling-house;

(b)  if the landlord does not own the freehold or if the dwelling-house is a flat (whether or not the landlord owns the freehold), to be granted a lease of the dwelling-house.

### 164. Secretary of State's general power to intervene.

(5)  While a notice under this section is in force the Secretary of State may do all such things as appear to him necessary or expedient to enable secure tenants of the landlord or landlords to which the notice was given to exercise the right to buy, the right to a mortgage and the right to be granted a shared ownership lease; and he is not bound to take the steps which the landlord would have been bound to take under this Part.

### 179. Provisions restricting right to buy etc. of no effect.

(1)  A provision of a lease held by the landlord or a superior landlord, or of an agreement (whenever made), is void in so far as it purports to prohibit or restrict—

(a)  the grant of a lease in pursuance of the right to buy or the right to be granted a shared ownership lease, or

(b)  the subsequent disposal (whether by way of assignment, sub-lease or otherwise) of a lease so granted,

or to authorise a forfeiture, or impose on the landlord or superior landlord a penalty or disability, in the event of such a grant or disposal.

# THE LANDLORD AND TENANT ACT 1985
## (1985, c. 70)

### 8.    Implied terms as to fitness for human habitation.
(1)    In a contract to which this section applies for the letting of a house for human habitation there is implied, notwithstanding any stipulation to the contrary—
(a)    a condition that the house is fit for human habitation at the commencement of the tenancy, and
(b)    an undertaking that the house will be kept by the landlord fit for human habitation during the tenancy.
(2)    The landlord, or a person authorised by him in writing, may at reasonable times of the day, on giving 24 hours' notice in writing to the tenant or occupier, enter premises to which this section applies for the purpose of viewing their state and condition.

# THE SURROGACY ARRANGEMENTS ACT 1985
## (1985, c. 49)

### 1.    Meaning of "surrogate mother", "surrogacy arrangement" and other terms.
(2)    "Surrogate mother" means a woman who carries a child in pursuance of an arrangement—
(a)    made before she began to carry the child, and
(b)    made with a view to any child carried in pursuance of it being handed over to, and the parental rights being exercised (so far as practicable) by, another person or other persons.
(3)    An arrangement is a surrogacy arrangement if, were a woman to whom the arrangement relates to carry a child in pursuance of it, she would be a surrogate mother.
(9)    This Act applies to arrangements whether or not they are lawful and whether or not they are enforceable by or against any of the persons making them.

### 2.    Negotiating surrogacy arrangements on a commercial basis, etc.
(1)    No person shall on a commercial basis do any of the following acts in the United Kingdom, that is—
(a)    initiate or take part in any negotiations with a view to the making of a surrogacy arrangement,
(b)    offer or agree to negotiate the making of a surrogacy arrangement, or
(c)    compile any information with a view to its use in making, or negotiating the making of, surrogacy arrangements;
and no person shall in the United Kingdom knowingly cause another to do any of those acts on a commercial basis.

# THE AGRICULTURAL HOLDINGS ACT 1986
## (1986, c. 5)

### 24.    Restriction of landlord's remedies for breach of contract of tenancy.
Notwithstanding any provision in a contract of tenancy of an agricultural holding making the tenant liable to pay a higher rent or other liquidated damages in the event of a breach or non-fulfilment of a term or condition of the contract, the landlord shall not be entitled to recover in consequence of any such breach or non-fulfilment, by distress or otherwise, any sum in excess of the damage actually suffered by him in consequence of the breach or non-fulfilment.

## THE EDUCATION (NO. 2) ACT 1986

### 22.   Discipline: general duties.

(1)   The articles of government for every county, voluntary and maintained special school shall provide—

(a)   for it to be the duty of the head teacher to determine measures (which may include the making of rules and provision for enforcing them) to be taken with a view to—

(i)   promoting, among pupils, self-discipline and proper regard for authority;

(ii)   encouraging good behaviour on the part of pupils;

(iii)   securing that the standard of behaviour of pupils is acceptable; and

(iv)   otherwise regulating the conduct of pupils; . . .

### 47.   Abolition of corporal punishment.

(1)   Where, in any proceedings, it is shown that corporal punishment has been given to a pupil by or on the authority of a member of the staff, giving the punishment cannot be justified on the ground that it was done in pursuance of a right exercisable by the member of the staff by virtue of his position as such.

(2)   Subject to subsection (3) below, references in this section to giving corporal punishment are references to doing anything for the purposes of punishing the pupil concerned (whether or not there are also other reasons for doing it) which, apart from any justification, would constitute battery.

(3)   A person is not to be taken for the purposes of this section as giving corporal punishment by virtue of anything done for reasons that include averting an immediate danger of personal injury to, or an immediate danger to the property of, any person (including the pupil concerned).

(4)   A person does not commit an offence by reason of any conduct relating to a pupil which would, apart from this section, be justified on the ground that it is done in pursuance of a right exercisable by a member of the staff by virtue of his position as such.

## THE FINANCIAL SERVICES ACT 1986

### PART I

### 3.   Persons entitled to carry on investment business.

No person shall carry on, or purport to carry on, investment business in the United Kingdom unless he is an authorised person under Chapter III or an exempted person under Chapter IV of this Part of this Act.

### 6.   Injunctions and restitution orders.

(1)   If on the application of the Secretary of State the court is satisfied—

(a)   that there is a reasonable likelihood that a person will contravene section 3 above; or

(b)   that any person has contravened that section and that there is a reasonable likelihood that the contravention will continue or be repeated,

the court may grant an injunction restraining the contravention . . .

(2)   If, on the application of the Secretary of State, the court is satisfied that a person has entered into any transaction in contravention of section 3 above the court may order that person and any other person who appears to the court to have been knowingly concerned in the contravention to take such steps as the court may direct for restoring the parties to the position in which they were before the transaction was entered into.

(3)   The court may, on the application of the Secretary of State, make an order under subsection (4) below . . . if satisfied that a person has been carrying on investment business in contravention of section 3 above and—

(a)   that profits have accrued to that person as a result of carrying on that business; or

(b)    that one or more investors have suffered loss or been otherwise adversely affected as a result of his contravention of section 47 or 56 below or failure to act substantially in accordance with any of the rules or regulations made under Chapter V of this Part of this Act.

(4)    The court may under this subsection order the person concerned to pay into court, or appoint a receiver to recover from him, such sum as appears to the court to be just having regard—

(a)    in a case within paragraph (a) of subsection (3) above, to the profits appearing to the court to have accrued;

(b)    in a case within paragraph (b) of that subsection, to the extent of the loss or other adverse effect; or

(c)    in a case within both paragraphs (a) and (b) of that subsection, to the profits and to the extent of the loss or other adverse effect.

## 63.    Gaming contracts.

No contract entered into by an authorised person in the course of carrying on investment business shall be void or unenforceable by reason of—

(a)    section 18 of the Gaming Act 1845, section 1 of the Gaming Act 1892 . . .

## 132.    Insurance contracts effected in contravention of s. 2 of Insurance Companies Act 1982.

(1)    Subject to subsection (3) below, a contract of insurance (not being an agreement to which section 5(1) above applies) which is entered into by a person in the course of carrying on insurance business in contravention of section 2 of the Insurance Companies Act 1982 shall be unenforceable against the other party; and that party shall be entitled to recover any money or other property paid or transferred by him under the contract, together with compensation for any loss sustained by him as a result of having parted with it.

(2)    The compensation recoverable under subsection (1) above shall be such as the parties may agree or as a court may, on the application of either party, determine.

(3)    A court may allow a contract to which subsection (1) above applies to be enforced or money or property paid or transferred under it to be retained if it is satisfied—

(a)    that the person carrying on insurance business reasonably believed that his entering into the contract did not constitute a contravention of section 2 of the said Act of 1982;

(b)    that it is just and equitable for the contract to be enforced or, as the case may be, for the money or property paid or transferred under it to be retained.

(4)    Where a person elects not to perform a contract which by virtue of this section is unenforceable against him or by virtue of this section recovers money or property paid or transferred under a contract he shall not be entitled to any benefits under the contract and shall repay any money and return any other property received by him under the contract.

(5)    Where any property transferred under a contract to which this section applies has passed to a third party the references to that property in this section shall be construed as references to its value at the time of its transfer under the contract.

(6)    A contravention of section 2 of the said Act of 1982 shall not make a contract of insurance illegal or invalid to any greater extent than is provided in this section; and a contravention of that section in respect of a contract of insurance shall not affect the validity of any re-insurance contract entered into in respect of that contract.

## 162.    Form and content of prospectus.

(1)    A prospectus shall contain such information and comply with such other requirements as may be prescribed by rules made by the Secretary of State for the purposes of this section.

**163.    General duty of disclosure in prospectus.**

(1)    In addition to the information required to be included in a prospectus by virtue of rules applying to it by virtue of section 162 above a prospectus shall contain all such information as investors and their professional advisers would reasonably require, and reasonably expect to find there, for the purpose of making an informed assessment of—

(a)    the assets and liabilities, financial position, profits and losses, and prospects of the issuer of the securities; and

(b)    the rights attaching to those securities.

**166.    Compensation for false or misleading prospectus.**

(1)    Subject to section 167 below, the person or persons responsible for a prospectus or supplementary prospectus shall be liable to pay compensation to any person who has acquired the securities to which the prospectus relates and suffered loss in respect of them as a result of any untrue or misleading statement in the prospectus or the omission from it of any matter required to be included by section 163 or 164 above.

## THE INSOLVENCY ACT 1986
### (1986, c. 45)

**238.    Transactions at an undervalue (England and Wales).**

(1)    This section applies in the case of a company where—

(a)    an administration order is made in relation to the company, or

(b)    the company goes into liquidation;

and "the office-holder" means the administrator or the liquidator, as the case may be.

(2)    Where the company has at a relevant time (defined in section 240) entered into a transaction with any person at an undervalue, the office-holder may apply to the court for an order under this section.

(3)    Subject as follows, the court shall, on such an application, make such order as it thinks fit for restoring the position to what it would have been if the company had not entered into that transaction.

(4)    For the purposes of this section and section 241, a company enters into a transaction with a person at an undervalue if—

(a)    the company makes a gift to that person or otherwise enters into a transaction with that person on terms that provide for the company to receive no consideration, or

(b)    the company enters into a transaction with that person for a consideration the value of which, in money or money's worth, is significantly less than the value, in money or money's worth, of the consideration provided by the company.

(5)    The court shall not make an order under this section in respect of a transaction at an undervalue if it is satisfied—

(a)    that the company which entered into the transaction did so in good faith and for the purpose of carrying on its business, and

(b)    that at the time it did so there were reasonable grounds for believing that the transaction would benefit the company.

## THE LATENT DAMAGE ACT 1986
### (1986, c. 37)

**1.    Time limits for negligence actions in respect of latent damage not involving personal injuries.**

The following sections shall be inserted in the Limitation Act 1980 (referred to below in this Act as the 1980 Act) . . .

**2.    Provisions consequential on section 1.**

. . .

**3.   Accrual of cause of action to successive owners in respect of latent damage to property.**

(1)    Subject to the following provisions of this section, where—

(a)    a cause of action ("the original cause of action") has accrued to any person in respect of any negligence to which damage to any property in which he has an interest is attributable (in whole or in part); and

(b)    another person acquires an interest in that property after the date on which the original cause of action accrued but before the material facts about the damage have become known to any person who, at the time when he first has knowledge of those facts, has any interest in the property;

a fresh cause of action in respect of that negligence shall accrue to that other person on the date on which he acquires his interest in the property.

(2)    A cause of action accruing to any person by virtue of subsection (1) above—

(a)    shall be treated as if based on breach of a duty of care at common law owed to the person to whom it accrues; and

(b)    shall be treated for the purposes of section 14A of the 1980 Act (special time limit for negligence actions where facts relevant to cause of action are not known at date of accrual) as having accrued on the date on which the original cause of action accrued.

(3)    Section 28 of the 1980 Act (extension of limitation period in case of disability) shall not apply in relation to any such cause of action.

(4)    Subsection (1) above shall not apply in any case where the person acquiring an interest in the damaged property is either—

(a)    a person in whom the original cause of action vests by operation of law; or

(b)    a person in whom the interest in that property vests by virtue of any order made by a court under section 538 of the Companies Act 1985 (vesting of company property in liquidator).

*[The Companies Act 1985, s. 538 has now been replaced by the Insolvency Act 1986, s. 145.]*

(5)    For the purposes of subsection (1)(b) above, the material facts about the damage are such facts about the damage as would lead a reasonable person who has an interest in the damaged property at the time when those facts become known to him to consider it sufficiently serious to justify his instituting proceedings for damages against a defendant who did not dispute liability and was able to satisfy a judgment.

(6)    For the purposes of this section a person's knowledge includes knowledge which he might reasonably have been expected to acquire—

(a)    from facts observable or ascertainable by him; or

(b)    from facts ascertainable by him with the help of appropriate expert advice which it is reasonable for him to seek;

but a person shall not be taken by virtue of this subsection to have knowledge of a fact ascertainable by him only with the help of expert advice so long as he has taken all reasonable steps to obtain (and, where appropriate, to act on) that advice.

(7)    This section shall bind the Crown, but as regards the Crown's liability in tort shall not bind the Crown further than the Crown is made liable in tort by the Crown Proceedings Act 1947.

**4.   Transitional provisions.**

(1)    Nothing in section 1 or 2 of this Act shall—

(a)    enable any action to be brought which was barred by the 1980 Act or (as the case may be) by the Limitation Act 1939 before this Act comes into force; or

(b)    affect any action commenced before this Act comes into force.

(2)    Subject to subsection (1) above, sections 1 and 2 of this Act shall have effect in relation to causes of action accruing before, as well as in relation to causes of action accruing after, this Act comes into force.

(3)    Section 3 of this Act shall only apply in cases where an interest in damaged property is acquired after this Act comes into force but shall so apply, subject to subsection

(4) below, irrespective of whether the original cause of action accrued before or after this Act comes into force.

(4)    Where—

(a)    a person acquires an interest in damaged property in circumstances to which section 3 would apart from this subsection apply; but

(b)    the original cause of action accrued more than six years before this Act comes into force;

a cause of action shall not accrue to that person by virtue of subsection (1) of that section unless section 32(1)(b) of the 1980 Act (postponement of limitation period in case of deliberate concealment of relevant facts) would apply to any action founded on the original cause of action.

## THE BANKING ACT 1987
## (1987, c. 22)

### 3.    Restriction on acceptance of deposits

(1)    Subject to section 4 below, no person shall in the United Kingdom accept a deposit in the course of carrying on (whether there or elsewhere) a business which for the purposes of this Act is a deposit-taking business unless that person is an institution for the time being authorised by the Bank under the following provisions of this Part of this Act.

(2)    Any persons who contravenes this section shall be guilty of an offence. . .

(3)    The fact that a deposit has been taken in contravention of this section shall not affect any civil liability arising in respect of the deposit or the money deposited.

## THE CONSUMER PROTECTION ACT 1987
## (1987, c. 43)

## PART I
## PRODUCT LIABILITY

### 1.    Purpose and construction of Part I.

(1)    This Part shall have effect for the purpose of making such provision as is necessary in order to comply with the product liability Directive and shall be construed accordingly.

(2)    In this Part, except in so far as the context otherwise requires—

"agricultural produce" means any produce of the soil, of stock-farming or of fisheries;

"dependant" and "relative" have the same meaning as they have in, respectively, the Fatal Accidents Act 1976 and the Damages (Scotland) Act 1976;

"producer", in relation to a product, means—

(a)    the person who manufactured it;

(b)    in the case of a substance which has not been manufactured but has been won or abstracted, the person who won or abstracted it;

(c)    in the case of a product which has not been manufactured, won or abstracted but essential characteristics of which are attributable to an industrial or other process having been carried out (for example, in relation to agricultural produce), the person who carried out that process;

"product" means any goods or electricity and (subject to subsection (3) below) includes a product which is comprised in another product, whether by virtue of being a component part or raw material or otherwise; and

"the product liability Directive" means the Directive of the Council of the European Communities, dated 25th July 1985, (No. 85/374/EEC) on the approximation of the laws, regulations and administrative provisions of the member States concerning liability for defective products.

(3)    For the purposes of this Part a person who supplies any product in which products are comprised, whether by virtue of being component parts or raw materials or otherwise, shall not be treated by reason only of his supply of that product as supplying any of the products so comprised.

## 2.    Liability for defective products.

(1)    Subject to the following provisions of this Part, where any damage is caused wholly or partly by a defect in a product, every person to whom subsection (2) below applies shall be liable for the damage.

(2)    This subsection applies to—

(a)    the producer of the product;

(b)    any person who, by putting his name on the product or using a trade mark or other distinguishing mark in relation to the product, has held himself out to be the producer of the product;

(c)    any person who has imported the product into a member State from a place outside the member States in order, in the course of any business of his, to supply it to another.

(3)    Subject as aforesaid, where any damage is caused wholly or partly by a defect in a product, any person who supplied the product (whether to the person who suffered the damage, to the producer of any product in which the product in question is comprised or to any other person) shall be liable for the damage if—

(a)    the person who suffered the damage requests the supplier to identify one or more of the persons (whether still in existence or not) to whom subsection (2) above applies in relation to the product;

(b)    that request is made within a reasonable period after the damage occurs and at a time when it is not reasonably practicable for the person making the request to identify all those persons; and

(c)    the supplier fails, within a reasonable period after receiving the request, either to comply with the request or to identify the person who supplied the product to him.

(4)    Neither subsection (2) nor subsection (3) above shall apply to a person in respect of any defect in any game or agricultural produce if the only supply of the game or produce by that person to another was at a time when it had not undergone an industrial process.

(5)    Where two or more persons are liable by virtue of this Part for the same damage, their liability shall be joint and several.

(6)    This section shall be without prejudice to any liability arising otherwise than by virtue of this Part.

## 3.    Meaning of "defect".

(1)    Subject to the following provisions of this section, there is a defect in a product for the purposes of this Part if the safety of the product is not such as persons generally are entitled to expect; and for those purposes "safety", in relation to a product, shall include safety with respect to products comprised in that product and safety in the context of risks of damage to property, as well as in the context of risks of death or personal injury.

(2)    In determining for the purposes of subsection (1) above what persons generally are entitled to expect in relation to a product all the circumstances shall be taken into account, including—

(a)    the manner in which, and purposes for which, the product has been marketed, its get-up, the use of any mark in relation to the product and any instructions for, or warnings with respect to, doing or refraining from doing anything with or in relation to the product;

(b)    what might reasonably be expected to be done with or in relation to the product; and

(c)    the time when the product was supplied by its producer to another;

and nothing in this section shall require a defect to be inferred from the fact alone that the safety of a product which is supplied after that time is greater than the safety of the product in question.

## 4. Defences.

(1)    In any civil proceedings by virtue of this Part against any person ("the person proceeded against") in respect of a defect in a product it shall be a defence for him to show—

    (a)    that the defect is attributable to compliance with any requirement imposed by or under any enactment or with any Community obligation; or

    (b)    that the person proceeded against did not at any time supply the product to another; or

    (c)    that the following conditions are satisfied, that is to say—

        (i)    that the only supply of the product to another by the person proceeded against was otherwise than in the course of a business of that person's; and

        (ii)    that section 2(2) above does not apply to that person or applies to him by virtue only of things done otherwise than with a view to profit; or

    (d)    that the defect did not exist in the product at the relevant time; or

    (e)    that the state of scientific and technical knowledge at the relevant time was not such that a producer of products of the same description as the product in question might be expected to have discovered the defect if it had existed in his products while they were under his control; or

    (f)    that the defect—

        (i)    constituted a defect in a product ("the subsequent product") in which the product in question had been comprised; and

        (ii)    was wholly attributable to the design of the subsequent product or to compliance by the producer of the product in question with instructions given by the producer of the subsequent product.

(2)    In this section "the relevant time", in relation to electricity, means the time at which it was generated, being a time before it was transmitted or distributed, and in relation to any other product, means—

    (a)    if the person proceeded against is a person to whom subsection (2) of section 2 above applies in relation to the product, the time when he supplied the product to another;

    (b)    if that subsection does not apply to that person in relation to the product, the time when the product was last supplied by a person to whom that subsection does apply in relation to the product.

## 5. Damage giving rise to liability.

(1)    Subject to the following provisions of this section, in this Part "damage" means death or personal injury or any loss of or damage to any property (including land).

(2)    A person shall not be liable under section 2 above in respect of any defect in a product for the loss of or any damage to the product itself or for the loss of or any damage to the whole or any part of any product which has been supplied with the product in question comprised in it.

(3)    A person shall not be liable under section 2 above for any loss of or damage to any property which, at the time it is lost or damaged, is not—

    (a)    of a description of property ordinarily intended for private use, occupation or consumption; and

    (b)    intended by the person suffering the loss or damage mainly for his own private use, occupation or consumption.

(4)    No damages shall be awarded to any person by virtue of this Part in respect of any loss of or damage to any property if the amount which would fall to be so awarded to that person, apart from this subsection and any liability for interest, does not exceed £275.

(5)    In determining for the purposes of this Part who has suffered any loss of or damage to property and when any such loss or damage occurred, the loss or damage shall be

regarded as having occurred at the earliest time at which a person with an interest in the property had knowledge of the material facts about the loss or damage.

(6)    For the purposes of subsection (5) above the material facts about any loss of or damage to any property are such facts about the loss or damage as would lead a reasonable person with an interest in the property to consider the loss or damage sufficiently serious to justify his instituting proceedings for damages against a defendant who did not dispute liability and was able to satisfy a judgment.

(7)    For the purposes of subsection (5) above a person's knowledge includes knowledge which he might reasonably have been expected to acquire—

(a)    from facts observable or ascertainable by him; or

(b)    from facts ascertainable by him with the help of appropriate expert advice which it is reasonable for him to seek;

but a person shall not be taken by virtue of this subsection to have knowledge of a fact ascertainable by him only with the help of expert advice unless he has failed to take all reasonable steps to obtain (and, where appropriate, to act on) that advice.

## 6.    Application of certain enactments etc.

(1)    Any damage for which a person is liable under section 2 above shall be deemed to have been caused—

(a)    for the purposes of the Fatal Accidents Act 1976, by that person's wrongful act, neglect or default; . . .

(2)    Where—

(a)    a person's death is caused wholly or partly by a defect in a product, or a person dies after suffering damage which has been so caused;

(b)    a request such as mentioned in paragraph (a) of subsection (3) of section 2 above is made to a supplier of the product by that person's personal representatives or, in the case of a person whose death is caused wholly or partly by the defect, by any dependant or relative of that person; and

(c)    the conditions specified in paragraphs (b) and (c) of that subsection are satisfied in relation to that request,

this Part shall have effect for the purposes of the Law Reform (Miscellaneous Provisions) Act 1934, the Fatal Accidents Act 1976 and the Damages (Scotland) Act 1976 as if liability of the supplier to that person under that subsection did not depend on that person having requested the supplier to identify certain persons or on the said conditions having been satisfied in relation to a request made by that person.

(3)    Section 1 of the Congenital Disabilities (Civil Liability) Act 1976 shall have effect for the purposes of this Part as if—

(a)    a person were answerable to a child in respect of an occurrence caused wholly or partly by a defect in a product if he is or has been liable under section 2 above in respect of any effect of the occurrence on a parent of the child, or would be so liable if the occurrence caused a parent of the child to suffer damage;

(b)    the provisions of this Part relating to liability under section 2 above applied in relation to liability by virtue of paragraph (a) above under the said section 1; and

(c)    subsection (6) of the said section 1 (exclusion of liability) were omitted.

(4)    Where any damage is caused partly by a defect in a product and partly by the fault of the person suffering the damage, the Law Reform (Contributory Negligence) Act 1945 and section 5 of the Fatal Accidents Act 1976 (contributory negligence) shall have effect as if the defect were the fault of every person liable by virtue of this Part for the damage caused by the defect.

(5)    In subsection (4) above "fault" has the same meaning as in the said Act of 1945.

(6)    Schedule 1 to this Act shall have effect for the purpose of amending the Limitation Act 1980 and the Prescription and Limitation (Scotland) Act 1973 in their application in relation to the bringing of actions by virtue of this Part.

(7)    It is hereby declared that liability by virtue of this Part is to be treated as liability in tort for the purposes of any enactment conferring jurisdiction on any court with respect to any matter.

(8)    Nothing in this Part shall prejudice the operation of section 12 of the Nuclear Installations Act 1965 (rights to compensation for certain breaches of duties confined to rights under that Act).

### 7.    Prohibition on exclusions from liability.

The liability of a person by virtue of this Part to a person who has suffered damage caused wholly or partly by a defect in a product, or to a dependant or relative of such a person, shall not be limited or excluded by any contract term, by any notice or by any other provision.

### 8.    Power to modify Part I.

(1)    Her Majesty may by Order in Council make such modifications of this Part and of any other enactment (including an enactment contained in the following Parts of this Act, or in an Act passed after this Act) as appear to Her Majesty in Council to be necessary or expedient in consequence of any modification of the product liability Directive which is made at any time after the passing of this Act.

### 9.    Application of Part I to Crown.

(1)    Subject to subsection (2) below, this Part shall bind the Crown.

(2)    The Crown shall not, as regards the Crown's liability by virtue of this Part, be bound by this Part further than the Crown is made liable in tort or in reparation under the Crown Proceedings Act 1947, as that Act has effect from time to time.

PART II
CONSUMER SAFETY

### 10.    The general safety requirement.

(1)    A person shall be guilty of an offence if he—

(a)    supplies any consumer goods which fail to comply with the general safety requirement;

(b)    offers or agrees to supply any such goods; or

(c)    exposes or possesses any such goods for supply.

(2)    For the purposes of this section consumer goods fail to comply with the general safety requirement if they are not reasonably safe having regard to all the circumstances, including—

(a)    the manner in which, and purposes for which, the goods are being or would be marketed, the get-up of the goods, the use of any mark in relation to the goods and any instructions or warnings which are given or would be given with respect to the keeping, use or consumption of the goods;

(b)    any standards of safety published by any person either for goods of a description which applies to the goods in question or for matters relating to goods of that description; and

(c)    the existence of any means by which it would have been reasonable (taking into account the cost, likelihood and extent of any improvement) for the goods to have been made safer.

(3)    For the purposes of this section consumer goods shall not be regarded as failing to comply with the general safety requirement in respect of—

(a)    anything which is shown to be attributable to compliance with any requirement imposed by or under any enactment or with any Community obligation;

(b)    any failure to do more in relation to any matter than is required by—

(i)    any safety regulations imposing requirements with respect to the matter;

(ii)    any standards of safety approved for the purposes of this subsection by or under any such regulations and imposing requirements with respect to that matter;

(iii)    any provision of any enactment or subordinate legislation imposing such requirements with respect to that matter as are designated for the purposes of this subsection by any such regulations.

(4)    In any proceedings against any person for an offence under this section in respect of any goods it shall be a defence for that person to show—

(a)    that he reasonably believed that the goods would not be used or consumed in the United Kingdom; or

(b)    that the following conditions are satisfied, that is to say—

(i)    that he supplied the goods, offered or agreed to supply them or, as the case may be, exposed or possessed them for supply in the course of carrying on a retail business; and

(ii)    that, at the time he supplied the goods or offered or agreed to supply them or exposed or possessed them for supply, he neither knew nor had reasonable grounds for believing that the goods failed to comply with the general safety requirement; or

(c)    that the terms on which he supplied the goods or agreed or offered to supply them or, in the case of goods which he exposed or possessed for supply, the terms on which he intended to supply them—

(i)    indicated that the goods were not supplied or to be supplied as new goods; and

(ii)    provided for, or contemplated, the acquisition of an interest in the goods by the persons supplied or to be supplied.

(5)    For the purposes of subsection (4)(b) above goods are supplied in the course of carrying on a retail business if—

(a)    whether or not they are themselves acquired for a person's private use or consumption, they are supplied in the course of carrying on a business of making a supply of consumer goods available to persons who generally acquire them for private use or consumption; and

(b)    the descriptions of goods the supply of which is made available in the course of that business do not, to a significant extent, include manufactured or imported goods which have not previously been supplied in the United Kingdom.

(6)    A person guilty of an offence under this section shall be liable on summary conviction to imprisonment for a term not exceeding six months or to a fine not exceeding level 5 on the standard scale or to both.

(7)    In this section "consumer goods" means any goods which are ordinarily intended for private use or consumption, not being—

(a)    growing crops or things comprised in land by virtue of being attached to it;

(b)    water, food, feeding stuff or fertiliser;

(c)    gas which is, is to be or has been supplied by a person authorised to supply it by or under section 6, 7 or 8 of the Gas Act 1986 (authorisation of supply of gas through pipes);

(d)    aircraft (other than hang-gliders) or motor vehicles;

(e)    controlled drugs or licensed medicinal products;

(f)    tobacco.

**11.    Safety regulations.**

(1)    The Secretary of State may by regulations under this section ("safety regulations") make such provision as he considers appropriate for the purposes of section 10(3) above and for the purpose of securing—

(a)    that goods to which this section applies are safe;

(b)    that goods to which this section applies which are unsafe, or would be unsafe in the hands of persons of a particular description, are not made available to persons generally or, as the case may be, to persons of that description; and

(c)    that appropriate information is, and inappropriate information is not, provided in relation to goods to which this section applies.

(2)    Without prejudice to the generality of subsection (1) above, safety regulations may contain provision—

(a)    with respect to the composition or contents, design, construction, finish or packing of goods to which this section applies, with respect to standards for such goods and with respect to other matters relating to such goods;

(b)    with respects to the giving, refusal, alteration or cancellation of approvals of such goods, of descriptions of such goods or of standards for such goods;

(c)    with respect to the conditions that may be attached to any approval given under the regulations;

(d)    for requiring such fees as may be determined by or under the regulations to be paid on the giving or alteration of any approval under the regulations and on the making of an application for such an approval or alteration;

(e)    with respect to appeals against refusals, alterations and cancellations of approvals given under the regulations and against the conditions contained in such approvals;

(f)    for requiring goods to which this section applies to be approved under the regulations or to conform to the requirements of the regulations or to descriptions or standards specified in or approved by or under the regulations;

(g)    with respect to the testing or inspection of goods to which this section applies (including provision for determining the standards to be applied in carrying out any test or inspection);

(h)    with respect to the ways of dealing with goods of which some or all do not satisfy a test required by or under the regulations or a standard connected with a procedure so required;

(i)    for requiring a mark, warning or instruction or any other information relating to goods to be put on or to accompany the goods or to be used or provided in some other manner in relation to the goods, and for securing that inappropriate information is not given in relation to goods either by means of misleading marks or otherwise;

(j)    for prohibiting persons from supplying, or from offering to supply, agreeing to supply, exposing for supply or possessing for supply, goods to which this section applies and component parts and raw materials for such goods;

(k)    for requiring information to be given to any such person as may be determined by or under the regulations for the purpose of enabling that person to exercise any function conferred on him by the regulations.

(3)    Without prejudice as aforesaid, safety regulations may contain provision—

(a)    for requiring persons on whom functions are conferred by or under section 27 below to have regard, in exercising their functions so far as relating to any provision of safety regulations, to matters specified in a direction issued by the Secretary of State with respect to that provision;

(b)    for securing that a person shall not be guilty of an offence under section 12 below unless it is shown that the goods in question do not conform to a particular standard;

(c)    for securing that proceedings for such an offence are not brought in England and Wales except by or with the consent of the Secretary of State or the Director of Public Prosecutions;

. . .

(e)    for enabling a magistrates' court in England and Wales or Northern Ireland to try an information or, in Northern Ireland, a complaint in respect of such an offence if the information was laid or the complaint made within twelve months from the time when the offence was committed;

. . .

(g)    for determining the persons by whom, and the manner in which, anything required to be done by or under the regulations is to be done.

(4)    Safety regulations shall not provide for any contravention of the regulations to be an offence.

(5)    Where the Secretary of State proposes to make safety regulations it shall be his duty before he makes them—

(a)    to consult such organisations as appear to him to be representative of interests substantially affected by the proposal;

(b)    to consult such other persons as he considers appropriate; and

(c)    in the case of proposed regulations relating to goods suitable for use at work, to consult the Health and Safety Commission in relation to the application of the proposed regulations to Great Britain;

but the preceding provisions of this subsection shall not apply in the case of regulations which provide for the regulations to cease to have effect at the end of a period of not more than twelve months beginning with the day on which they come into force and which contain a statement that it appears to the Secretary of State that the need to protect the public requires that the regulations should be made without delay.

(6)    The power to make safety regulations shall be exercisable by statutory instrument subject to annulment in pursuance of a resolution of either House of Parliament and shall include power—

(a)    to make different provision for different cases; and

(b)    to make such supplemental, consequential and transitional provision as the Secretary of State considers appropriate.

(7)    This section applies to any goods other than—

(a)    growing crops and things comprised in land by virtue of being attached to it;

(b)    water, food, feeding stuff and fertiliser;

(c)    gas which is, is to be or has been supplied by a person authorised to supply it by or under section 6, 7 or 8 of the Gas Act 1986 (authorisation of supply of gas through pipes);

(d)    controlled drugs and licensed medicinal products.

**12.    Offences against the safety regulations.**

(1)    Where safety regulations prohibit a person from supplying or offering or agreeing to supply any goods or from exposing or possessing any goods for supply, that person shall be guilty of an offence if he contravenes the prohibition.

(2)    Where safety regulations require a person who makes or processes any goods in the course of carrying on a business—

(a)    to carry out a particular test or use a particular procedure in connection with the making or processing of the goods with a view to ascertaining whether the goods satisfy any requirements of such regulations; or

(b)    to deal or not to deal in a particular way with a quantity of the goods of which the whole or part does not satisfy such a test or does not satisfy standards connected with such a procedure,

that person shall be guilty of an offence if he does not comply with the requirement.

(3)    If a person contravenes a provision of safety regulations which prohibits or requires the provision, by means of a mark or otherwise, of information of a particular kind in relation to goods, he shall be guilty of an offence.

(4)    Where safety regulations require any person to give information to another for the purpose of enabling that other to exercise any function, that person shall be guilty of an offence if—

(a)    he fails without reasonable cause to comply with the requirement; or

(b)    in giving the information which is required of him—

(i)    he makes any statement which he knows is false in a material particular; or

(ii)    he recklessly makes any statement which is false in a material particular.

(5)   A person guilty of an offence under this section shall be liable on summary conviction to imprisonment for a term not exceeding six months or to a fine not exceeding level 5 on the standard scale or to both.

### 13.   Prohibition notices and notices to warn.

(1)   The Secretary of State may—

(a)   serve on any person a notice ("a prohibition notice") prohibiting that person, except with the consent of the Secretary of State, from supplying, or from offering to supply, agreeing to supply, exposing for supply or possessing for supply, any relevant goods which the Secretary of State considers are unsafe and which are described in the notice;

(b)   serve on any person a notice ("a notice to warn") requiring that person at his own expense to publish, in a form and manner and on occasions specified in the notice, a warning about any relevant goods which the Secretary of State considers are unsafe, which that person supplies or has supplied and which are described in the notice.

(2)   Schedule 2 to this Act shall have effect with respect to prohibition notices and notices to warn; and the Secretary of State may by regulations make provision specifying the manner in which information is to be given to any person under that Schedule.

(3)   A consent given by the Secretary of State for the purposes of a prohibition notice may impose such conditions on the doing of anything for which the consent is required as the Secretary of State considers appropriate.

(4)   A person who contravenes a prohibition notice or a notice to warn shall be guilty of an offence and liable on summary conviction to imprisonment for a term not exceeding six months or to a fine not exceeding level 5 on the standard scale or to both.

(5)   The power to make regulations under subsection (2) above shall be exercisable by statutory instrument subject to annulment in pursuance of a resolution of either House of Parliament and shall include power—

(a)   to make different provision for different cases; and

(b)   to make such supplemental, consequential and transitional provision as the Secretary of State considers appropriate.

(6)   In this section "relevant goods" means—

(a)   in relation to a prohibition notice, any goods to which section 11 above applies; and

(b)   in relation to a notice to warn, any goods to which that section applies or any growing crops or things comprised in land by virtue of being attached to it.

### 14.   Suspension notices.

(1)   Where an enforcement authority has reasonable grounds for suspecting that any safety provision has been contravened in relation to any goods, the authority may serve a notice ("a suspension notice") prohibiting the person on whom it is served, for such period ending not more than six months after the date of the notice as is specified therein, from doing any of the following things without the consent of the authority, that is to say, supplying the goods, offering to supply them, agreeing to supply them or exposing them for supply.

(2)   A suspension notice served by an enforcement authority in respect of any goods shall—

(a)   describe the goods in a manner sufficient to identify them;

(b)   set out the grounds on which the authority suspects that a safety provision has been contravened in relation to the goods; and

(c)   state that, and the manner in which, the person on whom the notice is served may appeal against the notice under section 15 below.

(3)   A suspension notice served by an enforcement authority for the purpose of prohibiting a person for any period from doing the things mentioned in subsection (1) above in relation to any goods may also require that person to keep the authority informed

of the whereabouts throughout that period of any of those goods in which he has an interest.

(4)    Where a suspension notice has been served on any person in respect of any goods, no further such notice shall be served on that person in respect of the same goods unless—

(a)    proceedings against that person for an offence in respect of a contravention in relation to the goods of a safety provision (not being an offence under this section); or

(b)    proceedings for the forfeiture of the goods under section 16 or 17 below, are pending at the end of the period specified in the first-mentioned notice.

(5)    A consent given by an enforcement authority for the purposes of subsection (1) above may impose such conditions on the doing of anything for which the consent is required as the authority considers appropriate.

(6)    Any person who contravenes a suspension notice shall be guilty of an offence and liable on summary conviction to imprisonment for a term not exceeding six months or to a fine not exceeding level 5 on the standard scale or to both.

(7)    Where an enforcement authority serves a suspension notice in respect of any goods, the authority shall be liable to pay compensation to any person having an interest in the goods in respect of any loss or damage caused by reason of the service of the notice if—

(a)    there has been no contravention in relation to the goods of any safety provision; and

(b)    the exercise of the power is not attributable to any neglect or default by that person.

(8)    Any disputed question as to the right to or the amount of any compensation payable under this section shall be determined by arbitration . . .

## 15.    Appeals against suspension notices.

(1)    Any person having an interest in any goods in respect of which a suspension notice is for the time being in force may apply for an order setting aside the notice.

(2)    An application under this section may be made—

(a)    to any magistrates' court in which proceedings have been brought in England and Wales or Northern Ireland—

(i)    for an offence in respect of a contravention in relation to the goods of any safety provision; or

(ii)    for the forfeiture of the goods under section 16 below;

(b)    where no such proceedings have been so brought, by way of complaint to a magistrates' court; . . .

(3)    On an application under this section to a magistrates' court in England and Wales or Northern Ireland the court shall make an order setting aside the suspension notice only if the court is satisfied that there has been no contravention in relation to the goods of any safety provision.

(4)    On an application under this section to the sheriff he shall make an order setting aside the suspension notice only if he is satisfied that at the date of making the order—

(a)    proceedings for an offence in respect of a contravention in relation to the goods of any safety provision; or

(b)    proceedings for the forfeiture of the goods under section 17 below, have not been brought or, having been brought, have been concluded.

(5)    Any person aggrieved by an order made under this section by a magistrates' court in England and Wales or Northern Ireland, or by a decision of such a court not to make such an order, may appeal against that order or decision—

(a)    in England and Wales, to the Crown Court;

(b)    in Northern Ireland, to the county court;

and an order so made may contain such provision as appears to the court to be appropriate for delaying the coming into force of the order pending the making and determination of any appeal (including any application under section 111 of the Magistrates' Courts Act 1980 or Article 146 of the Magistrates' Courts (Northern Ireland) Order 1981 (statement of case)).

**16.    Forfeiture: England and Wales and Northern Ireland.**

(1)    An enforcement authority in England and Wales or Northern Ireland may apply under this section for an order for the forfeiture of any goods on the grounds that there has been a contravention in relation to the goods of a safety provision.

(2)    An application under this section may be made—

(a)    where proceedings have been brought in a magistrates' court for an offence in respect of a contravention in relation to some or all of the goods of any safety provision, to that court;

(b)    where an application with respect to some or all of the goods has been made to a magistrates' court under section 15 above or section 33 below, to that court; and

(c)    where no application for the forfeiture of the goods has been made under paragraph (a) or (b) above, by way of complaint to a magistrates' court.

(3)    On an application under this section the court shall make an order for the forfeiture of any goods only if it is satisfied that there has been a contravention in relation to the goods of a safety provision.

(4)    For the avoidance of doubt it is declared that a court may infer for the purposes of this section that there has been a contravention in relation to any goods of a safety provision if it is satisfied that any such provision has been contravened in relation to goods which are representative of those goods (whether by reason of being of the same design or part of the same consignment or batch or otherwise).

(5)    Any person aggrieved by an order made under this section by a magistrates' court, or by a decision of such a court not to make such an order, may appeal against that order or decision—

(a)    in England and Wales, to the Crown Court;

(b)    in Northern Ireland, to the county court;

and an order so made may contain such provision as appears to the court to be appropriate for delaying the coming into force of the order pending the making and determination of any appeal (including any application under section 111 of the Magistrates' Courts Act 1980 or Article 146 of the Magistrates' Courts (Northern Ireland) Order 1981 (statement of case)).

(6)    Subject to subsection (7) below, where any goods are forfeited under this section they shall be destroyed in accordance with such directions as the court may give.

(7)    On making an order under this section a magistrates' court may, if it considers it appropriate to do so, direct that the goods to which the order relates shall (instead of being destroyed) be released, to such person as the court may specify, on condition that that person—

(a)    does not supply those goods to any person otherwise than as mentioned in section 46(7)(a) or (b) below; and

(b)    complies with any order to pay costs or expenses (including any order under section 35 below) which has been made against that person in the proceedings for the order for forfeiture.

**18.    Power to obtain information.**

(1)    If the Secretary of State considers that, for the purpose of deciding whether—

(a)    to make, vary or revoke any safety regulations; or

(b)    to serve, vary or revoke a prohibition notice; or

(c)    to serve or revoke a notice to warn,

he requires information which another person is likely to be able to furnish, the Secretary of State may serve on the other person a notice under this section.

(2)    A notice served on any person under this section may require that person—

(a)    to furnish to the Secretary of State, within a period specified in the notice, such information as is so specified;

(b)    to produce such records as are specified in the notice at a time and place so specified and to permit a person appointed by the Secretary of State for the purpose to take copies of the records at that time and place.

(3)    A person shall be guilty of an offence if he—

(a)    fails, without reasonable cause, to comply with a notice served on him under this section; or

(b)    in purporting to comply with a requirement which by virtue of paragraph (a) of subsection (2) above is contained in such a notice—

(i)    furnishes information which he knows is false in a material particular; or

(ii)    recklessly furnishes information which is false in a material particular.

(4)    A person guilty of an offence under subsection (3) above shall—

(a)    in the case of an offence under paragraph (a) of that subsection, be liable on summary conviction to a fine not exceeding level 5 on the standard scale; and

(b)    in the case of an offence under paragraph (b) of that subsection be liable—

(i)    on conviction on indictment, to a fine;

(ii)    on summary conviction, to a fine not exceeding the statutory maximum.

**19.    Interpretation of Part II.**

(1)    In this Part—

"controlled drug" means a controlled drug within the meaning of the Misuse of Drugs Act 1971;

"feeding stuff" and "fertiliser" have the same meanings as in Part IV of the Agriculture Act 1970;

"food" does not include anything containing tobacco but, subject to that, has the same meaning as in the Food Act 1984 or, in relation to Northern Ireland, the same meaning as in the Food and Drugs Act (Northern Ireland) 1958;

"licensed medicinal product" means—

(a)    any medicinal product within the meaning of the Medicines Act 1968 in respect of which a product licence within the meaning of that Act is for the time being in force;

or

(b)    any other article or substance in respect of which any such licence is for the time being in force in pursuance of an order under section 104 or 105 of that Act (application of Act to other articles and substances);

"safe", in relation to any goods, means such that there is no risk, or no risk apart from one reduced to a minimum, that any of the following will (whether immediately or after a definite or indefinite period) cause the death of, or any personal injury to, any person whatsoever, that is to say—

(a)    the goods;

(b)    the keeping, use or consumption of the goods;

(c)    the assembly of any of the goods which are, or are to be, supplied unassembled;

(d)    any emission or leakage from the goods or, as a result of the keeping, use or consumption of the goods, from anything else; or

(e)    reliance on the accuracy of any measurement, calculation or other reading made by or by means of the goods,

and "safer" and "unsafe" shall be construed accordingly;

"tobacco" includes any tobacco produce within the meaning of the Tobacco Products Duty Act 1979 and any article or substance containing tobacco and intended for oral or nasal use.

(2)    In the definition of "safe" in subsection (1) above, references to the keeping, use or consumption of any goods are references to—

(a)    the keeping, use or consumption of the goods by the persons by whom, and in all or any of the ways or circumstances in which, they might reasonably be expected to be kept, used or consumed; and

(b)    the keeping, use or consumption of the goods either alone or in conjunction with other goods in conjunction with which they might reasonably be expected to be kept, used or consumed.

## PART III
## MISLEADING PRICE INDICATIONS

**20.    Offence of giving misleading indication.**

(1)    Subject to the following provisions of this Part, a person shall be guilty of an offence if, in the course of any business of his, he gives (by any means whatever) to any consumers an indication which is misleading as to the price at which any goods, services, accommodation or facilities are available (whether generally or from particular persons).

(2)    Subject as aforesaid, a person shall be guilty of an offence if—

(a)    in the course of any business of his, he has given an indication to any consumers which, after it was given, has become misleading as mentioned in subsection (1) above; and

(b)    some or all of those consumers might reasonably be expected to rely on the indication at a time after it has become misleading; and

(c)    he fails to take all such steps as are reasonable to prevent those consumers from relying on the indication.

(3)    For the purposes of this section it shall be immaterial—

(a)    whether the person who gives or gave the indication is or was acting on his own behalf or on behalf of another;

(b)    whether or not that person is the person, or included among the persons, from whom the goods, services, accommodation or facilities are available; and

(c)    whether the indication is or has become misleading in relation to all the consumers to whom it is or was given or only in relation to some of them.

(4)    A person guilty of an offence under subsection (1) or (2) above shall be liable  –

(a)    on conviction on indictment, to a fine;

(b)    on summary conviction, to a fine not exceeding the statutory maximum.

(5)    No prosecution for an offence under subsection (1) or (2) above shall be brought after whichever is the earlier of the following, that is to say—

(a)    the end of the period of three years beginning with the day on which the offence was committed; and

(b)    the end of the period of one year beginning with the day on which the person bringing the prosecution discovered that the offence had been committed.

(6)    In this Part—

"consumer"—

(a)    in relation to any goods, means any person who might wish to be supplied with the goods for his own private use or consumption;

(b)    in relation to any services or facilities, means any person who might wish to be provided with the services or facilities otherwise than for the purposes of any business of his; and

(c)      in relation to any accommodation, means any person who might wish to occupy the accommodation otherwise than for the purposes of any business of his; "price", in relation to any goods, services, accommodation or facilities, means—

(a)      the aggregate of the sums required to be paid by a consumer for or otherwise in respect of the supply of the goods or the provision of the services, accommodation or facilities;

(b)      except in section 21 below, any method which will be or has been applied for the purpose of determining that aggregate.

## 21.   Meaning of "misleading".

(1)   For the purposes of section 20 above an indication given to any consumers is misleading as to a price if what is conveyed by the indication, or what those consumers might reasonably be expected to infer from the indication or any omission from it, includes any of the following, that is to say—

(a)   that the price is less than in fact it is;

(b)   that the applicability of the price does not depend on facts or circumstances on which its applicability does in fact depend;

(c)   that the price covers matters in respect of which an additional charge is in fact made;

(d)   that a person who in fact has no such expectation—

(i)      expects the price to be increased or reduced (whether or not at a particular time or by a particular amount); or

(ii)      expects the price, or the price as increased or reduced, to be maintained (whether or not for a particular period); or

(e)   that the facts or circumstances by reference to which the consumers might reasonably be expected to judge the validity of any relevant comparison made or implied by the indication are not what in fact they are.

(2)   For the purposes of section 20 above, an indication given to any consumers is misleading as to a method of determining a price if what is conveyed by the indication, or what those consumers might reasonably be expected to infer from the indication or any omission from it, includes any of the following, that is to say—

(a)   that the method is not what in fact it is;

(b)   that the applicability of the method does not depend on facts or circumstances on which its applicability does in fact depend;

(c)   that the method takes into account matters in respect of which an additional charge will in fact be made;

(d)   that a person who in fact has no such expectation—

(i)      expects the method to be altered (whether or not at a particular time or in a particular respect); or

(ii)      expects the method, or that method as altered, to remain unaltered (whether or not for a particular period); or

(e)   that the facts or circumstances by reference to which the consumers might reasonably be expected to judge the validity of any relevant comparison made or implied by the indication are not what in fact they are.

(3)   For the purposes of subsections (1)(e) and (2)(e) above a comparison is a relevant comparison in relation to a price or method of determining a price if it is made between that price or that method, or any price which has been or may be determined by that method, and—

(a)   any price or value which is stated or implied to be, to have been or to be likely to be attributed or attributable to the goods, services, accommodation or facilities in question or to any other goods, services, accommodation or facilities; or

(b)   any method, or other method, which is stated or implied to be, to have been or to be likely to be applied or applicable for the determination of the price or value of the goods, services, accommodation or facilities in question or of the price or value of any other goods, services, accommodation or facilities.

**22.    Application to provision of services and facilities.**

(1)    Subject to the following provisions of this section, references in this Part to services or facilities are references to any services or facilities whatever including, in particular—

(a)    the provision of credit or of banking or insurance services and the provision of facilities incidental to the provision of such services;

(b)    the purchase or sale of foreign currency;

(c)    the supply of electricity;

(d)    the provision of a place, other than on a highway, for the parking of a motor vehicle;

(e)    the making or arrangements for a person to put or keep a caravan on any land other than arrangements by virtue of which that person may occupy the caravan as his only or main residence.

(2)    References in this Part to services shall not include references to services provided to an employer under a contract of employment.

(3)    References in this Part to services or facilities shall not include references to services or facilities which are provided by an authorised person or appointed representative in the course of the carrying on of an investment business.

(4)    In relation to a service consisting in the purchase or sale of foreign currency, references in this Part to the method by which the price of the service is determined shall include references to the rate of exchange.

(5)    In this section—

"appointed representative", "authorised person" and "investment business" have the same meanings as in the Financial Services Act 1986;

"caravan" has the same meaning as in the Caravan Sites and Control of Development Act 1960;

"contract of employment" and "employer" have the same meanings as in the Employment Protection (Consolidation) Act 1978;

"credit" has the same meaning as in the Consumer Credit Act 1974.

**23.    Application to provision of accommodation etc.**

(1)    Subject to subsection (2) below, references in this Part to accommodation or facilities being available shall not include references to accommodation or facilities being available to be provided by means of the creation or disposal of an interest in land except where—

(a)    the person who is to create or dispose of the interest will do so in the course of any business of his; and

(b)    the interest to be created or disposed of is a relevant interest in a new dwelling and is to be created or disposed of for the purpose of enabling that dwelling to be occupied as a residence, or one of the residences, of the person acquiring the interest.

(2)    Subsection (1) above shall not prevent the application of any provision of this Part in relation to—

(a)    the supply of any goods as part of the same transaction as any creation or disposal of an interest in land; or

(b)    the provision of any services or facilities for the purposes of, or in connection with, any transaction for the creation or disposal of such an interest.

(3)    In this section—

"new dwelling" means any building or part of a building in Great Britain which—

(a)    has been constructed or adapted to be occupied as a residence; and

(b)    has not previously been so occupied or has been so occupied only with other premises or as more than one residence,

and includes any yard, garden, out-houses or appurtenances which belong to that building or part or are to be enjoyed with it;
"relevant interest"—

(a)     in relation to a new dwelling in England and Wales, means the freehold estate in the dwelling or a leasehold interest in the dwelling for a term of years absolute of more than twenty-one years, not being a term of which twenty-one years or less remains unexpired;
. . .

## 24.   Defences.

(1)     In any proceedings against a person for an offence under subsection (1) or (2) of section 2 above in respect of any indication it shall be a defence for that person to show that his acts or omissions were authorised for the purposes of this subsection by regulations made under section 26 below.

(2)     In proceedings against a person for an offence under subsection (1) or (2) of section 20 above in respect of an indication published in a book, newspaper, magazine, film or radio or television broadcast or in a programme included in a cable programme service, it shall be a defence for that person to show that the indication was not contained in an advertisement.

(3)     In proceedings against a person for an offence under subsection (1) or (2) of section 20 above in respect of an indication published in an advertisement it shall be a defence for that person to show that—

(a)     he is a person who carries on a business of publishing or arranging for the publication of advertisements;

(b)     he received the advertisement for publication in the ordinary course of that business; and

(c)     at the time of publication he did not know and had no grounds for suspecting that the publication would involve the commission of the offence.

(4)     In any proceedings against a person for an offence under subsection (1) of section 20 above in respect of any indication, it shall be a defence for that person to show that—

(a)     the indication did not relate to the availability from him of any goods, services, accommodation or facilities;

(b)     a price had been recommended to every person from whom the goods, services, accommodation or facilities were indicated as being available;

(c)     the indication related to that price and was misleading as to that price only by reason of a failure by any person to follow the recommendation; and

(d)     it was reasonable for the person who gave the indication to assume that the recommendation was for the most part being followed.

(5)     The provisions of this section are without prejudice to the provisions of section 39 below.

(6)     In this section—
"advertisement" includes a catalogue, a circular and a price list;
"cable programme service" has the same meaning as in the Cable and Broadcasting Act 1984.

## 25.   Code of practice.

(1)     The Secretary of State may, after consulting the Director General of Fair Trading and such other persons as the Secretary of State considers it appropriate to consult, by order approve any code of practice issued (whether by the Secretary of State or another person) for the purpose of—

(a)     giving practical guidance with respect to any of the requirements of section 20 above; and

(b)     Promoting what appear to the Secretary of State to be desirable practices as to the circumstances and manner in which any person gives an indication as to the price at which any goods, services, accommodation or facilities are available or indicates any other matter in respect of which any such indication may be misleading.

(2)    A contravention of a code of practice approved under this section shall not of itself give rise to any criminal or civil liability, but in any proceedings against any person for an offence under section 20(1) or (2) above—

(a)    any contravention by that person of such a code may be relied on in relation to any matter for the purpose of establishing that that person committed the offence or of negativing any defence;

(b)    compliance by that person with such a code may be relied on in relation to any matter for the purpose of showing that the commission of the offence by that person has not been established or that that person has a defence.

(3)    Where the Secretary of State approves a code of practice under this section he may, after such consultation as is mentioned in subsection (1) above, at any time by order—

(a)    approve any modification of the code; or

(b)    withdraw his approval;

and references in subsection (2) above to a code of practice approved under this section shall be construed accordingly.

(4)    The power to make an order under this section shall be exercisable by statutory instrument subject to annulment in pursuance of a resolution of either House of Parliament.

## 26.    Power to make regulations.

(1)    The Secretary of State may, after consulting the Director General of Fair Trading and such other persons as the Secretary of State considers it appropriate to consult, by regulations make provision—

(a)    for the purpose of regulating the circumstances and manner in which any person—

(i)    gives any indication as to the price at which any goods, services, accommodation or facilities will be or are available or have been supplied or provided; or

(ii)    indicates any other matter in respect of which any such indication may be misleading;

(b)    for the purpose of facilitating the enforcement of the provisions of section 20 above or of any regulations made under this section.

(2)    The Secretary of State shall not make regulations by virtue of subsection (1)(a) above except in relation to—

(a)    indications given by persons in the course of business; and

(b)    such indications given otherwise than in the course of business as—

(i)    are given by or on behalf of persons by whom accommodation is provided to others by means of leases or licences; and

(ii)    relate to goods, services or facilities supplied or provided to those others in connection with the provision of the accommodation.

(3)    Without prejudice to the generality of subsection (1) above, regulations under this section may—

(a)    prohibit an indication as to a price from referring to such matters as may be prescribed by the regulations;

(b)    require an indication as to a price or other matter to be accompanied or supplemented by such explanation or such additional information as may be prescribed by the regulations;

(c)    require information or explanations with respect to a price or other matter to be given to an officer of an enforcement authority and to authorise such an officer to require such information or explanations to be given;

(d)    require any information or explanation provided for the purposes of any regulations made by virtue of paragraph (b) or (c) above to be accurate;

(e)    prohibit the inclusion in indications as to a price or other matter of statements that the indications are not to be relied upon;

(f)    provide that expressions used in any indication as to a price or other matter shall be construed in a particular way for the purposes of this Part;

(g)    provide that a contravention of any provision of the regulations shall constitute a criminal offence punishable—

(i)    on conviction on indictment, by a fine;

(ii)    on summary conviction, by a fine not exceeding the statutory maximum;

(h)    apply any provision of this Act which relates to a criminal offence to an offence created by virtue of paragraph (g) above.

(4)    The power to make regulations under this section shall be exercisable by statutory instrument . . .

## PART IV
## ENFORCEMENT OF PARTS II AND III

### 27.    Enforcement.

(1)    Subject to the following provisions of this section—

(a)    it shall be the duty of every weights and measures authority in Great Britain to enforce within their area the safety provisions and the provisions made by or under Part III of this Act; and

(b)    it shall be the duty of every district council in Northern Ireland to enforce within their area the safety provisions.

(2)    The Secretary of State may by regulations—

(a)    wholly or partly transfer any duty imposed by subsection (1) above on a weights and measures authority or a district council in Northern Ireland to such other person who has agreed to the transfer as is specified in the regulations;

(b)    relieve such an authority or council of any such duty so far as it is exercisable in relation to such goods as may be described in the regulations.

(3)    The power to make regulations under subsection (2) above shall be exercisable by statutory instrument . . .

### 28.    Test purchases.

(1)    An enforcement authority shall have power, for the purpose of ascertaining whether any safety provision or any provision made by or under Part III of this Act has been contravened in relation to any goods, services, accommodation or facilities—

(a)    to make, or to authorise an officer of the authority to make, any purchase of any goods; or

(b)    to secure, or to authorise an officer of the authority to secure, the provision of any services, accommodation or facilities.

(2)    Where—

(a)    any goods purchased under this section by or on behalf of an enforcement authority are submitted to a test; and

(b)    the test leads to—

(i)    the bringing of proceedings for an offence in respect of a contravention in relation to the goods of any safety provision or of any provision made by or under Part III of this Act or for the forfeiture of the goods under section 16 or 17 above; or

(ii)    the serving of a suspension notice in respect of any goods; and

(c)    the authority is requested to do so and it is practicable for the authority to comply with the request,

the authority shall allow the person from whom the goods were purchased or any person who is a party to the proceedings or has an interest in any goods to which the notice relates to have the goods tested.

(3)    The Secretary of State may by regulations provide that any test of goods purchased under this section by or on behalf of an enforcement authority shall—

(a)    be carried out at the expense of the authority in a manner and by a person prescribed by or determined under the regulations; or

(b)    be carried out either as mentioned in paragraph (a) above or by the authority in a manner prescribed by the regulations.

(4)    The power to make regulations under subsection (3) above shall be exercisable by statutory instrument . . .

(5)    Nothing in this section shall authorise the acquisition by or on behalf of an enforcement authority of any interest in land.

## 29.    Powers of search etc.

(1)    Subject to the following provisions of this Part, a duly authorised officer of an enforcement authority may at any reasonable hour and on production, if required, of his credentials exercise any of the powers conferred by the following provisions of this section.

(2)    The officer may, for the purpose of ascertaining whether there has been any contravention of any safety provision or of any provision made by or under Part III of this Act, inspect any goods and enter any premises other than premises occupied only as a person's residence.

(3)    The officer may, for the purpose of ascertaining whether there has been any contravention of any safety provision, examine any procedure '(including any arrangements for carrying out a test) connected with the production of any goods.

(4)    If the officer has reasonable grounds for suspecting that any goods are manufactured or imported goods which have not been supplied in the United Kingdom since they were manufactured or imported he may—

(a)    for the purpose of ascertaining whether there has been any contravention of any safety provision in relation to the goods, require any person carrying on a business, or employed in connection with the business, to produce any records relating to the business;

(b)    for the purpose of ascertaining (by testing or otherwise) whether there has been any such contravention, seize and detain the goods;

(c)    take copies of, or of any entry in, any records produced by virtue of paragraph (a) above.

(5)    If the officer has reasonable grounds for suspecting that there has been a contravention in relation to any goods of any safety provision or of any provision made by or under Part III of this Act, he may—

(a)    for the purpose of ascertaining whether there has been any such contravention, require any person carrying on a business, or employed in connection with a business, to produce any records relating to the business;

(b)    for the purpose of ascertaining (by testing or otherwise) whether there has been any such contravention, seize and detain the goods;

(c)    take copies of, or of any entry in, any records produced by virtue of paragraph (a) above.

(6)    The officer may seize and detain—

(a)    any goods or records which he has reasonable grounds for believing may be required as evidence in proceedings for an offence in respect of a contravention of any safety provision or of any provision made by or under Part III of this Act.

(b)    any goods which he has reasonable grounds for suspecting may be liable to be forfeited under section 16 or 17 above.

(7)    If and to the extent that it is reasonably necessary to do so to prevent a contravention of any safety provision or of any provision made by or under Part III of this Act, the officer may, for the purpose of exercising his power under subsection (4), (5) or (6) above to seize any goods or records—

(a)    require any person having authority to do so to open any container or to open any vending machine; and

(b)    himself open or break open any such container or machine where a requirement made under paragraph (a) above in relation to the container or machine has not been complied

## 30.    Provisions supplemental to s. 29.

(1)    An officer seizing any goods or records under section 29 above shall inform the following persons that the goods or records have been so seized, that is to say—

(a)    the person from whom they are seized; and

(b)    in the case of imported goods seized on any premises under the control of the Commissioners of Customs and Excise, the importer of those goods (within the meaning of the Customs and Excise Management Act 1979).

(2)    If a justice of the peace—

(a)    is satisfied by any written information on oath that there are reasonable grounds for believing either—

(i)    that any goods or records which any officer has power to inspect under section 29 above are on any premises and that their inspection is likely to disclose evidence that there has been a contravention of any safety provision or of any provision made by or under part III of this Act; or

(ii)    that such a contravention has taken place, is taking place or is about to take place on any premises; and

(b)    is also satisfied by any such information either—

(i)    that admission to the premises has been or is likely to be refused and that notice of intention to apply for a warrant under this subsection has been given to the occupier; or

(ii)    that an application for admission, or the giving of such a notice, would defeat the object of the entry or that the premises are unoccupied or that the occupier is temporarily absent and it might defeat the object of the entry to await his return, the justice may by warrant under his hand, which shall continue in force for a period of one month, authorise any officer of an enforcement authority to enter the premises, if need be by force.

(3)    An officer entering any premises by virtue of section 29 above or a warrant under subsection (2) above may take with him such other persons and such equipment as may appear to him necessary.

(4)    On leaving any premises which a person is authorised to enter by a warrant under subsection (2) above, that person shall, if the premises are unoccupied or the occupier is temporarily absent, leave the premises as effectively secured against trespassers as he found them.

(5)    If any person who is not an officer of an enforcement authority purports to act as such under section 29 above or this section he shall be guilty of an offence and liable on summary conviction to a fine not exceeding level 5 on the standard scale.

(6)    Where any goods seized by an officer under section 29 above are submitted to a test, the officer shall inform the persons mentioned in subsection (1) above of the result of the test and, if—

(a)    proceedings are brought for an offence in respect of a contravention in relation to the goods of any safety provision or of any provision made by or under Part III of this Act or for the forfeiture of the goods under section 16 or 17 above, or a suspension notice is served in respect of any goods; and

(b)    the officer is requested to do so and it is practicable to comply with the request, the officer shall allow any person who is a party to the proceedings or, as the case may be, has an interest in the goods to which the notice relates to have the goods tested.

(7)    The Secretary of State may by regulations provide that any test of goods seized under section 29 above by an officer of an enforcement authority shall—

(a)	be carried out at the expense of the authority in a manner and by a person prescribed by or determined under the regulations; or

(b)	be carried out either as mentioned in paragraph (a) above or by the authority in a manner prescribed by the regulations.

(8)	The power to make regulations under subsection (7) above shall be exercisable by statutory instrument . . .

## 31.	Power of customs officer to detain goods.

(1)	A customs officer may, for the purpose of facilitating the exercise by an enforcement authority or officer of such an authority of any functions conferred on the authority or officer by or under Part II of this Act, or by or under this Part in its application for the purposes of the safety provisions, seize any imported goods and detain them for not more than two working days.

(2)	Anything seized and detained under this section shall be dealt with during the period of its detention in such manner as the Commissioners of Customs and Excise may direct.

## 32.	Obstruction of authorised officer.

(1)	Any person who—

(a)	intentionally obstructs any officer of an enforcement authority who is acting in pursuance of any provision of this Part or any customs officer who is so acting; or

(b)	intentionally fails to comply with any requirement made of him by any officer of any enforcement authority under any provision of this Part; or

(c)	without reasonable cause fails to give any officer of an enforcement authority who is so acting any other assistance or information which the officer may reasonably require of him for the purposes of the exercise of the officer's functions under any provision of this Part,

shall be guilty of an offence and liable on summary conviction to a fine not exceeding level 5 on the standard scale.

(2)	A person shall be guilty of an offence if, in giving any information which is required of him by virtue of subsection (1)(c) above—

(a)	he makes any statement which he knows is false in a material particular; or

(b)	he recklessly makes a statement which is false in a material particular.

(3)	A person guilty of an offence under subsection (2) above shall be liable—

(a)	on conviction on indictment, to a fine;

(b)	on summary conviction, to a fine not exceeding the statutory maximum.

## 33.	Appeals against detention of goods.

(1)	Any person having an interest in any goods which are for the time being detained under any provision of this Part by an enforcement authority or by an officer of such an authority may apply for an order requiring the goods to be released to him or to another person.

(2)	An application under this section may be made—

(a)	to any magistrates' court in which proceedings have been brought in England and Wales or Northern Ireland—

(i)	for an offence in respect of a contravention in relation to the goods of any safety provision or of any provision made by or under Part III of this Act; or

(ii)	for the forfeiture of the goods under section 16 above;

(b)	where no such proceedings have been so brought, by way of complaint to a magistrates' court . . .

(3)	On an application under this section to a magistrates' court . . ., an order requiring goods to be released shall be made only if the court . . . is satisfied—

(a)	that proceedings—

(i)	for an offence in respect of a contravention in relation to the goods of any safety provision or of any provision made by or under Part III of this Act; or

(ii)      for the forfeiture of the goods under section 16 or 17 above,
have not been brought or, having been brought, have been concluded without the goods being forfeited; and
(b)      where no such proceedings have been brought, that more than six months have elapsed since the goods were seized.
(4)      Any person aggrieved by an order made under this section by a magistrates' court in England and Wales or Northern Ireland, or by a decision of such a court not to make such an order, may appeal against that order or decision—
(a)      in England and Wales, to the Crown Court;
(b)      in Northern Ireland, to the county court;
and an order so made may contain such provision as appears to the court to be appropriate for delaying the coming into force of the order pending the making and determination of any appeal (including any application under section 111 of the Magistrates' Courts Act 1980 or Article 146 of the Magistrates' Courts (Northern Ireland) Order 1981 (statement of case)).

**34.      Compensation for seizure and detention.**
(1)      Where an officer of an enforcement authority exercises any power under section 29 above to seize and detain goods, the enforcement authority shall be liable to pay compensation to any person having an interest in the goods in respect of any loss or damage caused by reason of the exercise of the power if—
(a)      there has been no contravention in relation to the goods of any safety provision or of any provision made by or under Part III of this Act; and
(b)      the exercise of the power is not attributable to any neglect or default by that person.
(2)      Any disputed question as to the right to or the amount of any compensation payable under this section shall be determined by arbitration . . .

**35.      Recovery of expenses of enforcement.**
(1)      This section shall apply where a court—
(a)      convicts a person of an offence in respect of a contravention in relation to any goods of any safety provision or of any provision made by or under Part III of this Act; or
(b)      makes an order under section 16 or 17 above for the forfeiture of any goods.
(2)      The court may (in addition to any other order it may make as to costs or expenses) order the person convicted or, as the case may be, any person having an interest in the goods to reimburse an enforcement authority for an expenditure which has been or may be incurred by that authority—
(a)      in connection with any seizure or detention of the goods by or on behalf of the authority; or
(b)      in connection with any compliance by the authority with directions given by the court for the purposes of any order for the forfeiture of the goods.

PART V
MISCELLANEOUS AND SUPPLEMENTAL

**37.      Power of Commissioners of Customs and Excise to disclose information.**
(1)      If they think it appropriate to do so for the purpose of facilitating the exercise by any person to whom subsection (2) below applies of any functions conferred on that person by or under Part II of this Act, or by or under Part IV of this Act in its application for the purposes of the safety provisions, the Commissioners of Customs and Excise may authorise the disclosure to that person of any information obtained for the purposes of the exercise by the Commissioners of their functions in relation to imported goods.
(2)      This subsection applies to an enforcement authority and to any officer of an enforcement authority.

(3)     A disclosure of information made to any person under subsection (1) above shall be made in such manner as may be directed by the Commissioners of Customs and Excise and may be made through such person acting on behalf of that person as may be so directed.

(4)     Information may be disclosed to a person under subsection (1) above whether or not the disclosure of the information has been requested by or on behalf of that person.

### 38.     Restrictions on disclosure of information.

(1)     Subject to the following provisions of this section, a person shall be guilty of an offence if he discloses any information—

(a)     which was obtained by him in consequence of its being given to any person in compliance with any requirement imposed by safety regulations or regulations under section 26 above;

(b)     which consists in a secret manufacturing process or a trade secret and was obtained by him in consequence of the inclusion of the information—

(i)     in written or oral representations made for the purposes of Part I or II of Schedule 2 to this Act; or

(ii)     in a statement of a witness in connection with any such oral representations;

(c)     which was obtained by him in consequence of the exercise by the Secretary of State of the power conferred by section 18 above;

(d)     which was obtained by him in consequence of the exercise by any person of any power conferred by Part IV of this Act; or

(e)     which was disclosed to or through him under section 37 above.

(2)     Subsection (1) above shall not apply to a disclosure of information if the information is publicised information or the disclosure is made—

(a)     for the purpose of facilitating the exercise of a relevant person's functions under this Act or any enactment or subordinate legislation mentioned in subsection (3) below;

(b)     for the purposes of compliance with a Community obligation; or

(c)     in connection with the investigation of any criminal offence or for the purposes of any civil or criminal proceedings.

(3)     The enactments and subordinate legislation referred to in subsection (2)(a) above are—

(a)     the Trade Descriptions Act 1968;

(b)     Parts II and III and section 125 of the Fair Trading Act 1973;

(c)     the relevant statutory provisions within the meaning of Part I of the Health and Safety at Work etc. Act 1974 or within the meaning of the Health and Safety at Work (Northern Ireland) Order 1978;

(d)     the Consumer Credit Act 1974;

(e)     The Restrictive Trade Practices Act 1976;

(f)     the Resale Prices Act 1976;

(g)     the Estate Agents Act 1979;

(h)     the Competition Act 1980;

(i)     the Telecommunications Act 1984;

(j)     the Airports Act 1986;

(k)     The Gas Act 1986;

(l)     any subordinate legislation made (whether before or after the passing of this Act) for the purpose of securing compliance with the Directive of the Council of the European Communities, dated 10th September 1984 (No. 84/450/EEC) on the approximation of the laws, regulations and administrative provisions of the member States concerning misleading advertising.

(4)     In subsection (2)(a) above the reference to a person's functions shall include a reference to any function of making, amending or revoking any regulations or order.

(5)    A person guilty of an offence under this section shall be liable—
(a)    on summary conviction, to a fine not exceeding the statutory maximum;
(b)    on conviction on indictment, to imprisonment for a term not exceeding two years or to a fine or to both.
(6)    In this section—
"publicised information" means any information which has been disclosed in any civil or criminal proceedings or is or has been required to be contained in a warning published in pursuance of a notice to warn; and
"relevant person" means any of the following, that is to say—
(a)    a Minister of the Crown, Government department or Northern Ireland department;
(b)    the Monopolies and Mergers Commission, the Director General of Fair Trading, the Director General of Telecommunications or the Director General of Gas Supply;
(c)    the Civil Aviation Authority;
(d)    any weights and measures authority, any district council in Northern Ireland or any person on whom functions are conferred by regulations under section 27(2) above;
(e)    any person who is an enforcing authority for the purposes of Part I of the Health and Safety at Work etc. Act 1974 or for the purposes of Part II of the Health and Safety at Work (Northern Ireland) Order 1978.

**39.    Defence of due diligence.**
(1)    Subject to the following provisions of this section, in proceedings against any person for an offence to which this section applies it shall be a defence for that person to show that he took all reasonable steps and exercised all due diligence to avoid committing the offence.
(2)    Where in any proceedings against any person for such an offence the defence provided by subsection (1) above involves an allegation that the commission of the offence was due—
(a)    to the act or default of another; or
(b)    to reliance on information given by another,
that person shall not, without the leave of the court, be entitled to rely on the defence unless, not less than seven clear days before the hearing of the proceedings, he has served a notice under subsection (3) below on the person bringing the proceedings.
(3)    A notice under this subsection shall give such information identifying or assisting in the identification of the person who committed the act or default or gave the information as is in the possession of the person serving the notice at the time he serves it.
(4)    It is hereby declared that a person shall not be entitled to rely on the defence provided by subsection (1) above by reason of his reliance on information supplied by another, unless he shows that it was reasonable in all the circumstances for him to have relied on the information, having regard in particular—
(a)    to the steps which he took, and those which might reasonably have been taken, for the purpose of verifying the information; and
(b)    to whether he had any reason to disbelieve the information.
(5)    This section shall apply to an offence under section 10, 12(1), (2) or (3), 13(4), 14(6) or 20(1) above.

**40.    Liability of persons other than principal offender.**
(1)    Where the commission by any person of an offence to which section 39 above applies is due to an act or default committed by some other person in the course of any business of his, the other person shall be guilty of the offence and may be proceeded against and punished by virtue of this subsection whether or not proceedings are taken against the first mentioned person.

(2)    Where a body corporate is guilty of an offence under this Act (including where it is so guilty by virtue of subsection (1) above) in respect of any act or default which is shown to have been committed with the consent or connivance of, or to be attributable to any neglect on the part of, any director, manager, secretary or other similar office of the body corporate or any person who was purporting to act in any such capacity he, as well as the body corporate, shall be guilty of that offence and shall be liable to be proceeded against and punished accordingly.

(3)    Where the affairs of a body corporate are managed by its members, subsection (2) above shall apply in relation to the acts and defaults of a member in connection with his functions of management as if he were a director of the body corporate.

### 41.    Civil proceedings.

(1)    An obligation imposed by safety regulations shall be a duty owed to any person who may be affected by a contravention of the obligation and, subject to any provision to the contrary in the regulations and to the defences and other incidents applying to actions for breach of statutory duty, a contravention of any such obligation shall be actionable accordingly.

(2)    This Act shall not be construed as conferring any other right of action in civil proceedings, apart from the right conferred by virtue of Part I of this Act, in respect of any loss or damage suffered in consequence of a contravention of a safety provision or of a provision made by or under Part III of this Act.

(3)    Subject to any provision to the contrary in the agreement itself, an agreement shall not be void or unenforceable by reason only of a contravention of a safety provision or of a provision made by or under Part III of this Act.

(4)    Liability by virtue of subsection (1) above shall not be limited or excluded by any contract term, by any notice or (subject to the power contained in subsection (1) above to limit or exclude it in safety regulations) by any other provision.

(5)    Nothing in subsection (1) above shall prejudice the operation of section 12 of the Nuclear Installations Act 1965 (rights to compensation for certain breaches of duties confined to rights under that Act).

(6)    In this section "damage" includes personal injury and death.

### 42.    Reports etc.

(1)    It shall be the duty of the Secretary of State at least once in every five years to lay before each House of Parliament a report on the exercise during the period to which the report relates of the functions which under Part II of this Act, or under Part IV of this Act in its application for the purposes of the safety provisions, are exercisable by the Secretary of State, weights and measures authorities, district councils in Northern Ireland and persons on whom functions are conferred by regulations made under section 27(2) above.

(2)    The Secretary of State may from time to time prepare and lay before each House of Parliament such other reports on the exercise of those functions as he considers appropriate.

(3)    Every weights and measures authority, every district council in Northern Ireland and every person on whom functions are conferred by regulations under subsection (2) of section 27 above shall, whenever the Secretary of State so directs, make a report to the Secretary of State on the exercise of the functions exercisable by the authority or council under that section or by that person by virtue of any such regulations.

### 45.    Interpretation.

(1)    In this Act, except in so far as the context otherwise requires—
"aircraft" includes gliders, balloons and hovercraft;
"business" includes a trade or profession and the activities of a professional or trade association or of a local authority or other public authority;

"conditional sale agreement", "credit—sale agreement" and "hire-purchase agreement" have the same meanings as in the Consumer Credit Act 1974 but as if in the definitions in that Act "goods" had the same meaning as in this Act;

"contravention" includes a failure to comply and cognate expressions shall be construed accordingly;

"enforcement authority" means the Secretary of State, any other Minister of the Crown in charge of a Government department, any such department and any authority, council or other person on whom functions under this Act are conferred by or under section 27 above;

"gas" has the same meaning as in Part I of the Gas Act 1986;

"goods" includes substances, growing crops and things comprised in land by virtue of being attached to it and any ship, aircraft or vehicle;

"information" includes accounts, estimates and returns;

"magistrates' court" in relation to Northern Ireland, means a court of summary jurisdiction;

"mark" and "trade mark" have the same meanings as in the Trade Marks Act 1938;

"modifications" includes additions, alterations and omissions, and cognate expressions shall be construed accordingly;

"motor vehicle" has the same meaning as in [the Road Traffic Act 1988];

"notice" means a notice in writing;

"notice to warn" means a notice under section 13(1)(b) above;

"officer", in relation to an enforcement authority, means a person authorised in writing to assist the authority in carrying out its functions under or for the purposes of the enforcement of any of the safety provisions or of any of the provisions made by or under Part III of this Act;

"personal injury" includes any disease and any other impairment of a person's physical or mental condition;

"premises" includes any place and any ship, aircraft or vehicle;

"prohibition notice" means a notice under section 13(1)(a) above;

"records" includes any books or documents and any records in non-documentary form;

"safety provision" means the general safety requirement in section 10 above or any provision of safety regulations, a prohibition notice or a suspension notice;

"safety regulations" means regulations under section 11 above;

"ship" includes any boat and any other description of vessel used in navigation;

"subordinate legislation" has the same meaning as in the Interpretation Act 1978;

"substance" means any natural or artificial substance, whether in solid, liquid or gaseous form or in the form of a vapour, and includes substances that are comprised in or mixed with other goods;

"supply" and cognate expressions shall be construed in accordance with section 46 below;

"suspension notice" means a notice under section 14 above.

(2)    Except in so far as the context otherwise requires, references in this Act to a contravention of a safety provision shall, in relation to any goods, include references to anything which would constitute such a contravention if the goods were supplied to any person.

(3)    References in this Act to any goods in relation to which any safety provision has been or may have been contravened shall include references to any goods which it is not reasonably practicable to separate from any such goods.

## 46.    Meaning of "supply".

(1)    Subject to the following provisions of this section, references in this Act to supplying goods shall be construed as references to doing any of the following, whether as principal or agent, that is to say—

(a)    selling, hiring out or lending the goods;
(b)    entering into a hire-purchase agreement to furnish the goods;
(c)    the performance of any contract for work and materials to furnish the goods;
(d)    providing the goods in exchange for any consideration (including trading stamps) other than money;
(e)    providing the goods in or in connection with the performance of any statutory function; or
(f)    giving the goods as a prize or otherwise making a gift of the goods;
and, in relation to gas or water, those references shall be construed as including references to providing the service by which the gas or water is made available for use.

(2)    For the purpose of any reference in this Act to supplying goods, where a person ("the ostensible supplier") supplies goods to another person ("the customer") under a hire-purchase agreement, conditional sale agreement or credit-sale agreement or under an agreement for the hiring of goods (other than a hire-purchase agreement) and the ostensible supplier—

(a)    carries on the business of financing the provision of goods for others by means of such agreements; and
(b)    in the course of that business acquired his interest in the goods supplied to the customer as a means of financing the provision of them for the customer by a further person ("the effective supplier"),
the effective supplier and not the ostensible supplier shall be treated as supplying the goods to the customer.

(3)    Subject to subsection (4) below, the performance of any contract by the erection of any building or structure on any land or by the carrying out of any other building works shall be treated for the purposes of this Act as a supply of goods in so far as, but only in so far as, it involves the provision of any goods to any person by means of their incorporation into the building, structure or works.

(4)    Except for the purposes of, and in relation to, notices to warn or any provision made by or under Part III of this Act, references in this Act to supplying goods shall not include references to supplying goods comprised in land where the supply is effected by the creation or disposal of an interest in the land.

(5)    Except in Part I of this Act references in this Act to a person's supplying goods shall be confined to references to that person's supplying goods in the course of a business of his, but for the purposes of this subsection it shall be immaterial whether the business is a business of dealing in the goods.

(6)    For the purposes of subsection (5) above goods shall not be treated as supplied in the course of a business if they are supplied, in pursuance of an obligation arising under or in connection with the insurance of the goods, to the person with whom they were insured.

(7)    Except for the purposes of, and in relation to, prohibition notices or suspension notices, references in Parts II to IV of this Act to supplying goods shall not include—

(a)    references to supplying goods where the person supplied carries on a business of buying goods of the same description as those goods and repairing or reconditioning them;
(b)    references to supplying goods by a sale of articles as scrap (that is to say, for the value of materials included in the articles rather than for the value of the articles themselves).

(8)    Where any goods have at any time been supplied by being hired out or lent to any person, neither a continuation or renewal of the hire or loan (whether on the same or different terms) nor any transaction for the transfer after that time of any interest in the goods to the person to whom they were hired or lent shall be treated for the purposes of this Act as a further supply of the goods to that person.

(9)    A ship, aircraft or motor vehicle shall not be treated for the purposes of this Act as supplied to any person by reason only that services consisting in the carriage of goods or

passengers in that ship, aircraft or vehicle, or in its use for any other purpose, are provided to that person in pursuance of an agreement relating to the use of the ship, aircraft or vehicle for a particular period or for particular voyages, flights or journeys.

**Section 13.**                          SCHEDULE 2
PROHIBITION NOTICES AND NOTICES TO WARN

PART I
PROHIBITION NOTICES

1.   A prohibition notice in respect of any goods shall—
    (a)   state that the Secretary of State considers that the goods are unsafe;
    (b)   set out the reasons why the Secretary of State considers that the goods are unsafe;
    (c)   specify the day on which the notice is to come into force; and
    (d)   state that the trader may at any time make representations in writing to the Secretary of State for the purpose of establishing that the goods are safe.

2.—(1)   If representations in writing about a prohibition notice are made by the trader to the Secretary of State, it shall be the duty of the Secretary of State to consider whether to revoke the notice and—
    (a)   if he decides to revoke it, to do so;
    (b)   in any other case, to appoint a person to consider those representations, any further representations made (whether in writing or orally) by the trader about the notice and the statements of any witnesses examined under this Part of this Schedule.

    (2)   Where the Secretary of State has appointed a person to consider representations about a prohibition notice, he shall serve a notification on the trader which—
    (a)   states that the trader may make oral representations to the appointed person for the purpose of establishing that the goods to which the notice relates are safe; and
    (b)   specifies the place and time at which the oral representations may be made.

    (3)   The time specified in a notification served under sub-paragraph (2) above shall not be before the end of the period of twenty-one days beginning with the day on which the notification is served, unless the trader otherwise agrees.

    (4)   A person on whom a notification has been served for the purposes of sub-paragraph (2)(b) above or his representative may, at the place and time specified in the notification—
    (a)   make oral representations to the appointed person for the purpose of establishing that the goods in question are safe; and
    (b)   call and examine witnesses in connection with the representations.

4.—(1)   Where a person is appointed to consider representations about a prohibition notice, it shall be his duty to consider—
    (a)   any written representations made by the trader about the notice, other than those in respect of which a notification is served under paragraph 3(2)(a) above;
    (b)   any oral representations made under paragraph 2(4) or 3(4) above; and
    (c)   any statements made by witnesses in connection with the oral representations, and, after considering any matters under this paragraph, to make a report (including recommendations) to the Secretary of State about the matters considered by him and the notice.

    (2)   It shall be the duty of the Secretary of State to consider any report made to him under sub-paragraph (1) above and, after considering the report, to inform the trader of his decision with respect to the prohibition notice to which the report relates

5.—(1)   The Secretary of State may revoke or vary a prohibition notice by serving on the trader a notification stating that the notice is revoked or, as the case may be, is varied as specified in the notification.

(2)   The Secretary of State shall not vary a prohibition notice so as to make the effect of the notice more restrictive for the trader.

(3)   Without prejudice to the power conferred by section 13(2) of this Act, the service of a notification under sub-paragraph (1) above shall be sufficient to satisfy the requirement of paragraph 4(2) above that the trader shall be informed of the Secretary of State's decision.

## PART II
## NOTICES TO WARN

6.—(1)   If the Secretary of State proposes to serve a notice to warn on any person in respect of any goods, the Secretary of State, before he serves the notice, shall serve on that person a notification which—

(a)   contains a draft of the proposed notice;

(b)   states that the Secretary of State proposes to serve a notice in the form of the draft on that person;

(c)   states that the Secretary of State considers that the goods described in the draft are unsafe;

(d)   sets out the reasons why the Secretary of State considers that those goods are unsafe; and

(e)   states that that person may make representations to the Secretary of State for the purpose of establishing that the goods are safe if, before the end of the period of fourteen days beginning with the day on which the notification is served, he informs the Secretary of State—

(i)       of his intention to make representations; and

(ii)      whether the representations will be made only in writing or both in writing and orally.

(2)   Where the Secretary of State has served a notification containing a draft of a proposed notice to warn on any person, he shall not serve a notice to warn on that person in respect of the goods to which the proposed notice relates unless—

(a)   the period of fourteen days beginning with the day on which the notification was served expires without the Secretary of State being informed as mentioned in sub-paragraph (1)(e) above;

(b)   the period of twenty-eight days beginning with that day expires without any written representations being made by that person to the Secretary of State about the proposed notice; or

(c)   the Secretary of State has considered a report about the proposed notice by a person appointed under paragraph 7(1) below.

7.—(1)   Where a person on whom a notification containing a draft of a proposed notice to warn has been served—

(a)   informs the Secretary of State as mentioned in paragraph 6(1)(e) above before the end of the period of fourteen days beginning with the day on which the notification was served; and

(b)   makes written representations to the Secretary of State about the proposed notice before the end of the period of twenty-eight days beginning with that day,

the Secretary of State shall appoint a person to consider those representations, any further representations made by that person about the draft notice and the statements of any witnesses examined under this Part of this Schedule.

(2)   Where—

(a)   the Secretary of State has appointed a person to consider representations about a proposed notice to warn; and

(b)   the person whose representations are to be considered has informed the Secretary of State for the purposes of paragraph 6(1)(e) above that the representations he intends to make will include oral representations, the Secretary of State shall inform the person intending to make the representations of the place and time at which oral representations may be made to the appointed person.

(3)    Where a person on whom a notification containing a draft of a proposed notice to warn has been served is informed of a time for the purposes of sub-paragraph (2) above, that time shall not be—

(a)    before the end of the period of twenty-eight days beginning with the day on which the notification was served; or

(b)    before the end of the period of seven days beginning with the day on which that person is informed of the time.

(4)    A person who has been informed of a place and time for the purposes of sub-paragraph (2) above or his representative may, at that place and time—

(a)    make oral representations to the appointed person for the purpose of establishing that the goods to which the proposed notice relates are safe; and

(b)    call and examine witnesses in connection with the representations.

8.—(1)    Where a person is appointed to consider representations about a proposed notice to warn, it shall be his duty to consider—

(a)    any written representations made by the person on whom it is proposed to serve the notice; and

(b)    in a case where a place and a time has been appointed under paragraph 7(2) above for oral representations to be made by that person or his representative, any representations so made and any statements made by witnesses in connection with those representations,

and, after considering those matters, to make a report (including recommendations) to the Secretary of State about the matters considered by him and the proposal to serve the notice.

(2)    It shall be the duty of the Secretary of State to consider any report made to him under sub-paragraph (1) above and, after considering the report, to inform the person on whom it was proposed that a notice to warn should be served of his decision with respect to the proposal.

(3)    If at any time after serving a notification on a person under paragraph 6 above the Secretary of State decides not to serve on that person either the proposed notice to warn or that notice with modifications, the Secretary of State shall inform that person of the decision; and nothing done for the purposes of any of the preceding provisions of this Part of this Schedule before that person was so informed shall—

(a)    entitle the Secretary of State subsequently to serve the proposed notice or that notice with modifications; or

(b)    require the Secretary of State, or any person appointed to consider representations about the proposed notice, subsequently to do anything in respect of, or in consequence of, any such representations.

(4)    Where a notification containing a draft of a proposed notice to warn is served on a person in respect of any goods, a notice to warn served on him in consequence of a decision made under sub-paragraph (2) above shall either be in the form of the draft or shall be less onerous than the draft.

9.    The Secretary of State may revoke a notice to warn by serving on the person on whom the notice was served a notification stating that the notice is revoked.

## PART III
## GENERAL

10.—(1)    Where in a notification served on any person under this Schedule the Secretary of State has appointed a time for the making of oral representations or the examination of witnesses, he may, by giving that person such notification as the Secretary of State considers appropriate, change that time to a later time or appoint further times at which further representations may be made or the examination of witnesses may be continued; and paragraphs 2(4), 3(4) and 7(4) above shall have effect accordingly.

(2) For the purposes of this Schedule the Secretary of State may appoint a person (instead of the appointed person) to consider any representations or statements, if the person originally appointed, or last appointed under this sub-paragraph, to consider those representations or statements has died or appears to the Secretary of State to be otherwise unable to act.

11. In this Schedule—

"the appointed person" in relation to a prohibition notice or a proposal to serve a notice to warn, means the person for the time being appointed under this Schedule to consider representations about the notice or, as the case may be, about the proposed notice;

"notification" means a notification in writing;

"trader", in relation to a prohibition notice, means the person on whom the notice is or was served.

## THE MINORS' CONTRACTS ACT 1987
### (1987, c. 13)

### 2. Guarantees.

Where—

(a) a guarantee is given in respect of an obligation of a party to a contract made after the commencement of this Act, and

(b) the obligation is unenforceable against him (or he repudiates the contract) because he was a minor when the contract was made,

the guarantee shall not for that reason alone be unenforceable against the guarantor.

### 3. Restitution.

(1) Where—

(a) a person ("the plaintiff") has after the commencement of this Act entered into a contract with another ("the defendant"), and

(b) the contract is unenforceable against the defendant (or he repudiates it) because he was a minor when the contract was made,

the court may, if it is just and equitable to do so, require the defendant to transfer to the plaintiff any property acquired by the defendant under the contract, or any property representing it.

(2) Nothing in this section shall be taken to prejudice any other remedy available to the plaintiff.

## THE PILOTAGE ACT 1987
### (1987, c. 21)

### 16. Liability for ships under compulsory pilotage.

The fact that a ship is being navigated in an area and in circumstances in which pilotage is compulsory for it shall not affect any liability of the owner or master of the ship for any loss or damage caused by the ship or by the manner in which it is navigated.

### 22. Limitation of liability in respect of pilots.

(8) A competent harbour authority shall not be liable for any loss or damage caused by any act or omission of a pilot authorised by it under section 3 above by virtue only of that authorisation.

## THE CONSUMER ARBITRATION AGREEMENTS ACT 1988
### (1988, c. 21)

*England, Wales and Northern Ireland*

**1.    Arbitration agreements.**

(1)    Where a person (referred to in section 4 below as "the consumer") enters into a contract as a consumer, an agreement that future differences arising between parties to the contract are to be referred to arbitration cannot be enforced against him in respect of any cause of acting so arising to which this section applies except—

(a)    with his written consent signified after the differences in question have arisen; or

(b)    where he has submitted to arbitration in pursuance of the agreement, whether in respect of those or any other differences; or

(c)    where the court makes an order under section 4 below in respect of that cause of action.

(2)    This section applies to a cause of action—

(a)    if proceedings in respect of it would be within the jurisdiction of a county court; or

(b)    if it satisfies such other conditions as may be prescribed for the purposes of this paragraph in an order under section 5 below.

(3)    Neither section 4(1) of the Arbitration Act 1950 nor section 4 of the Arbitration Act (Northern Ireland) 1937 (which provide for the staying of court proceedings where an arbitration agreement is in force) shall apply to an arbitration agreement to the extent that it cannot be enforced by virtue of this section.

**2.    Exclusions.**

Section 1 above does not affect—

(a)    the enforcement of an arbitration agreement to which section 1 of the Arbitration Act 1975 applies, that is, an arbitration agreement other than a domestic arbitration agreement within the meaning of that section;

(b)    the resolution of differences arising under any contract so far as it is, by virtue of section 1(2) of, and Schedule 1 to, the Unfair Contract Terms Act 1977 ("the Act of 1977"), excluded from the operation of section 2, 3, 4 or 7 of that Act.

**3.    Contracting "as a consumer".**

(1)    For the purposes of section 1 above a person enters into a contract "as a consumer" if—

(a)    he neither makes the contract in the course of a business nor holds himself out as doing so; and

(b)    the other party makes the contract in the course of a business; and

(c)    in the case of a contract governed by the law of sale of goods or hire-purchase, or by section 7 of the Act of 1977, the goods passing under or in pursuance of the contract are of a type ordinarily supplied for private use or consumption;
but on a sale by auction or by competitive tender the buyer is not in any circumstances to be regarded as entering into the contract as a consumer.

(2)    In subsection (1) above—

"business" includes a profession and the activities of any government department, Northern Ireland Department or local or public authority; and

"goods" has the same meaning as in the Sale of Goods Act 1979.

(3)    It is for those claiming that a person entered into a contract otherwise than as a consumer to show that he did so.

**4. Power of courts to disapply section 1 where no detriment to consumer.**

(1) The High Court or a county court may, on an application made after the differences in question have arisen, order that a cause of action to which this section applies shall be treated as one to which section 1 above does not apply.

(2) Before making an order under this section the court must be satisfied that it is not detrimental to the interests of the consumer for the differences in question to be referred to arbitration in pursuance of the arbitration agreement instead of being determined by proceedings before a court.

(3) In determining for the purposes of subsection (2) above whether a reference to arbitration is or is not detrimental to the interests of the consumer, the court shall have regard to all factors appearing to be relevant, including, in particular, the availability of legal aid and the relative amount of any expense which may result to him—

(a) if the differences in question are referred to arbitration in pursuance of the arbitration agreement; and

(b) if they are determined by proceedings before a court.

(4) This section applies to a cause of action—

(a) if proceedings in respect of it would be within the jurisdiction of a county court and would not fall within the small claims limit; or

(b) if it satisfies the conditions referred to in section 1(2)(b) above and the order under section 5 below prescribing the conditions in question provides for this section to apply to causes of action which satisfy them.

(5) For the purposes of subsection (4)(a) above proceedings "fall within the small claims limit"—

(a) in England and Wales, if in a county court they would stand referred to arbitration (without any order of the court) under rules made by virtue of section 64(1)(a) of the County Courts Act 1984;

(6) Where the consumer submits to arbitration in consequence of an order under this section, he shall not be regarded for the purposes of section 1(1)(b) above as submitting to arbitration in pursuance of the agreement there mentioned.

**5. Orders adding to the causes of action to which section 1 applies.**

(1) Orders under this section may prescribe the conditions referred to in section 1(2)(b) above; and any such order may provide that section 4 above shall apply to a cause of action which satisfies the conditions so prescribed.

(2) Orders under this section may make different provision for different cases and for different purposes.

(3) The power to make orders under this section for England and Wales shall be exercisable by statutory instrument made by the Secretary of State with the concurrence of the Lord Chancellor; but no such order shall be made unless a draft of it has been laid before, and approved by resolution of, each House of Parliament.

*Supplementary*

**9. Short title, commencement, interpretation and extent.**

(3) In this Act "the Act of 1977" means the Unfair Contract Terms Act 1977.

## THE CRIMINAL JUSTICE ACT 1988
### (1988, c. 33)

### PART VI
### CONFISCATION OF THE PROCEEDS OF AN OFFENCE

**71. Confiscation orders.**

(1) The Crown Court and a magistrates' court shall each have power, in addition to dealing with an offender in any other way, to make an order under this section requiring him to pay such sum as the court thinks fit.

(2)    The Crown Court may make such an order against an offender where—
    (a)    he is found guilty of any offence to which this Part of this Act applies; and
    (b)    it is satisfied—
        (i)        that he has benefited from that offence or from that offence taken together with some other offence of which he is convicted in the same proceedings, or which the court takes into consideration in determining his sentence, and which is not a drug trafficking offence; and
        (ii)       that his benefit is at least the minimum amount.

(4)    For the purposes of this Part of this Act a person benefits from an offence if he obtains property as a result of or in connection with its commission and his benefit is the value of the property so obtained.

(5)    Where a person derives a pecuniary advantage as a result of or in connection with the commission of an offence, he is to be treated for the purposes of this Part of this Act as if he had obtained as a result of or in connection with the commission of the offence a sum of money equal to the value of the pecuniary advantage.

(6)    The sum which an order made by a court under this section requires an offender to pay must be at least the minimum amount, but must not exceed—
    (a)    the benefit in respect of which it is made; or
    (b)    the amount appearing to the court to be the amount that might be realised at the time the order is made,
whichever is the less.

(7)    For the purposes of this Part of this Act the minimum amount is £10,000 or such other amount as the Secretary of State may specify by order made by statutory instrument.

## 72.    Making of confiscation orders.

(3)    When considering whether to make a confiscation order the court may take into account any information that has been placed before it showing that a victim of an offence to which the proceedings relate has instituted, or intends to institute, civil proceedings against the defendant in respect of loss, injury or damage sustained in connection with the offence.

(5)    Where a court makes a confiscation order against a defendant in any proceedings, it shall be its duty, in respect of any offence of which he is convicted in those proceedings, to take account of the order before—
    (a)    imposing any fine on him;
    (b)    making any order involving any payment by him, other than an order under section 35 of the Powers of Criminal Courts Act 1973 (compensation orders); or
    (c)    making any order under—
        (i)        section 27 of the Misuse of Drugs Act 1971 (forfeiture orders); or
        (ii)       section 43 of the Powers of Criminal Courts Act 1973 (deprivation orders),
but subject to that shall leave the order out of account in determining the appropriate sentence or other manner of dealing with him.

(7)    Where—
    (a)    a court makes both a confiscation order and an order for the payment of compensation under section 35 of the Powers of Criminal Courts Act 1973 against the same person in the same proceedings; and
    (b)    it appears to the court that he will not have sufficient means to satisfy both the orders in full,
it shall direct that so much of the compensation as will not in its opinion be recoverable because of the insufficiency of his means shall be paid out of any sums recovered under the confiscation order.

## 98.    Disclosure of information subject to contractual restriction upon disclosure.

(1)    Where a person discloses to a constable—

(a)    a suspicion or belief that any property—
    (i)        has been obtained as a result of or in connection with the commission or an offence to which this Part of this Act applies; or
    (ii)       derives from property so obtained; or
(b)    any matter on which such a suspicion or belief is based,
the disclosure shall not be treated as a breach of any restriction upon the disclosure of information imposed by contract.

PART VII

**108.    The Criminal Injuries Compensation Board and the administration of the scheme.**
(1)    The Criminal Injuries Compensation Board ("the Board") shall by that name be a body corporate.
(2)    The Board shall administer the scheme for the payment of compensation for criminal injuries established by the following provisions of this Part of this Act (in this Act referred to as "the scheme") and shall be responsible for determining claims for compensation under the scheme and for paying compensation due under it.

**109.    Criminal injuries.**
(1)    In this Part of this Act "criminal injury" means any personal injury caused by—
(a)    conduct constituting—
    (i)        an offence which is specified in subsection (3) below; or
    (ii)       an offence which is not so specified but which requires proof of intent to cause death or personal injury or recklessness as to whether death or personal injury is caused; or
(b)    any of the following activities—
    (i)        the apprehension or attempted apprehension of an offender or suspected offender;
    (ii)       the prevention or attempted prevention of the commission of an offence; or
    (iii)      assisting a constable engaged in any of the activities mentioned in sub-paragraph (i) or (ii) above;
and "personal injury" includes any disease, any harm to a person's physical or mental condition and pregnancy.
(2)    Harm to a person's mental condition is only a criminal injury if it is attributable—
(a)    to his having been put in fear of immediate physical injury to himself or another; or
(b)    to his being present when another sustained a criminal injury other than harm to his mental condition.
(3)    The offences mentioned in subsection (1)(a)(i) above are—
(a)    rape;
(b)    assault;
(c)    an offence which falls to be charged as arson;
(d)    wilful fireraising;
(e)    any offence under section 2 (causing explosion likely to endanger life or property) or 3 (attempt to cause explosion, or making or keeping explosive with intent to endanger life or property) of the Explosive Substances Act 1883;
(f)    an offence under section 16 (possession of firearm with intent to injure), 17 (use of firearm to resist arrest), 18 (carrying firearm with criminal intent), 19 (carrying firearm in a public place) or 20 (trespassing with firearm) of the Firearms Act 1968;
(g)    an offence under section 1 (riot), 2 (violent disorder) or 3 (affray) of the Public Order Act 1986;
(h)    mobbing;
(j)    kidnapping;

    (k)    false imprisonment;
    (l)    abduction;
    (m)   trespass on a railway; and
    (n)   any attempt to commit an offence mentioned in this subsection.
   (4)   For the purposes of this Part of this Act, a person's conduct shall be treated as constituting an offence notwithstanding that he may not be convicted of the offence by reason of age, insanity or diplomatic immunity.

## 110.   Qualifying injuries.

   (1)   Compensation for a criminal injury shall only be payable under this Part of this Act if the injury is a qualifying injury. . .

## 111.   Awards of compensation.

   (1)   An award of compensation may be made—
    (a)   to any person who satisfies the Board that he has sustained a qualifying injury;
    (b)   to any person who satisfies the Board that he is a dependant of a person who died after sustaining a qualifying injury (whether or not he died as a result of it);
and in this subsection "satisfies" means satisfies on a balance of probabilities.
   (2)   The heads of compensation are those specified in subsections (3) to (6) below.
   (3)   An award may be made under subsection (1)(a) above—
    (a)   for the injury; and
    (b)   for any loss of or damage to property of the claimant which occurred in the course of his sustaining the injury,
but compensation shall only be payable under paragraph (b) above if he relied on the property as a physical aid and for damage only if the damage impaired the utility of the property as a physical aid and shall only be for the cost of replacing it with other property of equal utility as a physical aid or carrying out repairs to restore its utility as a physical aid.
   (4)   If a person dies as a result of a qualifying injury—
    (a)   an award of compensation for funeral expenses may be made to any person other than a public authority but shall not exceed a reasonable amount;
    (b)   where a claim falls to be determined in accordance with the rules of the law of England and Wales, an award of compensation for bereavement may be made to any person falling within section 1A(2) of the Fatal Accidents Act 1976;
    (d)   an award may be made to a dependant of the deceased (whether or not an award is made to him or to any other person under paragraph (a), (b) or (c) above) in respect of any loss of support suffered by the dependant.
   (5)   Subject to subsection (8) below, if a person who has sustained a qualifying injury dies otherwise than as a result of it, the Board may award compensation to a dependant of his in respect of any loss which he has suffered by reason—
    (a)   of any reduction in earnings (not being prospective earnings) by the deceased; and
    (b)   of any expenses and liabilities incurred by the deceased as a result of the injury.
   (6)   If—
    (a)   a woman is awarded compensation for rape; and
    (b)   she has given birth to a child conceived as a result of the rape; and
    (c)   at the time of the award she intends to keep the child, the Board shall award her the additional statutory sum in respect of each child so conceived that she then intends to keep.
   (7)   The Board may make an interim award, but without prejudice to their powers on a final determination.
   (8)   If a person who has sustained a qualifying injury dies otherwise than as a result of it, the Board may not award compensation to a dependant of his if before he died he became entitled, otherwise than on an interim award, to a payment of compensation in respect of it.

(9)   If—
(a)    a deceased person was entitled to payment of compensation for an injury; and
(b)    a claim for compensation for the same injury is made by one of his dependants,
any compensation awarded to the dependant shall be reduced by the amount of the
compensation to payment of which the deceased was entitled; and proportionate
reductions shall be made on awards to two or more dependants.

(10)   Where a person has been awarded compensation by the Board in respect of a
qualifying injury sustained by him, he may be awarded further compensation in respect of
the injury if the Board are satisfied—
(a)    that since the date of the previous award his medical condition has
deteriorated as a result of having sustained the injury; and
(b)    that the extent to which his condition has so deteriorated is such that it would
be unjust not to make an award of further compensation to him in respect of the injury.

(11)   In this Part of this Act—
"the additional statutory sum" means £5,000 or such other sum as may for the time
being be specified by virtue of an order under subsection (12) below; and
"dependant"—
(a)    where the appropriate law for the determination of a claim is the law of
England and Wales, has the same meaning as in the Fatal Accidents Act 1976;

(12)   The Secretary of State may by order made by statutory instrument substitute a
different sum for the sum specified in subsection (11) above.

## 115   Reimbursement and recovery.
(1)   Where—
(a)    a person has been convicted in England or Wales of an offence; and
(b)    the Board have made an award of compensation in respect of an injury which is
a criminal injury by virtue of the offence,
proceedings may be brought by the Board in a county court for an order for the repayment
by the offender to the Board of the whole of the award or such part of it as the court thinks
fit.

(2)   The Board shall only make an application for an order under subsection (1) above
if they have reason to believe that the offender is able to pay the whole or a substantial part
of the award.

(3)   In considering whether to make an order under subsection (1) above, the court
shall have regard to the financial position of the offender and to such other matters (not
including the question whether he was properly convicted) as the court considers relevant.

(4)   Where after an award of compensation under this Part of this Act has been made
to a person he receives any payment which, had he received it before the making of the
award, would, under any provision contained in Schedule 7 to this Act, have led to any
reduction in the amount of compensation payable to him he shall be liable to repay to the
Board a sum equal to the amount of that reduction.

(5)   The Board may set-off any sum owed to them by any person by virtue of
subsection (4) above against any compensation under this Part of this Act to which that
person is or becomes entitled.

(6)   Where by virtue of any order under section 35 of the Powers of Criminal Courts
Act 1973 (compensation orders against convicted persons) compensation is required to be
paid for any personal injury, loss or damage which the Board are satisfied has been the
subject of compensation under this Part of this Act, they may by notice require the
magistrates' court for the time being having functions in relation to the enforcement of that
order to pay to them any amount recovered in pursuance of that order in respect of any such
personal injury, loss or damage.

PART XI

### 133.   Compensation for miscarriages of justice.

(1)   Subject to subsection (2) below, when a person has been convicted of a criminal offence and when subsequently his conviction has been reversed or he has been pardoned on the ground that a new or newly discovered fact shows beyond reasonable doubt that there has been a miscarriage of justice, the Secretary of State shall pay compensation for the miscarriage of justice to the person who has suffered punishment as a result of such conviction or, if he is dead, to his personal representatives, unless the non-disclosure of the unknown fact was wholly or partly attributable to the person convicted.

### 134.   Torture.

(1)   A public official or person acting in an official capacity, whatever his nationality, commits the offence of torture if in the United Kingdom or elsewhere he intentionally inflicts severe pain or suffering on another in the performance or purported performance of his official duties.

(2)   A person not falling within subsection (1) above commits the offence of torture, whatever his nationality, if—

(a)   in the United Kingdom or elsewhere he intentionally inflicts severe pain or suffering on another at the instigation or with the consent or acquiescence—

(i)   of a public official; or

(ii)   of a person acting in an official capacity; and

(b)   the official or other person is performing or purporting to perform his official duties when he instigates the commission of the offence or consents to or acquiesces in it.

(3)   It is immaterial whether the pain or suffering is physical or mental and whether it is caused by an act or an omission.

(4)   It shall be a defence for a person charged with an offence under this section in respect of any conduct of his to prove that he had lawful authority, justification or excuse for that conduct.

### THE HOUSING ACT 1988
### (1988, c. 50)

### 16.   Access for repairs.

It shall be an implied term of every assured tenancy that the tenant shall afford to the landlord access to the dwelling-house let on the tenancy and all reasonable facilities for executing therein any repairs which the landlord is entitled to execute.

### 27.   Damages for unlawful eviction.

(1)   This section applies if, at any time after 9th June 1988, a landlord (in this section referred to as "the landlord in default") or any person acting on behalf of the landlord in default unlawfully deprives the residential occupier of any premises of his occupation of the whole or part of the premises.

(2)   This section also applies if, at any time after 9th June 1988, a landlord (in this section referred to as "the landlord in default") or any person acting on behalf of the landlord in default—

(a)   attempts unlawfully to deprive the residential occupier of any premises of his occupation of the whole or part of the premises, or

(b)   knowing or having reasonable cause to believe that the conduct is likely to cause the residential occupier of any premises—

(i)   to give up his occupation of the premises or any part thereof, or

(ii)   to refrain from exercising any right or pursuing any remedy in respect of the premises or any part thereof, does acts likely to interfere with the peace or comfort of the residential occupier or members of his household, or persistently withdraws or withholds services reasonably required for the occupation of the premises as a residence,

and, as a result, the residential occupier gives up his occupation of the premises as a residence.

(3) Subject to the following provisions of this section, where this section applies, the landlord in default shall, by virtue of this section, be liable to pay to the former residential occupier, in respect of his loss of the right to occupy the premises in question as his residence, damages assessed on the basis set out in section 28 below.

(4) Any liability arising by virtue of subsection (3) above—

(a) shall be in the nature of a liability in tort; and

(b) subject to subsection (5) below, shall be in addition to any liability arising apart from this section (whether in tort, contract or otherwise).

(5) Nothing in this section affects the right of a residential occupier to enforce any liability which arises apart from this section in respect of his loss of the right to occupy premises as his residence; but damages shall not be awarded both in respect of such a liability and in respect of a liability arising by virtue of this section on account of the same loss.

(6) No liability shall arise by virtue of subsection (3) above if—

(a) before the date on which proceedings to enforce the liability are finally disposed of, the former residential occupier is reinstated in the premises in question in such circumstances that he becomes again the residential occupier of them; or

(b) at the request of the former residential occupier, a court makes an order (whether in the nature of an injunction or otherwise) as a result of which he is reinstated as mentioned in paragraph (a) above;

and, for the purposes of paragraph (a) above, proceedings to enforce a liability are finally disposed of on the earliest date by which the proceedings (including any proceedings on or in consequence of an appeal) have been determined and any time for appealing or further appealing has expired, except that if any appeal is abandoned, the proceedings shall be taken to be disposed of on the date of the abandonment.

(7) If, in proceedings to enforce a liability arising by virtue of subsection (3) above, it appears to the court—

(a) that, prior to the event which gave rise to the liability, the conduct of the former residential occupier or any person living with him in the premises concerned was such that it is reasonable to mitigate the damages for which the landlord in default would otherwise be liable, or

(b) that, before the proceedings were begun, the landlord in default offered to reinstate the former residential occupier in the premises in question and either it was unreasonable of the former residential occupier to refuse that offer or, if he had obtained alternative accommodation before the offer was made, it would have been unreasonable of him to refuse that offer if he had not obtained that accommodation,

the court may reduce the amount of damages which would otherwise be payable to such amount as it thinks appropriate.

(8) In proceedings to enforce a liability arising by virtue of subsection (3) above, it shall be a defence for the defendant to prove that he believed, and had reasonable cause to believe—

(a) that the residential occupier had ceased to reside in the premises in question at the time when he was deprived of occupation as mentioned in subsection (1) above or, as the case may be, when the attempt was made or the acts were done as a result of which he gave up his occupation of those premises; or

(b) that, where the liability would otherwise arise by virtue only of the doing of acts or the withdrawal or withholding of services, he had reasonable grounds for doing the acts or withdrawing or withholding the services in question.

**28.    The measure of damages.**

(1)    The basis for the assessment of damages referred to in section 27(3) above is the difference in value, determined as at the time immediately before the residential occupier ceased to occupy the premises in question as his residence, between—

(a)    the value of the interest of the landlord in default determined on the assumption that the residential occupier continues to have the same right to occupy the premises as before that time; and

(b)    the value of that interest determined on the assumption that the residential occupier has ceased to have that right.

(2)    In relation to any premises, any reference in this section to the interest of the landlord in default is a reference to his interest in the building in which the premises in question are comprised (whether or not that building contains any other premises) together with its curtilage.

(3)    For the purposes of the valuations referred to in subsection (1) above, it shall be assumed—

(a)    that the landlord in default is selling his interest on the open market to a willing buyer;

(b)    that neither the residential occupier nor any member of his family wishes to buy; and

(c)    that it is unlawful to carry out any substantial development of any of the land in which the landlord's interest subsists or to demolish the whole or part of any building on that land.

## THE LANDLORD AND TENANT ACT 1988
### (1988, c. 26)

**1.    Qualified duty to consent to assigning, underletting etc. of premises.**

(1)    This section applies in any case where—

(a)    a tenancy includes a covenant on the part of the tenant not to enter into one or more of the following transactions, that is—

(i)        assigning,

(ii)       underletting,

(iii)      charging, or

(iv)      parting with the possession of,

the premises comprised in the tenancy or any part of the premises without the consent of the landlord or some other person, but

(b)    the covenant is subject to the qualification that the consent is not to be unreasonably withheld (whether or not it is also subject to any other qualification).

(2)    In this section and section 2 of this Act—

(a)    references to a proposed transaction are to any assignment, underletting, charging or parting with possession to which the covenant relates, and

(b)    references to the person who may consent to such a transaction are to the person who under the covenant may consent to the tenant entering into the proposed transaction.

(3)    Where there is served on the person who may consent to a proposed transaction a written application by the tenant for consent to the transaction, he owes a duty to the tenant within a reasonable time—

(a)    to give consent, except in a case where it is reasonable not to give consent,

(b)    to serve on the tenant written notice of his decision whether or not to give consent specifying in addition—

(i)        if the consent is given subject to conditions, the conditions,

(ii)       if the consent is withheld, the reasons for withholding it.

(4)    Giving consent subject to any condition that is not a reasonable condition does not satisfy the duty under subsection (3)(a) above.

**4.    Breach of duty.**
A claim that a person has broken any duty under this Act may be made the subject of civil proceedings in like manner as any other claim in tort for breach of statutory duty.

**6.    Application to Crown.**
This Act binds the Crown; but as regards the Crown's liability in tort shall not bind the Crown further than the Crown is made liable in tort by the Crown Proceedings Act 1947.

## THE MALICIOUS COMMUNICATIONS ACT 1988
### (1988, c. 27)

**1.    Offence of sending letters etc. with intent to cause distress or anxiety.**
  (1)    Any person who sends to another person—
      (a)    a letter or other article which conveys—
            (i)        a message which is indecent or grossly offensive;
            (ii)       a threat; or
            (iii)      information which is false and known or believed to be false by the
sender; or
      (b)    any other article which is, in whole or part, of an indecent or grossly offensive
nature,
is guilty of an offence if his purpose, or one of his purposes, in sending it is that it should, so far as falling within paragraph (a) or (b) above, cause distress or anxiety to the recipient or to any other person to whom he intends that it or its contents or nature should be communicated.
  (2)    A person is not guilty of an offence by virtue of subsection (1)(a)(ii) above if he shows—
      (a)    that the threat was used to reinforce a demand which he believed he had reasonable grounds for making; and
      (b)    that he believed that the use of the threat was a proper means of reinforcing the demand.
  (3)    In this section references to sending include references to delivering and to causing to be sent or delivered and "sender" shall be construed accordingly.
  (4)    A person guilty of an offence under this section shall be liable on summary conviction to a fine not exceeding level 4 on the standard scale.

## THE ROAD TRAFFIC ACT 1988
### (1988, c. 52)

**16.    Wearing of protective headgear.**
  (1)    The Secretary of State may make regulations requiring, subject to such exceptions as may be specified in the regulations, persons driving or riding (otherwise than in side-cars) on motor cycles of any class specified in the regulations to wear protective headgear of such description as may be so specified.
  (2)    A requirement imposed by regulations under this section shall not apply to any follower of the Sikh religion while he is wearing a turban.
  (3)    Regulations under this section may make different provision in relation to different circumstances.
  (4)    A person who drives or rides on a motor cycle in contravention of regulations under this section is guilty of an offence. . .

**38.    The Highway Code.**
  (7)    A failure on the part of a person to observe a provision of the Highway Code shall not of itself render that person liable to criminal proceedings of any kind but any such failure may in any proceedings (whether civil or criminal, and including proceedings for an

offence under the Traffic Acts, the Public Passenger Vehicles Act 1981 or sections 18 to 23 of the Transport Act 1985) be relied upon by any party to the proceedings as tending to establish or negative any liability which is in question in those proceedings.

**143.    Users of motor vehicles to be insured or secured against third-party risks.**
(1)    Subject to the provisions of this Part of this Act—
(a)    a person must not use a motor vehicle on a road unless there is in force in relation to the use of the vehicle by that person such a policy of insurance or such a security in respect of third party risks as complies with the requirements of this Part of this Act, and
(b)    a person must not cause or permit any other person to use a motor vehicle on a road unless there is in force in relation to the use of the vehicle by that other person such a policy of insurance or such a security in respect of third party risks as complies with the requirements of this Part of this Act.
(2)    If a person acts in contravention of subsection (1) above he is guilty of an offence.
(3)    A person charged with using a motor vehicle in contravention of this section shall not be convicted if he proves—
(a)    that the vehicle did not belong to him and was not in his possession under a contract of hiring or of loan,
(b)    that he was using the vehicle in the course of his employment, and
(c)    that he neither knew nor had reason to believe that there was not in force in relation to the vehicle such a policy of insurance or security as is mentioned in subsection (1) above.
(4)    This Part of this Act does not apply to invalid carriages.

**144.    Exceptions from requirement of third-party insurance or security.**
(1)    Section 143 of this Act does not apply to a vehicle owned by a person who has deposited and keeps deposited with the Accountant General of the Supreme Court the sum of £15,000, at a time when the vehicle is being driven under the owner's control.
(2)    Section 143 does not apply—
(a)    to a vehicle owned—
(i)      by the council of a county or county district in England and Wales, the Common Council of the City of London, the council of a London borough, the Inner London Education Authority, or a joint authority (other than a police authority) established by Part IV of the Local Government Act 1985,
(ii)      by a regional, islands or district council in Scotland, or
(iii)      by a joint board or committee in England or Wales, or joint committee in Scotland, which is so constituted as to include among its members representatives of any such council,
at a time when the vehicle is being driven under the owner's control,
(b)    to a vehicle owned by a police authority or the Receiver for the Metropolitan Police district, at a time when it is being driven under the owner's control, or to a vehicle at a time when it is being driven for police purposes by or under the direction of a constable, or by a person employed by a police authority, or employed by the Receiver, or
(c)    to a vehicle at a time when it is being driven on a journey to or from any place undertaken for salvage purposes pursuant to Part IX of the Merchant Shipping Act 1894,
(d)    to the use of a vehicle for the purpose of its being provided in pursuance of a direction under section 166(2)(b) of the Army Act 1955 or under the corresponding provision of the Air Force Act 1955,
(e)    to a vehicle which is made available by the Secretary of State to any person, body or local authority in pursuance of section 23 or 26 of the National Health Service Act 1977 at a time when it is being used in accordance with the terms on which it is so made available.

**145.    Requirements in respect of policies of insurance.**

(1)    In order to comply with the requirements of this Part of this Act, a policy of insurance must satisfy the following conditions.

(2)    The policy must be issued by an authorised insurer.

(3)    Subject to subsection (4) below, the policy—

(a)    must insure such person, persons or classes of persons as may be specified in the policy in respect of any liability which may be incurred by him or them in respect of the death of or bodily injury to any person or damage to property caused by, or arising out of, the use of the vehicle on a road in Great Britain, and

(b)    must insure him or them in respect of any liability which may be incurred by him or them in respect of the use of the vehicle and of any trailer, whether or not coupled, in the territory other than Great Britain and Gibraltar of each of the member States of the Communities according to the law on compulsory insurance against civil liability in respect of the use of vehicles of the State where the liability may be incurred, and

(c)    must also insure him or them in respect of any liability which may be incurred by him or them under the provisions of this Part of this Act relating to payment for emergency treatment.

(4)    The policy shall not, by virtue of subsection (3)(a) above, be required—

(a)    to cover liability in respect of the death, arising out of and in the course of his employment, of a person in the employment of a person insured by the policy or of bodily injury sustained by such a person arising out of and in the course of his employment, or

(b)    to provide insurance of more than £250,000 in respect of all such liabilities as may be incurred in respect of damage to property caused by, or arising out of, any one accident involving the vehicle, or

(c)    to cover liability in respect of damage to the vehicle, or

(d)    to cover liability in respect of damage to goods carried for hire or reward in or on the vehicle or in or on any trailer (whether or not coupled) drawn by the vehicle, or

(e)    to cover any liability of a person in respect of damage to property in his custody or under his control, or

(f)    to cover any contractual liability.

**148.    Avoidance of certain exceptions to policies or securities.**

(1)    Where a certificate of insurance or certificate of security has been delivered under section 147 of this Act to the person by whom a policy has been effected or to whom a security has been given, so much of the policy or security as purports to restrict—

(a)    the insurance of the persons insured by the policy, or

(b)    the operation of the security,

(as the case may be) by reference to any of the matters mentioned in subsection (2) below shall, as respects such liabilities as are required to be covered by a policy under section 145 of this Act, be of no effect.

(2)    Those matters are—

(a)    the age or physical or mental condition of persons driving the vehicle,

(b)    the condition of the vehicle,

(c)    the number of persons that the vehicle carries,

(d)    the weight or physical characteristics of the goods that the vehicle carries,

(e)    the time at which or the areas within which the vehicle is used,

(f)    the horsepower or cylinder capacity or value of the vehicle,

(g)    the carrying on the vehicle of any particular apparatus, or

(h)    the carrying on the vehicle of any particular means of identification other than any means of identification required to be carried by or under the Vehicles (Excise) Act 1971.

(3)    Nothing in subsection (1) above requires an insurer or the giver of a security to pay any sum in respect of the liability of any person otherwise than in or towards the discharge of that liability.

(4)    Any sum paid by an insurer or the giver of a security in or towards the discharge of any liability of any person which is covered by the policy or security by virtue only of subsection (1) above is recoverable by the insurer or giver of the security from that person.

(5)    A condition in a policy or security issued or given for the purposes of this Part of this Act providing—

(a)    that no liability shall arise under the policy or security, or

(b)    that any liability so arising shall cease,

in the event of some specified thing being done or omitted to be done after the happening of the event giving rise to a claim under the policy or security, shall be of no effect in connection with such liabilities as are required to be covered by a policy under section 145 of this Act.

(6)    Nothing in subsection (5) above shall be taken to render void any provision in a policy or security requiring the person insured or secured to pay to the insurer or the giver of the security any sums which the latter may have become liable to pay under the policy or security and which have been applied to the satisfaction of the claims of third parties.

(7)    Notwithstanding anything in any enactment, a person issuing a policy of insurance under section 145 of this Act shall be liable to indemnify the persons or classes of persons specified in the policy in respect of any liability which the policy purports to cover in the case of those persons or classes of persons.

**149.    Avoidance of certain agreements as to liability towards passengers.**

(1)    This section applies where a person uses a motor vehicle in circumstances such that under section 143 of this Act there is required to be in force in relation to his use of it such a policy of insurance or such a security in respect of third-party risks as complies with the requirements of this Part of this Act.

(2)    If any other person is carried in or upon the vehicle when the user is so using it, any antecedent agreement or understanding between them (whether intended to be legally binding or not) shall be of no effect so far as it purports or might be held—

(a)    to negative or restrict any such liability of the user in respect of persons carried in or upon the vehicle as is required by section 145 of this Act to be covered by a policy of insurance, or

(b)    to impose any conditions with respect to the enforcement of any such liability of the user.

(3)    The fact that a person so carried has willingly accepted as his the risk of negligence on the part of the user shall not be treated as negativing any such liability of the user.

(4)    For the purposes of this section—

(a)    references to a person being carried in or upon a vehicle include references to a person entering or getting on to, or alighting from, the vehicle, and

(b)    the reference to an antecedent agreement is to one made at any time before the liability arose.

**151.    Duty of insurers of persons giving security to satisfy judgment against persons insured or secured against third-party risks.**

(1)    This section applies where, after a certificate of insurance or certificate of security has been delivered under section 147 of this Act to the person by whom a policy has been effected or to whom a security has been given, a judgment to which this subsection applies is obtained.

(2)    Subsection (1) above applies to judgments relating to a liability with respect to any matter where liability with respect to that matter is required to be covered by a policy of insurance under section 145 of this Act and either—

(a)    it is a liability covered by the terms of the policy or security to which the certificate relates, and the judgment is obtained against any person who is insured by the policy or whose liability is covered by the security, as the case may be, or

(b)    it is a liability, other than an excluded liability, which would be so covered if the policy insured all persons or, as the case may be, the security covered the liability of all persons, and the judgment is obtained against any person other than one who is insured by the policy or, as the case may be, whose liability is covered by the security.

(3)    In deciding for the purposes of subsection (2) above whether a liability is or would be covered by the terms of a policy or security, so much of the policy or security as purports to restrict, as the case may be, the insurance of the persons insured by the policy or the operation of the security by reference to the holding by the driver of the vehicle of a licence authorising him to drive it shall be treated as of no effect.

(4)    In subsection (2)(b) above "excluded liability" means a liability in respect of the death of, or bodily injury to, or damage to the property of any person who, at the time of the use which gave rise to the liability, was allowing himself to be carried in or upon the vehicle and knew or had reason to believe that the vehicle had been stolen or unlawfully taken, not being a person who—

(a)    did not know and had no reason to believe that the vehicle had been stolen or unlawfully taken until after the commencement of his journey, and

(b)    could not reasonably have been expected to have alighted from the vehicle.

In this subsection the reference to a person being carried in or upon a vehicle includes a reference to a person entering or getting on to, or alighting from, the vehicle.

(5)    Notwithstanding that the insurer may be entitled to avoid or cancel, or may have avoided or cancelled, the policy or security, he must, subject to the provisions of this section, pay to the persons entitled to the benefit of the judgment—

(a)    as regards liability in respect of death or bodily injury, any sum payable under the judgment in respect of the liability, together with any sum which, by virtue of any enactment relating to interest on judgments, is payable in respect of interest on that sum,

(b)    as regards liability in respect of damage to property, any sum required to be paid under subsection (6) below, and

(c)    any amount payable in respect of costs.

(6)    This subsection requires—

(a)    where the total of any amounts paid, payable or likely to be payable under the policy or security in respect of damage to property caused by, or arising out of, the accident in question does not exceed £250,000, the payment of any sum payable under the judgment in respect of the liability, together with any sum which, by virtue of any enactment relating to interest on judgments, is payable in repect of interest on that sum,

(b)    where that total exceeds £250,000, the payment of either—

(i)    such proportion of any sum payable under the judgment in respect of the liability as £250,000 bears to that total, together with the same proportion of any sum which, by virtue of any enactment relating to interest on judgments, is payable in respect of interest on that sum, or

(ii)    the difference between the total of any amounts already paid under the policy or security in respect of such damage and £250,000, together with such proportion of any sum which, by virtue of any enactment relating to interest on judgments, is payable in respect of interest on any sum payable under the judgment in respect of the liability as the difference bears to that sum,

whichever is the less, unless not less than £250,000 has already been paid under the policy or security in respect of such damage (in which case nothing is payable).

(7)    Where an insurer becomes liable under this section to pay an amount in respect of a liability of a person who is insured by a policy or whose liability is covered by a security, he is entitled to recover from that person—

(a)    that amount, in a case where he became liable to pay it by virtue only of subsection (3) above, or

(b)    in a case where that amount exceeds the amount for which he would, apart from the provisions of this section, be liable under the policy or security in respect of that liability, the excess.

(8)    Where an insurer becomes liable under this section to pay an amount in respect of a liability of a person who is not insured by a policy or whose liability is not covered by a security, he is entitled to recover the amount from that person or from any person who—

(a)    is insured by the policy, or whose liability is covered by the security, by the terms of which the liability would be covered if the policy insured all persons or, as the case may be, the security covered the liability of all persons, and

(b)    caused or permitted the use of the vehicle which gave rise to the liability.

(9)    In this section—

(a)    "insurer" includes a person giving a security,

(b)    "material" means of such a nature as to influence the judgment of a prudent insurer in determining whether he will take the risk and, if so, at what premium and on what conditions, and

(c)    "liability covered by the terms of the policy or security" means a liability which is covered by the policy or security or which would be so covered but for the fact that the insurer is entitled to avoid or cancel, or has avoided or cancelled, the policy or security.

**153.    Bankruptcy, etc., of insured or secured persons not to affect claims by third parties.**

(1)    Where, after a certificte of insurance or certificate of security has been delivered under section 147 of this Act to the person by whom a policy has been effected or to whom a security as been given, any of the events mentioned in subsection (2) below happens, the happening of that event shall, notwithstanding anything in the Third Parties (Rights Against Insurers) Act 1930, not affect any such liability of that person as is required to be covered by a policy of insurance under section 145 of this Act.

(2)    In the case of the person by whom the policy was effected or to whom the security was given, the events referred to in subsection (1) above are—

(a)    that he becomes bankrupt or makes a composition or arrangement with his creditors or that his estate is sequestrated or he grants a trust deed for his creditors,

(b)    that he dies and—

(i)    his estate falls to be administered in accordance with an order under section 421 of the Insolvency Act 1986,

(ii)    an award of sequestration of his estate is made, or

(iii)    a judicial factor is appointed to administer his estate under section 11A of the Judicial Factors (Scotland) Act 1889,

(c)    that if that person is a company—

(i)    a winding-up order or an administration order is made with respect of the company,

(ii)    a resolution for a voluntary winding-up is passed with respect to the company,

(iii)    a receiver or manager of the company's business or undertaking is duly appointed, or

(iv)    possession is taken, by or on behalf of the holders of any debentures secured by a floating charge, of any property comprised in or subject to the charge.

(3)    Nothing in subsection (1) above affects any rights conferred by the Third Parties (Rights Against Insurers) Act 1930 on the person to whom the liability was incurred, being rights so conferred against the person by whom the policy was issued or the security was given.

**157.    Payment for hospital treatment of traffic casualties.**

(1)    Subject to subsection (2) below, where—

(a)    a payment, other than a payment under section 158 of this Act, is made (whether or not with an admission of liability) in respect of the death of, or bodily injury to, any person arising out of the use of a motor vehicle on a road or in a place to which the public have a right of access, and

(b)    the payment is made—

(i)    by an authorised insurer, the payment being made under or in consequence of a policy issued under section 145 of this Act, or

(ii)    by the owner of a vehicle in relation to the use of which a security under this Part of this Act is in force, or

(iii)    by the owner of a vehicle who has made a deposit under this Part of this Act, and

(c)    the person who has so died or been bodily injured has to the knowledge of the insurer or owner, as the case may be, received treatment at a hospital, whether as an in-patient or as an out-patient, in respect of the injury so arising,

the insurer or owner must pay the expenses reasonably incurred by the hospital in affording the treatment, after deducting from the expenses any moneys actually received in payment of a specific charge for the treatment, not being moneys received under any contributory scheme.

(2)    The amount to be paid shall not exceed £2,000.37 for each person treated as an in-patient or £200.04 for each person treated as an out-patient.

(3)    For the purposes of this section "expenses reasonably incurred" means—

(a)    in relation to a person who receives treatment at a hospital as an in-patient, an amount for each day he is maintained in the hospital representing the average daily cost, for each in-patient, of the maintenance of the hospital and the staff of the hospital and the maintenance and treatment of the in-patients in the hospital, and

(b)    in relation to a person who receives treatment at a hospital as an out-patient, reasonable expenses actually incurred.

### 158.    Payment for emergency treatment of traffic casualties.

(1)    Subsection (2) below applies where—

(a)    medical or surgical treatment or examination is immediately required as a result of bodily injury (including fatal injury) to a person caused by, or arising out of, the use of a motor vehicle on a road, and

(b)    the treatment or examination so required (in this Part of this Act referred to as "emergency treatment") is effected by a legally qualified medical practitioner.

(2)    The person who was using the vehicle at the time of the event out of which the bodily injury arose must, on a claim being made in accordance with the provisions of section 159 of this Act, pay to the practitioner (or, where emergency treatment is effected by more than one practitioner, to the practitioner by whom it is first effected)—

(a)    a fee of £15.00 in respect of each person in whose case the emergency treatment is effected by him, and

(b)    a sum, in respect of any distance in excess of two miles which he must cover in order—

(i)    to proceed from the place from which he is summoned to the place where the emergency treatment is carried out by him, and

(ii)    to return to the first mentioned place,

equal to 29 pence for every complete mile and additional part of a mile of that distance.

(3)    Where emergency treatment is first effected in a hospital, the provisions of subsections (1) and (2) above with respect to payment of a fee shall, so far as applicable, but subject (as regards the recipient of a payment) to the provisions of section 159 of this Act, have effect with the substitution of references to the hospital for references to a legally qualified medical practitioner.

(4)    Liability incurred under this section by the person using a vehicle shall, where the event out of which it arose was caused by the wrongful act of another person, be treated for the purposes of any claim to recover damage by reason of that wrongful act as damage sustained by the person using the vehicle.

**159.    Supplementary provisions as to payments for treatment.**

(2)    A claim for a payment under section 158 of this Act may be made at the time when the emergency treatment is effected, by oral request to the person who was using the vehicle, and if not so made must be made by request in writing served on him within seven days from the day on which the emergency treatment was effected.

(4)    A payment made under section 158 of this Act shall operate as a discharge, to the extent of the amount paid, of any liability of the person who was using the vehicle, or of any other person, to pay any sum in respect of the expenses of remuneration of the practitioner or hospital concerned of or for effecting the emergency treatment.

## THE ROAD TRAFFIC (CONSEQUENTIAL PROVISIONS) ACT 1988
### (1988, c. 54)

**7.    Saving for law of nuisance.**

Nothing in the Road Traffic Acts authorises a person to use on a road a vehicle so constructed or used as to cause a public or private nuisance . . . or affects the liability, whether under statute or common law, of the driver or owner so using a vehicle.

## THE EMPLOYERS' LIABILITY (COMPULSORY INSURANCE) GENERAL REGULATIONS 1971
### (SI 1971, No. 1117)

*[Made under the Employers' Liability (Compulsory Insurance) Act 1969, ss. 1(2), (3)(a), 2(2), 4(1), (2) and 6.]*

**2.    Prohibition of certain conditions in policies of insurance.**

(1)    Any condition in a policy of insurance issued or renewed in accordance with the requirements of the Act after the coming into operation of this Regulation which provides (in whatever terms) that no liability (either generally or in respect of a particular claim) shall arise under the policy, or that any such liability so arising shall cease—

(a)    in the event of some specified thing being done or omitted to be done after the happening of the event giving rise to a claim under the policy;

(b)    unless the policy holder takes reasonable care to protect his employees risk of bodily injury or disease in the course of their employment;

(c)    unless the policy holder complies with the requirements of any enactment for the protection of employees against the risk of bodily injury or disease in the course of their employment; and

(d)    unless the policy holder keeps specified records or provides the insurer with or makes available to him information therefrom,

is hereby prohibited for the purposes of the Act.

(2)    Nothing in this Regulation shall be taken as prejudicing any provision in a policy requiring the policy holder to pay to the insurer any sums which the latter may have become liable to pay under the policy and which have been applied to the satisfaction of claims in respect of employees or any costs and expenses incurred in relation to such claims.

**3.    Limit of amount of compulsory insurance.**

The amount for which an employer is required by the Act to insure and maintain insurance shall be two million pounds in respect of claims relating to any one or more of his employees arising out of any one occurrence.

## THE CONSUMER TRANSACTIONS (RESTRICTIONS ON STATEMENTS) ORDER 1976
### (SI 1976, No. 1813)
*[As amended by the Consumer Transactions (Restrictions on Statements) (Amendment) Order 1978: SI 1978, No. 127.]*

**3.**    A person shall not, in the course of a business—

(a)    display, at any place where consumer transactions are effected (whether wholly or partly), a notice containing a statement which purports to apply, in relation to consumer transactions effected there, a term which would—

[(i)    be void by virtue of section 6 or 20 of the Unfair Contract Terms Act 1977]

(ii)    be inconsistent with a warranty . . . implied by section 4(1)(c) of the Trading Stamps Act 1964 . . . as amended by the Act of 1973,
if applied to some or all such consumer transactions;

(b)    publish or cause to be published any advertisement which is intended to induce persons to enter into consumer transactions and which contains a statement purporting to apply in relation to such consumer transactions such a term as is mentioned in paragraph (a)(i) or (ii), being a term which would be void by virtue of, or as the case may be, inconsistent with, the provisions so mentioned if applied to some or all of those transactions;

(c)    supply to a consumer pursuant to a consumer transaction goods bearing, or goods in a container bearing, a statement which is a term of that consumer transaction and which is void by virtue of, or inconsistent with, the said provisions, or if it were a term of that transaction, would be so void or inconsistent;

(d)    furnish to a consumer in connection with the carrying out of a consumer transaction or to a person likely, as a consumer, to enter into such a transaction, a document which includes a statement which is a term of that transaction and is void or inconsistent as aforesaid, or, if it were a term of that transaction or were to become a term of a prospective transaction, would be so void or inconsistent.

**4.**    A person shall not in the course of a business—

(i)    supply to a consumer pursuant to a consumer transaction goods bearing, or goods in a container bearing, a statement about the rights that the consumer has against that person or about the obligations to the consumer accepted by that person in relation to the goods (whether legally enforceable or not), being rights or obligations that arise if the goods are defective or are not fit for a purpose or do not correspond with a description;

(ii)    furnish to a consumer in connection with the carrying out of a consumer transaction or to a person likely, as a consumer, to enter into such a transaction with him or through his agency a document containing a statement about such rights and obligations, unless there is in close proximity to any such statement another statement which is clear and conspicuous and to the effect that the first mentioned statement does not or will not affect the statutory rights of a consumer.

**5.**—(1)    This Article applies to goods which are supplied in the course of a business by one person ("the supplier") to another where, at the time of the supply, the goods were intended by the supplier to be, or might reasonably be expected by him to be, the subject of a subsequent consumer transaction.

(2)    A supplier shall not—

(a)    supply goods to which this Article applies if the goods bear, or are in a container bearing, a statement which sets all or describes or limits obligations (whether legally enforceable or not) accepted or to be accepted by him in relation to the goods, or

(b)    furnish a document in relation to the goods which contains such a statement, unless there is in close proximity to any such statement another statement which is clear and conspicuous and to the effect that the first mentioned statement does not or will not affect the statutory rights of a consumer.

(3)    A person does not contravene paragraph (2) above—

(i)    in a case to which sub-paragraph (a) of that paragraph applies, unless the goods have become the subject of a consumer transaction;

(ii)    in a case to which sub-paragraph (b) applies unless the document has been furnished to a consumer in relation to goods which were the subject of a consumer transaction, or to a person likely to become a consumer pursuant to such a transaction; or

(iii)    by virtue of any statement if before the date on which this Article comes into operation the document containing, or the goods or container bearing, the statement has ceased to be in his possession.

## THE TRANSFER OF UNDERTAKINGS (PROTECTION OF EMPLOYMENT) REGULATIONS 1981
### (SI 1981, No. 1794)
*[Made under the European Communities Act 1972, s. 2(2).]*

**5.    Effect of relevant transfer on contracts of employment, etc.**

(1)    A relevant transfer shall not operate so as to terminate the contract of employment of any person employed by the transferor in the undertaking or part transferred but any such contract which would otherwise have been terminated by the transfer shall have effect after the transfer as if originally made between the person so employed and the transferee.

## TREATY
### establishing
## THE EUROPEAN ECONOMIC COMMUNITY
### (Rome, 25 March 1957)

**Art. 85.**    1.    The following shall be prohibited as incompatible with the common market: all agreements between undertakings, decisions by associations of undertakings and concerted practices which may affect trade between Member States and which have as their object or effect the prevention, restriction or distortion of competition within the common market, and in particular those which:

(a)    directly or indirectly fix purchase or selling prices or any other trading conditions;

(b)    limit or control production, markets, technical development, or investment;

(c)    share markets or sources of supply;

(d)    apply dissimilar conditions to equivalent transactions with other trading parties, thereby placing them at a competitive disadvantage;

(e)    make the conclusion of contracts subject to acceptance by the other parties of supplementary obligations which, by their nature or according to commercial usage, have no connection with the subject of such contracts.

2.    Any agreements or decisions prohibited pursuant to this Article shall be automatically void.

3.    The provisions of paragraph 1 may, however, be declared inapplicable in the case of:

—any agreement or category of agreements between undertakings;

—any decision or category of decisions by associations of undertakings;

—any concerted practice or category of concerted practices;

which contributes to improving the production or distribution of goods or to promoting technical or economic progress, while allowing consumers a fair share of the resulting benefit, and which does not:

(a)    impose on the undertakings concerned restrictions which are not indispensable to the attainment of these objectives;

(b)    afford such undertakings the possibility of eliminating competition in respect of a substantial part of the products in question.

**Art. 86.**    Any abuse by one or more undertakings of a dominant position within the common market or in a substantial part of it shall be prohibited as incompatible with the common market in so far as it may affect trade between Member States. Such abuse may, in particular, consist in:

(a)    directly or indirectly imposing unfair purchase or selling prices or other unfair trading conditions;

(b)    limiting production, markets or technical development to the prejudice of consumers;

(c)    applying dissimilar conditions to equivalent transactions with other trading parties, thereby placing them at a competitive disadvantage;

(d)    making the conclusion of contracts subject to acceptance by the other parties of supplementary obligations which, by their nature or according to commercial usage, have no connection with the subject of such contracts.

**COUNCIL DIRECTIVE**
**of 25 July 1985**
**on the approximation of the laws, regulations and administrative provisions of the Member States concerning liability for defective products**
**(85/374/EEC:L 210/29)**

THE COUNCIL OF THE EUROPEAN COMMUNITIES,

Having regard to the Treaty establishing the European Economic Community, and in particular Article 100 thereof,

Having regard to the proposal from the Commission,

Having regard to the opinion of the European Parliament,

Having regard to the opinion of the Economic and Social Committee,

Whereas approximation of the laws of the Member States concerning the liability of the producer for damage caused by the defectiveness of his products is necessary because the existing divergences may distort competition and affect the movement of goods within the common market and entail a differing degree of protection of the consumer against damage caused by a defective product to his health or property;

Whereas liability without fault on the part of the producer is the sole means of adequately solving the problem, peculiar to our age of increasing technicality, of a fair apportionment of the risks inherent in modern technological production;

Whereas liability without fault should apply only to movables which have been industrially produced; whereas, as a result, it is appropriate to exclude liability for agricultural products and game, except where they have undergone a processing of an industrial nature which could cause a defect in these products; whereas the liability provided for in this Directive should also apply to movables which are used in the construction of immovables or are installed in immovables;

Whereas protection of the consumer requires that all producers involved in the production process should be made liable, in so far as their finished product, component part or any raw material supplied by them was defective; whereas, for the same reason, liability should extend to importers of products into the Community and to persons who present themselves as producers by affixing their name, trade mark or other distinguishing feature or who supply a product the producer of which cannot be identified;

Whereas, in situations where several persons are liable for the same damage, the protection of the consumer requires that the injured person should be able to claim full compensation for the damage from any one of them;

Whereas, to protect the physical well-being and property of the consumer, the defectiveness of the product should be determined by reference not to its fitness for use but to the lack of the safety which the public at large is entitled to expect; whereas the safety is assessed by excluding any misuse of the product not reasonable under the circumstances;

Whereas a fair apportionment of risk between the injured person and the producer implies that the producer should be able to free himself from liability if he furnishes proof as to the existence of certain exonerating circumstances;

Whereas the protection of the consumer requires that the liability of the producer remains unaffected by acts or omissions of other persons having contributed to cause the damage; whereas, however, the contributory negligence of the injured person may be taken into account to reduce or disallow such liability;

Whereas the protection of the consumer requires compensation for death and personal injury as well as compensation for damage to property; whereas the latter should nevertheless be limited to goods for private use or consumption and be subject to a deduction of a lower threshold of a fixed amount in order to avoid litigation in an excessive number of cases; whereas this Directive should not prejudice compensation for pain and suffering and other non-material damages payable, where appropriate, under the law applicable to the case;

Whereas a uniform period of limitation for the bringing of action for compensation is in the interests both of the injured person and of the producer;

Whereas products age in the course of time, higher safety standards are developed and the state of science and technology progresses; whereas, therefore, it would not be reasonable to make the producer liable for an unlimited period for the defectiveness of his product; whereas therefore, liability should expire after a reasonable length of time, without prejudice to claims pending at law;

Whereas, to achieve effective protection of consumers, no contractual derogation should be permitted as regards the liability of the producer in relation to the injured person;

Whereas under the legal systems of the Member States an injured party may have a claim for damages based on grounds of contractual liability or on grounds of non-contractual liability other than that provided for in this Directive; in so far as these provisions also serve to attain the objective of effective protection of consumers, they should remain unaffected by this Directive; whereas, in so far as effective protection of consumers in the sector of pharmaceutical products is already also attained in a Member State under a special liability system, claims based on this system should similarly remain possible;

Whereas, to the extent that liability for nuclear injury or damage is already covered in all Member States by adequate special rules, it has been possible to exclude damage of this type from the scope of this Directive;

Whereas, since the exclusion of primary agricultural products and game from the scope of this Directive may be felt, in certain Member States, in view of what is expected for the protection of consumers, to restrict unduly such protection, it should be possible for a Member State to extend liability to such products;

Whereas, for similar reasons, the possibility offered to a producer to free himself from liability if he proves that the state of scientific and technical knowledge at the time when he put the product into circulation was not such as to enable the existence of a defect to be discovered may be felt in certain Member States to restrict unduly the protection of the consumer; whereas it should therefore be possible for a Member State to maintain in its legislation or to provide by new legislation that this exonerating circumstance is not admitted; whereas, in the case of new legislation, making use of this derogation should, however, be subject to a Community stand-still procedure, in order to raise, if possible, the level of protection in a uniform manner throughout the Community;

Whereas, taking into account the legal traditions in most of the Member States, it is inappropriate to set any financial ceiling on the producer's liability without fault; whereas, in so far as there are, however, differing traditions, it seems possible to admit that a Member State may derogate from the principle of unlimited liability by providing a limit for the total liability of the producer for damage resulting from a death or personal injury and caused by identical items with the same defect, provided that this limit is established at a level sufficiently high to guarantee adequate protection of the consumer and the correct functioning of the common market;

Whereas the harmonization resulting from this cannot be total at the present stage, but opens the way towards greater harmonization; whereas it is therefore necessary that the Council receive at regular intervals, reports from the Commission on the application of this Directive, accompanied, as the case may be, by appropriate proposals;

Whereas it is particularly important in this respect that a re-examination be carried out of those parts of the Directive relating to the derogations open to the Member States, at the expiry of a period of sufficient length to gather practical experience on the effects of these derogations on the protection of consumers and on the functioning of the common market,

## HAS ADOPTED THIS DIRECTIVE:

**Art. 1.** The producer shall be liable for damage caused by a defect in his product.

**Art. 2.** For the purpose of this Directive 'product' means all movables, with the exception of primary agricultural products and game, even though incorporated into another movable or into an immovable. 'Primary agricultural products' means the products of the soil, of stock-farming and of fisheries, excluding products which have undergone initial processing. 'Product' includes electricity.

**Art. 3.** 1. 'Producer' means the manufacturer of a finished product, the producer of any raw material or the manufacturer of a component part and any person who, by putting his name, trade mark or other distinguishing feature on the product presents himself as its producer.

Without prejudice to the liability of the producer, any person who imports into the Community a product for sale, hire, leasing or any form of distribution in the course of his business shall be deemed to be a producer within the meaning of this Directive and shall be responsible as a producer.

3. Where the producer of the product cannot be identified, each supplier of the product shall be treated as its producer unless he informs the injured person, within a reasonable time, of the identity of the producer or of the person who supplied him with the product. The same shall apply, in the case of an imported product, if this product does not indicate the identity of the importer referred to in paragraph 2, even if the name of the producer is indicated.

**Art. 4.** The injured person shall be required to prove the damage, the defect and the causal relationship between defect and damage.

**Art. 5.** Where, as a result of the provisions of this Directive, two or more persons are liable for the same damage, they shall be liable jointly and severally, without prejudice to the provisions of national law concerning the rights of contribution or recourse.

**Art. 6.** 1. A product is defective when it does not provide the safety which a person is entitled to expect, taking all circumstances into account, including:

(a) the presentation of the product;

(b) the use to which it could reasonably be expected that the product would be put;

(c) the time when the product was put into circulation.

2. A product shall not be considered defective for the sole reason that a better product is subsequently put into circulation.

**Art. 7.**    The producer shall not be liable as a result of this Directive if he proves:

(a)    that he did not put the product into circulation; or

(b)    that, having regard to the circumstances, it is probable that the defect which caused the damage did not exist at the time when the product was put into circulation by him or that this defect came into being afterwards; or

(c)    that the product was neither manufactured by him for sale or any form of distribution for economic purpose nor manufactured or distributed by him in the course of his business; or

(d)    that the defect is due to compliance of the product with mandatory regulations issued by the public authorities; or

(e)    that the state of scientific and technical knowledge at the time when he put the product into circulation was not such as to enable the existence of the defect to be discovered; or

(f)    in the case of a manufacturer of a component, that the defect is attributable to the design of the product in which the component has been fitted or to the instructions given by the manufacturer of the product.

**Art. 8.**    1.    Without prejudice to the provisions of national law concerning the right of contribution or recourse, the liability of the producer shall not be reduced when the damage is caused both by a defect in product and by the act or omission of a third party.

2.    The liability of the producer may be reduced or disallowed when, having regard to all the circumstances, the damage is caused both by a defect in the product and by the fault of the injured person or any person for whom the injured person is responsible.

**Art. 9.**    For the purpose of Article 1, 'damage' means:

(a)    damage caused by death or by personal injuries;

(b)    damage to, or destruction of, any item of property other than the defective product itself, with a lower threshold of 500 ECU, provided that the item of property:

(i)    is of a type ordinarily intended for private use or consumption, and

(ii)    was used by the injured person mainly for his own private use or consumption.

This Article shall be without prejudice to national provisions relating to non-material damage.

**Art. 10.**    1.    Member States shall provide in their legislation that a limitation period of three years shall apply to proceedings for the recovery of damages as provided for in this Directive. The limitation period shall begin to run from the day on which the plaintiff became aware, or should reasonably have become aware, of the damage, the defect and the identity of the producer.

2.    The laws of Member States regulating suspension or interruption of the limitation period shall not be affected by this Directive.

**Art. 11.**    Member States shall provide in their legislation that the rights conferred upon the injured person pursuant to this Directive shall be extinguished upon the expiry of a period of 10 years from the date on which the producer put into circulation the actual product which caused the damage, unless the injured person has in the meantime instituted proceedings against the producer.

**Art. 12.**    The liability of the producer arising from this Directive may not, in relation to the injured person, be limited or excluded by a provision limiting his liability or exempting him from liability.

**Art. 13.**    This Directive shall not affect any rights which an injured person may have according to the rules of the law of contractual or non-contractual liability or a special liability system existing at the moment when this Directive is notified.

**Art. 14.**    This Directive shall not apply to injury or damage arising from nuclear accidents and covered by international conventions ratified by the Member States.

**Art. 15.**    1.    Each Member State may:

(a)    by way of derogation from Article 2, provide in its legislation that within the meaning of Article 1 of this Directive 'product' also means primary agricultural products and game;

(b)    by way of derogation from Article 7(e), maintain or, subject to the procedure set out in paragraph 2 of this Article, provide in this legislation that the producer shall be liable even if he proves that the state of scientific and technical knowledge at the time when he put the product into circulation was not such as to enable the existence of a defect to be discovered.

2.    A Member State wishing to introduce the measure specified in paragraph 1(b) shall communicate the text of the proposed measure to the Commission. The Commission shall inform the other Member States thereof.

The Member State concerned shall hold the proposed measure in abeyance for nine months after the Commission is informed and provided that in the meantime the Commission has not submitted to the Council a proposal amending this Directive on the relevant matter. However, if within three months of receiving the said information, the Commission does not advise the Member State concerned that it intends submitting such a proposal to the Council, the Member State may take the proposed measure immediately.

If the Commission does submit to the Council such a proposal amending this Directive within the aforementioned nine months, the Member State concerned shall hold the proposed measure in abeyance for a further period of 18 months from the date on which the proposal is submitted.

3.    Ten years after the date of notification of this Directive, the Commission shall submit to the Council a report on the effect that rulings by the courts as to the application of Article 7(e) and of paragraph 1(b) of this Article have on consumer protection and the functioning of the common market. In the light of this report the Council, acting on a proposal from the Commission and pursuant to the terms of Article 100 of the Treaty, shall decide whether to repeal Article 7(e).

**Art. 16.**    1.    Any Member State may provide that a producer's total liability for damage resulting from a death or personal injury and caused by identical items with the same defect shall be limited to an amount which may not be less than 70 million ECU.

2.    Ten years after the date of notification of this Directive, the Commission shall submit to the Council a report on the effect on consumer protection and the functioning of the common market of the implementation of the financial limit on liability by those Member States which have used the option provided for in paragraph 1. In the light of this report the Council, acting on a proposal from the Commission and pursuant to the terms of Article 100 of the Treaty, shall decide whether to repeal paragraph 1.

**Art. 17.**    This Directive shall not apply to products put into circulation before the date on which the provisions referred to in Article 19 enter into force.

**Art. 18.**    1.    For the purposes of this Directive, the ECU shall be that defined by Regulation (EEC) No. 3180/78, as amended by Regulation (EEC) No. 2626/84. The equivalent in national currency shall initially be calculated at the rate obtaining on the date of adoption of this Directive.

2.    Every five years the Council, acting on a proposal from the Commission, shall examine and, if need be, revise the amounts in this Directive, in the light of economic and monetary trends in the Community.

**Art. 19.**    1.    Member States shall bring into force, not later than three years from the date of notification of this Directive, the laws, regulations and administrative provisions necessary to comply with this Directive. They shall forthwith inform the Commission thereof.

2.    The procedure set out in Article 15(2) shall apply from the date of notification of this Directive.

**Art. 20.**    Member States shall communicate to the Commission the texts of the main provisions of national law which they subsequently adopt in the field governed by this Directive.

**Art. 21.**    Every five years the Commission shall present a report to the Council on the application of this Directive and, if necessary, shall submit appropriate proposals to it.

**Art. 22.**    This Directive is addressed to the Member States.

Done at Brussels, 25 July 1985.

# INDEX

# BLACKSTONE'S STATUTES

## TITLES IN THE SERIES

Contract & Tort Statutes
Public Law Statutes
Employment Law Statutes
Criminal Law Statutes
Criminal Procedure: Evidence and Sentencing Statutes
Family Law Statutes
Property Law Statutes
Commercial Law Statutes
Company Law Statutes
English Legal System Statutes